P9-EJI-646

ACTION FIGURE!

Doonesbury Books by G.B. Trudeau

Still a Few Bugs in the System
The President Is a Lot Smarter Than You Think
But This War Had Such Promise
Call Me When You Find America
Guilty, Guilty, Guilty!
"What Do We Have for the Witnesses, Johnnie?"
Dare to Be Great, Ms. Caucus
Wouldn't a Gremlin Have Been More Sensible?
"Speaking of Inalienable Rights, Amy..."
You're Never Too Old for Nuts and Berries
An Especially Tricky People
As the Kid Goes for Broke
Stalking the Perfect Tan
"Any Grooming Hints for Your Fans, Rollie?"
But the Pension Fund Was Just Sitting There
We're Not Out of the Woods Yet
A Tad Overweight, But Violet Eyes to Die For
And That's My Final Offer!
He's Never Heard of You, Either
In Search of Reagan's Brain
Ask for May, Settle for June
Unfortunately, She Was Also Wired for Sound
The Wreck of the "Rusty Nail"
You Give Great Meeting, Sid
Doonesbury: A Musical Comedy
Check Your Egos at the Door
That's Doctor Sinatra, You Little Bimbo!
Death of a Party Animal
Downtown Doonesbury
Calling Dr. Whoopee
Talkin' About My G-G-Generation
We're Eating More Beets!
Read My Lips, Make My Day, Eat Quiche and Die!
Give Those Nymphs Some Hooters!
You're Smokin' Now, Mr. Butts!
I'd Go With the Helmet, Ray
Welcome to Club Scud!
What Is It, Tink, Is Pan in Trouble?

In Large Format

The Doonesbury Chronicles
Doonesbury's Greatest Hits
The People's Doonesbury
Doonesbury Dossier: The Reagan Years
Doonesbury Deluxe: Selected Glances Askance
Recycled Doonesbury: Second Thoughts on a Gilded Age

ACTION FIGURE!

ANDREWS AND McMEEL A UNIVERSAL PRESS SYNDICATE COMPANY KANSAS CITY

DOONESBURY is distributed internationally by Universal Press Syndicate.
Action Figure! The Adventures of Doonesbury's Uncle Duke copyright © 1992 by G.B. Trudeau. All rights reserved. Printed in the United States of America. No part of this book may be used or reproduced in any manner whatsoever without written permission except in the case of reprints in the context of reviews.
For information write Andrews and McMeel, a Universal Press Syndicate Company, 4900 Main Street, Kansas City, Missouri 64112.

ISBN: 0-8362-1702-0

Library of Congress Catalog Card Number: 92-72255

ATTENTION: SCHOOLS AND BUSINESSES

Andrews and McMeel books are available at quantity discounts with bulk purchase for educational, business, or sales promotional use. For information, please write to: Special Sales Department, Andrews and McMeel, 4900 Main Street, Kansas City, Missouri 64112.

"Just waking up in the morning means a lot to me."

— Keith Richards

1 PHGU PHGU

1974-1976

YOUR TIMING COULDN'T HAVE BEEN BETTER, SON — YOUR MOTHER HAS QUITE A HOME-COMING FEAST WHIPPED UP..
GREAT! LEMME JUST PUT MY STUFF UP IN MY ROOM..
OH.. UH.. I FORGOT TO TELL YOU..
HEY! UNCLE DUKE! WHAT'S HE DOING HERE?!
SAME AS USUAL — CONVALESCING. HE GOT INTO SOME PARTICULARLY VICIOUS HALLUCINOGENS OVER THANKSGIVING.
OH, WOW... WHAT'S THE PROGNOSIS? YOU GOT A TARGET?
UP AND ABOUT BY EASTER.
HMM..
NO WAY!
DAD! MOM! SIGNS OF LIFE FROM UNCLE DUKE!
A BREAK-THROUGH, SON?!
COULD BE!.. C'MON, UNCLE DUKE — YOU CAN DO IT! SHAKE IT OFF, MAN, SHAKE IT OFF!
C'MON, DUKE! HANG IN THERE, MAN!
I CAN SEE HIS PUPILS! YES.. YES.. HE'S GOT IT! THAT'S IT! HE'S CONSCIOUS!
YEA!!
MERRY CHRISTMAS, UNCLE DUKE!
OH, WOW! A GIANT LIZARD!
HOW YOU FEELIN', UNCLE DUKE?
HEY, WHAT GOES ON HERE?.. WHERE AM I?
UNCLE DUKE, YOU'RE COMING OUT OF ONE OF YOUR CLASSIC, MASSIVE ACID ROMPS!
WHAT UTTER NONSENSE! I NEVER TOUCH THE STUFF — GAVE IT UP YEARS AGO!
NOW, YOU DID NOT, UNCLE DUKE! THAT'S JUST NOT TRUE!
YOU TWISTED MANIAC! I'VE BEEN CLEAN FOR YEARS! ASK ANYONE — I HAVEN'T SO MUCH AS TAKEN AN ASPIRIN!
ASPIRIN!? WHY, YOU OLD FOOL..
THIS IS RIDICULOUS! — WHY AM I ARGUING WITH A LIZARD?

HEY! YOU'RE NOT A LIZARD— YOU'RE.. YOU'RE.. ZONKER!
RIGHT! NOW YOU'VE GOT IT!
SO WHAT THE DEVIL DID I..OH..OH, I REMEMBER NOW—I TOOK A LITTLE SOMETHING TO GET READY FOR YOUR MOTHER'S THANKSGIVING FEAST...
HEE, HEE..OH, WELL! SAY, WHAT TIME IS IT ANYWAY? I SUPPOSE EVERY-ONE'S ALREADY FINISHED EATING..
GEE, UNCLE DUKE, I DON'T KNOW HOW TO TELL YOU THIS..
WHAT?—YOU DIDN'T LEAVE ME ANY TURKEY!? IS THAT IT?! WHY, YOU GREEDY LITTLE..
DUKE!—NOW, JUST WAIT A MINUTE..
GBTrudeau
DECEMBER 27TH! YOU'RE KIDDING! I MISSED MY DEADLINE AGAIN!
DEADLINE FOR WHAT, UNCLE DUKE?
MY PIECE! MY PIECE FOR THE CHRISTMAS ISSUE OF "ROLLING STONE"! THE FINEST, MOST SAVAGE ARTICLE I'VE EVER CRANKED OUT!
OH, DEAR.. WHAT WAS IT ON?..
MY SHOPLIFTING CONVICTION!! I'VE BEEN WRITING THE THING FOR MONTHS! I'D FINALLY BEATEN IT INTO SHAPE!!
LET'S SEE..
IT WAS MY MAJOR OPUS!!
"FEAR AND LOATHING AT MACY'S MEN'S WEAR"?
GBTrudeau
YOU KNOW, UNCLE DUKE, I THINK YOU OUGHT TO START GIVING SOME SERIOUS THOUGHT SOME-TIME TO STRAIGHTENING YOURSELF OUT..
RIGHT YOU ARE, ZONK— I DAMN NEAR BLEW OUT ALL MY TUBES ON THAT LAST NUMBER, DIDN'T I?.. THAT KIND OF DERANGED BEHAVIOR JUST CAN'T GO ON!
IN FACT, I'M THINKING THAT IN A FEW DAYS I MIGHT JUST GO BACK TO ASPEN AND TRY TO TURN OVER A NEW LEAF— YOU KNOW, SETTLE DOWN, RAISE A FAMILY, BUY A LABRADOR..
..OPEN UP A LITTLE MASSAGE PARLOR.
OH, DUKE...
GBTrudeau

SURE, UNCLE DUKE, I'D LOVE TO COME! I HAVEN'T BEEN TO COLORADO IN AGES!
GOOD! WE'LL LEAVE TONIGHT! YOUR AUNT SANDY WILL BE DELIGHTED!

YOU KNOW, SHE SENT ME A CARD RECENTLY. SHE SAID JOHN DENVER HAS MOVED NEXT DOOR TO YOU!
DON'T REMIND ME! THE LITTLE TWERP'S ALWAYS SINGING HIS GUTS OUT DOWN BY MY CREEK!

REALLY? THAT MUST BE GREAT!
ARE YOU KIDDING?! HE'S MURDERING MY SOCIAL LIFE! NONE OF MY FRIENDS WILL COME OVER TO THE HOUSE ANYMORE!

OH, DEAR..
HE'S SCARING THE TROUT, TOO..
GBTrudeau

I DUNNO.. I MEAN, WHAT WOULD YOU DO IF JOHN DENVER KEPT SINGING BY YOUR CREEK?
WHY DON'T YOU JUST LEVEL WITH HIM? ASK HIM TO PLAY ELSEWHERE.

I HAVE, ZONK! I'VE TRIED EVERYTHING TO DISCOURAGE HIM! ONE DAY, I EVEN SET MY DOGS ON HIM! AS YOU KNOW, I'VE GOT TWO OF THE UGLIEST, MOST SAVAGE DOBERMANS THIS SIDE OF HAITI!

SIR? WE'VE GOT YOUR BLOODY MARY'S..
BUT, OF COURSE, THEY BOTH TURNED OUT TO BE COUNTRY MUSIC FANS!

THAT'S $1.67 EACH. WE'D APPRECIATE EXACT CHANGE..
JUST A SECOND... SO THE DUMB BRUTES JUST SAT IN THE CREEK WAGGING THEIR TAILS IN TIME!
GBTrudeau

GEE, DUKE, IT'S CERTAINLY NICE TO HAVE YOU HOME AGAIN. THIS OLD PLACE SURE SEEMS EMPTY WITHOUT YOU..
US MAIL

WELL, SANDY, MAYBE THIS TIME I'LL STAY AWHILE. I KEEP FORGETTING HOW SEDUCTIVE OUR LIFE OUT HERE REALLY IS..
US MAIL

I GUESS IT'S THE PERFECT, ABSOLUTE STILLNESS OF THE MOUNTAINS! AFTER ALL THE BAD CRAZINESS OF L.A., I SURELY LOVE JUST SITTING HERE ON MY PORCH, SIPPING WILD TURKEY, AND CLEANING MY OL' GUN..
US MAIL

ROCKY MOUNTAIN HIIIIGH...
SAY, HONEY, HAND ME THOSE CARTRIDGES, WILL YA?
US MAIL
GBTrudeau

ROCKY MOUN-TAIN HIIIGH...
GEE, AUNT SANDY, DOES JOHN DENVER REALLY PLAY DOWN BY YOUR CREEK EVERY NIGHT?
YES, HE DOES, ZONKER...
US MAIL

COLO-RAADO! ROCKY MOUN...
WOW, IT SURE SOUNDS PRETTY..
IT SURE DOES! DUKE, DEAR, IN ALL FAIR-NESS, YOU'VE GOT TO ADMIT..
US MAIL

LISTEN, DENVER!! YOU BETTER ROCKY MOUNTAIN HIGH-TAIL YOUR FANNY OFF MY PROPERTY RIGHT NOW, OR YOUR GUITAR AIN'T GONNA BE THE ONLY THING WITH A BIG HOLE IN IT!!
US MAIL

DUKE! THE MAN'S A STAR!
YOU HEAR ME, BOY?! YOU GOT TEN SECONDS!
US MAIL
©B Trudeau

HI YA, DUKE! WHEN JA GET HOME?
TEN MINUTES AGO! AND THE LAST THING I WANTED TO HEAR WAS A FRESH-AIR FREAK HOWLING DOWN BY MY CREEK!
US MAIL

AW, C'MON, DUKE, IT'S SUCH A FAR-OUT CREEK! LOTS OF SUNSHINE AND WATER AND ANIMALS AND LOVE AND PEACE AND PROMISES!
HEY, DENVER-HAVE YOU EVER CONSIDERED CHANGING YOUR NAME TO AKRON, AND MOVING TO OHIO?!
US MAIL

LOOK, DUKE-I'LL MAKE YOU A DEAL IF I CAN PLAY HERE...
A DEAL?! YOU THINK I'D MAKE A DEAL WITH A PINE NEEDLE JUNKIE AN ADOLESCENT COWBOY WITH..
US MAIL

500 CASES OF COORS BEER!
I'LL BRING YOU DOWN A CHAIR.
US MAIL
©B Trudeau

WELL, WELL! LOOK WHO'S BACK!
HOWDY, YAWN! YOUR FAVORITE WORD WIZARD HAS RETURNED FOR SOME HEAVY DUTY WRITING!

I HOPE SO! THANKS TO YOUR VARIOUS INDUL-GENCES, YOU'VE PUNTED NO LESS THAN SIX CONTRACTS!
SIX? GOODNESS, HOW THEY DO MOUNT UP! CHIEF, I PROMISE YOU ALL THOSE ARTICLES BY NEXT ISSUE!

I'LL SETTLE FOR ONE! PICK A CONTRACT, ANY CON-TRACT!
EENIE, MEENIE, MINIE, MOE!

15,000 WORDS ON SNORKLING.
PIECE OF CAKE! HAVE IT FOR YOU IN THE MORNING!
©B Trudeau

HEY, CHIEF! I FINISHED THE ARTICLE!
WHAT?! HOW'D THAT HAPPEN?
WELL, I GOT GOOD AND WIRED LAST NIGHT, AND THE WORDS JUST POURED OUT!
"GLIPPER. PPTPLE PI ZIP. XXPLT COPA LIPZZ."
WHAT?! LET ME SEE THAT!
"PXXT? NOOB... PHLAP-SLABBLE KPPT SALMOKK! LIPPY. GORPLER."
I DIDN'T WRITE THIS! THIS IS THE WORK OF AN IMPOSTOR!
SOUNDS LIKE YOUR STUFF TO ME..
Nat. Affairs
GBTrudeau

ALL RIGHT, DAN- I GUESS WE'RE READY TO..
YAWN! DON'T CLOSE THE PAPER! I'M FINISHED! I GOT MY ARTICLE ON TAPE!
HOLD IT A SEC, DAN..
WAIT'LL YOU HEAR THIS, CHIEF! I STAYED UP ALL NIGHT DICTATING! REALLY POWERFUL STUFF! ALL YOU HAVE TO DO IS TRANSCRIBE IT! LISTEN..
CLIK!
COUGH! HEE! HEE! HEE.. SNIFF! HEE.. UH.. HEE, HEE! HEE... HEE, HEE! HEE! HEE!
OKAY, DAN- PUT IT TO BED.
HEE, HEE! HEE! HEE! HEE, HEE, HEE!
I CAN'T UNDER-STAND IT..
GBTrudeau

CHEER UP, DUKE! THERE'LL BE ANOTHER ISSUE. YOU'LL GET INTO PRINT YET..
YOU KNOW, FENDER, MAYBE I'M JUST NOT READY YET TO BE-COME A MAJOR WRIT-ER... PERHAPS MY MOVE TO SAMOA WILL BE A GOOD THING!
YOUR MOVE TO WHERE, DUKE?
YOU MEAN YOU HAVEN'T HEARD? I'VE APPLIED FOR THE POST OF GOVERNOR OF AMERICAN SAMOA!
WHAT ARE YOU TALKING ABOUT, MAN?
HEY, I'M SERIOUS! I WROTE THE PRES-IDENT A FORMAL REQUEST! EVEN SENT HIM MY PICTURE AND RESUME!
YOUR RESUME?! DUKE, YOUR RESUME READS LIKE A POLICE BLOTTER!
YEAH, BUT THE PICTURE'S SENSATIONAL!
GBTrudeau

OR
CHIEF, I HAVEN'T BEEN FEELING MYSELF LATELY — I'M MOVING THE NATIONAL AFFAIRS DESK BACK TO COLORADO FOR A WHILE..

OR
SUIT YOURSELF, DUKE. JUST SO LONG AS YOU DON'T BLOW ANOTHER DEADLINE..
ME? BLOW A DEADLINE? WHY, I'D SOONER STOMP MY ARTHRITIC GRANDMOTHER!

OR
I KNOW THAT, DUKE. BUT THE PRINTERS AREN'T QUITE SO UNDERSTANDING.
THE PRINTERS!? YOU KNOW, THAT GANG OF PHILISTINES IS REALLY BEGINNING TO GET TO ME! MY NEW JOB IS COMING NONE TOO SOON!

OR
NEW JOB, DUKE?
WHAT? YOU MEAN YOU HAVEN'T HEARD?—ANY DAY NOW, I'M GOING TO BE APPOINTED GOVERNOR OF AMERICAN SAMOA! HOW 'BOUT THAT, HUH?

OR
LOOK, DUKE, I'M AWFUL BUSY RIGHT NOW, SO IF YOU DON'T...
SEE, I READ THE JOB WAS OPENING UP OUT THERE, SO I SENT IN MY RESUME TO FORD! I'M VERY HOPEFUL!

HMMM...IS HE A REPUBLICAN?
NO, SIR. HE IS A MANIAC.
GBTrudeau

UH.. DUKE, WOULD I BE OUT OF LINE IF I INQUIRED WHY YOU'RE NOT WEARING YOUR USUAL TACKY SPORTSWEAR TODAY?
A GOVERNOR HAS TO LOOK HIS BEST, SON!
GOVERNOR? DUKE, DON'T YOU THINK YOU'RE KIND OF JUMPING THE GUN?
RING! RING!
DUKE! WHITE HOUSE ON LINE TWO!
DO YOU THINK THE CUT'S RIGHT?
HELLO?.. OH, HI, DUKE! .. WHAT'S UP NOW?
YES, YES, DUKE – I GAVE ZONKER YOUR MESSAGE – AS SOON AS HE CAME HOME!
WHAT?.. YES, DUKE, HE KNOWS YOU HAVE TO HAVE AN ANSWER TODAY – HE'S DOWN TALKING TO THE DEAN RIGHT THIS MOMENT!
YOU'RE BECOMING THE AMERICAN SAMOAN WHAT?!
UH.. LIEUTENANT GOVERNOR, SIR.
SO HOW'D YOUR NEW APPOINTMENT AS LIEUTENANT-GOVERNOR OF SAMOA GO DOWN AT THE DEAN'S OFFICE?
OKAY, I GUESS. I JUST EXPLAINED THAT IT WAS SOMETHING I HAD TO DO. I KNOW IT SOUNDS CRAZY, BUT I THINK I'M FINALLY READY FOR SOME RESPONSIBILITY IN MY LIFE..
ALSO, I GUESS I'M.. WELL.. LOOKING FOR SOMETHING! CALL IT A QUEST!
A QUEST? A QUEST FOR WHAT, AMIGO ?
THE... THE PERFECT TAN!
YOU'LL FIND IT, BOY! I JUST KNOW YOU WILL!

GOVERNOR?.. I'M MACARTHUR, SIR – YOUR ADMINISTRATIVE AIDE. I'VE GOT A CAR WAITING TO TAKE YOU TO YOUR RESIDENCE, SIR!

WELL, I'M GLAD TO MEET YOU, MACARTHUR! BUT BEFORE WE GO ANYWHERE, I REALLY THINK I NEED A..
YES, SIR. HERE YOU ARE, SIR.

WHAT'S THIS?
A THERMOS OF FROZEN DAIQUIRIS, EXCELLENCY.

MACARTHUR, YOU ARE A WONDER!
NOT REALLY, SIR – WASHINGTON WIRED AHEAD ABOUT YOU.

MACARTHUR, MR. HARRIS HERE IS MY LIEUTENANT-GOVERNOR. HE'LL BE HELPING ME IMPLEMENT SOME OF MY SWEEPING REFORM PROGRAMS!

YOU'VE GOT SOME SWEEPING REFORMS, SIR?
YUP – MADE A LIST COMING IN ON THE PLANE! I'LL GIVE YOU A QUICK RUN-DOWN.. "1) RELEASE ALL POLITICAL PRISONERS."

GOT ANY POLITICAL PRISONERS, MACARTHUR?
YES, SIR – TWO. THE PREVIOUS GOVERNOR LOCKED UP A COUPLE VACATIONING MONDALE SUPPORTERS. HE WAS A HUMPHREY MAN.

RELEASE THEM AT ONCE!
YES, SIR!
"2) BURN ALL JOHN DENVER RECORDS.."

TELL ME, AMIGO – HOW'D YOU WIND UP WITH A NAME LIKE "MACARTHUR"?
SIMPLE – I WAS A WAR BABY – BORN IN '42!

ACTUALLY, I ALMOST GOT NAMED "HIROHITO". BUT FORTUNATELY, MY PARENTS HELD OFF ON NAMING ME UNTIL AFTER THE BATTLE OF MIDWAY.

AS YOU KNOW, THE JAPS REALLY GOT STOMPED THERE – LOST FOUR CARRIERS! SO AFTER THAT, SAMOAN PARENTS BEGAN NAMING ALL THEIR NEW CHILDREN AFTER GENERAL MACARTHUR! CAN YOU IMAGINE?!

OH, WELL – AT LEAST IT'S A NICE NAME!
TRY TELLING THAT TO MY SISTER DOUG..

QUITE A VIEW, MACARTHUR, QUITE A VIEW! IS THE VOLCANO STILL ACTIVE?
SEMI-ACTIVE, SIR. BUT YOU NEEDN'T WORRY- WE'VE GOT IT ON A STEADY DIET OF SACRIFICIAL VIRGINS!
SACRIFICIAL VIRGINS! YOU'RE KIDDING!
NO, SIR – IT'S A TIME-HONORED CUSTOM! I HOPE YOU DON'T DISAPPROVE, SIR.
DISAPPROVE?! WE'RE APPALLED! HOW LONG HAS THIS BEEN GOING ON, MACARTHUR?!
2,000 YEARS! BUT WE HAVEN'T HAD A SINGLE ERUPTION!
CAN'T ARGUE WITH THAT.
DUKE!
THEN IT'S OKAY, SIR?
MACARTHUR, YOU DON'T REALLY STILL SACRIFICE VIRGINS TO THE VOLCANO, DO YOU?
OH, YES, SIR! – THE VOLCANO HAS BEEN VERY GOOD TO US- NO ERUPTIONS IN 2,000 YEARS! IT'S OUR LITTLE WAY OF SAYING THANKS!
AND THE PEOPLE CAN STILL RELATE TO SUCH A BRUTAL CUSTOM?
WELL, A FEW OF THE KIDS ARE A BIT PUT OFF BY IT. BUT MOST OLDER SAMOANS STILL VIEW THE SACRIFICE AS A MAJOR EVENT ON THEIR SOCIAL CALENDARS!
HMM... HOW OFTEN IS IT HELD?
GENERALLY SPEAKING, WE LIMIT IT TO ONE SACRIFICIAL VIRGIN A MONTH. OF COURSE, THERE ARE EXCEPTIONS.
FOR INSTANCE?
WELL, LIKE, THE NIGHT NIXON RESIGNED, WE HAD A DOUBLE-HEADER.
WAIT'LL YOU SEE HER IN THAT DRESS, FRANK! SHE'LL BE THE PRETTIEST VOLCANO VIRGIN ON THE ISLAND!
WELL, I HOPE IT DOESN'T NEED ANY ALTERATIONS- HER SACRIFICE IS ON FRIDAY!
TA-DA!
MY LORD! YOU CALL THAT A DRESS!? YOU CAN SEE RIGHT THROUGH IT!!
OH, DADDY! FOR PETE'S SAKE! I'LL BE WEARING A BODY STOCKING UNDER IT!
NO WAY!
FRANK, YOU'RE SHOWING YOUR AGE! TRANSPARENT VESTMENTS ARE ALL THE RAGE NOW!
BUT IT'S... IT'S.. SACRILEGIOUS!!
HEEY.. FRANKIE.. C'MON, TRUST ME!

NORMAN, STOP SULKING AND WAVE GOOD-BYE TO YOUR SISTER! YOU'RE NEVER GOING TO SEE HER AGAIN, POOR LAMB!
BUT, MA, IT'S JUST NOT FAIR! HOW COME SUZY GETS TO BE A VOLCANO VIRGIN AND I DON'T?!
BOYS AREN'T ALLOWED TO BE VOLCANO VIRGINS, NORMAN! YOU KNOW THAT!
BUT WHY NOT?! I COULD DO IT, I COULD QUALIFY! EASY!
NORMAN, WILL YOU STOP MAKING SUCH A FUSS AND WAVE GOOD-BYE TO YOUR SISTER?! SHE'S AT THE RIM ALREADY!
I CAN BE JUST AS CHASTE AS ANY DUMB GIRL!!
LAST CHANCE, NORMAN— SHE'S GETTING INTO HER CROUCH!
©BTrudeau
JUST A MINUTE DADDY. I'VE GOT TO ADJUST MY SACRIFICIAL VESTMENTS, I WANT TO LOOK MY BEST..
YOU LOOK FINE, DAUGHTER, JUST FINE! NOW, COME ON, THE GODS ARE WAITING..
DO MY SHOES LOOK RIGHT? I WASN'T SURE IF I SHOULD WEAR BEIGE OR WHITE..
DAUGHTER, WILL YOU JUST JUMP?!—YOUR MOTHER'S EXPECTING ME HOME FOR DINNER!
OKAY, OKAY—IN JUST A SECOND..
NOW WHAT?!
I'VE GOT TO MAKE A WISH.
OH, FOR GOD'S SAKE...
©BTrudeau
COME ON, DAUGHTER, IT'S TIME TO JUMP! LET'S GET IT OVER WITH.
HOLD YOUR HORSES, DADDY. I HAVE TO COMB MY HAIR FOR THE GODS.
DAUGHTER! WE HAVEN'T TIME FOR THAT! WE'RE BEHIND SCHEDULE AS IT IS! NOW, COME ON—LET'S GO!
JUST A SEC—I'M ALMOST THROUGH..
RRRUUMBLLE!!
JUMP, ALREADY!
STOP PUSHING, DADDY!
©BTrudeau

SHE WOULDN'T JUMP?
NO, SIR. AT THE LAST MINUTE, SHE JUST CHANGED HER MIND. HER FATHER'S TERRIBLY EMBARRASSED!
HAVE YOU FOUND ANOTHER VOLCANO VIRGIN TO SUB FOR HER?
WE'RE LOOKING, SIR, BUT IT'S NOT EASY. LIKE WITH EVERYTHING ELSE THERE'S A SHORTAGE. IN RECENT YEARS WE'VE HAD TO CUT BACK TO ONE SACRIFICE A MONTH.
IT'S REALLY A VERY TRAGIC DEVELOPMENT, EXCELLENCY. IN THE OLD DAYS, WE USED TO HAVE QUITE A LINEUP — SOME REALLY GREAT TALENT, I'LL TELL YOU!
I'LL NEVER FORGET MOPSY DEBEERS, CLASS OF '62 — SHE DID A TRIPLE GAINER ON THE WAY DOWN! WHAT A GAL! SHE WAS REALLY A VIRGIN'S VIRGIN!
BUT NOW, YOU JUST CAN'T GET THE YOUNG GIRLS TO GO INTO IT. THEY THINK SELF-SACRIFICE IS OLD-FASHIONED. THEY'RE JUST OUT FOR A GOOD TIME!
AH, YES, BUT WHAT CAN YOU DO, MACARTHUR? — THE KIDS TODAY...
YES, SIR. IT'S A DIFFERENT WORLD.
©Brucker

A LOCUST PLAGUE?! WELL, DON'T JUST STAND THERE MACARTHUR—GET OUT THE FLAME THROWERS! BURN THE MONSTERS IN THEIR TRACKS!

WE ALREADY DID THAT, YOUR EXCELLENCY, BUT WE STARTED A BRUSH FIRE BY MISTAKE.
A WHAT?!
NO PROBLEM! THERE'S ANOTHER HURRICANE ALERT. IT'LL PUT OUT THE BRUSH FIRE!

IT'LL BE TOO LATE! THE ISLAND'S CROPS ARE ALREADY BURNED UP! LOOKS LIKE WE'RE IN FOR A FAMINE.
NO WAY! WE'VE GOT FOOD RESERVES!
NO, WE DON'T, DUKE—THEY WERE RUINED IN THE FLOOD LAST NIGHT..

DID WE HAVE A FLOOD LAST NIGHT? I DIDN'T NOTICE, ON ACCOUNT OF THE PROBLEMS WE'RE HAVING WITH THE VOLCANO..
THE VOLCANO!! I THOUGHT YOU HAD IT ON A DIET OF VIRGINS!

UH... WE RAN OUT.
RAN OUT?! MACARTHUR, THAT'S JUST CARELESS! HOW MANY TIMES DO I... HEY... THAT WRETCHED THING ISN'T ACTUALLY ERUPTING, IS IT?!

YEAH, SORT OF...
THAT DOES IT—I'M GOING HOME.
EXCUSE ME, SIR—THERE'S SOME LAVA HERE TO SEE YOU.

SUZY?.. SUZY WILLOWMAKER? THIS IS YOUR GOVERNOR SPEAKING!
C'MON, UNCLE DUKE, IT WASN'T HER FAULT!
OKAY, SUZY, WHAT'S THE BIG IDEA OF BACKING OUT ON YOUR SACRIFICE?! DO YOU REALIZE THAT BECAUSE OF YOU, WE'VE GOT A MAJOR ERUPTION ON OUR HANDS?!
NOW, LISTEN TO ME, SUZY!! I WANT YOU TO GO UP THERE THIS AFTERNOON AND SACRIFICE YOURSELF – BEFORE THE WHOLE ISLAND'S DESTROYED!!..WHADDA YA MEAN YOU CAN'T?!..
WHY NOT?!
SHE'S GOT A DENTIST APPOINTMENT.
FAIR ENOUGH – NOW LET HER BE!
A TYPHOON?! WE'RE GOING TO HAVE A TYPHOON, TOO?!
YES, SIR. SHOULD HIT US IN ABOUT AN HOUR..
WELL, THAT'S THE BIG FOUR, ISN'T IT?! I MEAN, ALONG WITH THE EARTHQUAKE, THE FLOOD, AND THE VOLCANO ERUPTION, WE'VE HAD THE GRAND SLAM OF NATURAL DISASTERS!
YES, SIR – IT'S BEEN QUITE A WEEK!
AND YOU PEOPLE BILL THIS GOD-FORSAKEN ISLAND AS A PARADISE?!
MACARTHUR, I CAN'T TAKE MUCH MORE OF THIS..
I KNOW, SIR – THAT'S WHY I'M NOT GOING TO EVEN MENTION THE CHOLERA EPIDEMIC.
TAKE A CABLE, MACARTHUR! "TO: THE SECRETARY OF THE INTERIOR, WASHINGTON, D.C. RE: CURRENT SITUATION IN THE TINY, TROPICAL TERRITORY OF AMERICAN SAMOA."
"DEAR MR. SECRETARY: IN THE PAST WEEK THE DENIZENS OF THIS ISLAND HAVE ENDURED A HURRICANE, A LOCUST PLAGUE, A FAMINE, A VOLCANO ERUPTION... .. AND... UH..
I'M A REASONABLE MAN, MACARTHUR, SO I KNOW THIS ISN'T SNOW.
PAY IT NO MIND, EXCELLENCY – IT NEVER STICKS.

FINALLY DECIDED TO MAKE TIME FOR A BATH, MACARTHUR!
YES, SIR. YOU'RE VERY GOOD WITH THE HARD DECISIONS, SIR.

SO WHAT'S ON YOUR MIND, MAC?..
WELL, SIR, TOMORROW'S YOUR INAUGURATION — AND THE INAUGURAL BALL! I WAS GOING TO SUGGEST YOU SCRUB EXTRA HARD.

INDEED I WILL, MACARTHUR! I'VE BEEN LOOKING FORWARD TO THIS!
DO YOU HAVE ANY INSTRUCTIONS FOR ME, SIR?

UH... YEAH! WRITE ME A SPEECH, ORDER THE BOOZE, AND SEND AN INVITE TO MY OLD LADY!
I'M ON IT!
G B Trudeau

WHAT IS IT, MACARTHUR?
YOUR EXCELLENCY, I HAVE YOUR INAUGURAL SPEECH HERE FOR YOU..

GOOD MAN! — YOU DO FAST WORK!
ACTUALLY, SIR, I DIDN'T WRITE IT. IT'S THE SAME INAUGURAL SPEECH USED BY EVERY PREVIOUS GOVERNOR OF THE ISLAND.

IT'S SORT OF AN OLD TRADITION — SAMOANS FEEL VERY SECURE WITH THIS SPEECH. IT'S GOT SOME REALLY GREAT PROMISES, AND SOME VERY NICE REFERENCES TO OUR PLACE IN THE WORLD COMMUNITY!

"MEN OF SAMOA! I BRING YOU GREETINGS FROM PRESIDENT McKINLEY..."
..OR WHOEVER..
G B Trudeau

..AND WITH YOUR HELP, MY FELLOW CITIZENS, THE TERRITORY OF AMERICAN SAMOA WILL RISE, PHOENIX-LIKE, TO TAKE HER PLACE AS THE PRIDE OF THE PACIFIC!

DOWN WITH AMERICAN COLONIALISM!
HEY, HEY! LET'S HAVE NONE OF THAT! WHERE DO YOU THINK YOU ARE — PUERTO RICO?!

LONG LIVE INDEPENDENT SAMOA!
I'M WARNING YOU, SWEETHEART! ONE MORE OUTBURST AND..
G B Trudeau

KAA-BLAM!
MACARTHUR! START A FILE ON THAT MAN!!

HIT IT, MACARTHUR— THEY'RE BEGINNING TO ARRIVE EN MASSE!
THE MOST HONORABLE TINA SLIMS, MINISTER OF WOMEN!
GOVERNOR! MAY I WELCOME YOU TO SAMOA!
YOU'RE BARKING UP THE WRONG TREE, HONEY. I'M MARRIED.
THE MOST HONORABLE ANTHONY HAYDEN-JONES, MINISTER OF SURFING AFFAIRS!
A REAL HONOR, SIR.
THANKS, TONY. SURF'S UP, I TRUST?
THE HONORABLE BOBBY VALDEZ, MINISTER OF MARIJUANA AND CENTRAL NERVOUS SYSTEM DEPRESSANTS!
GOOD EVENING, MAN!
MACARTHUR, CANCEL MY APPOINTMENTS FOR TOMORROW!
EXCELLENCY, MACARTHUR TELLS ME YOU HAD A SPOT OF LAVA TROUBLE IN YOUR GARDEN LAST WEEK..
MORE LIKE A TOTAL WIPEOUT, TONY! WE GOT HIT SOMETHIN' FIERCE!
IT REALLY TICKED ME OFF! WE LOST EVERYTHING! — THE ROSES, THE PETUNIAS, THE BEGONIAS, SOME SENSATIONAL ORCHIDS AND AFRICAN VIOLETS THAT JUST KNOCKED YOUR EYES OUT!!
NOT TO MENTION A DAMN FINE GARDENER!
OH, REALLY? YOU LOST RALPHIE?
GOVERNOR, WE ALL THINK YOU'VE DONE A MARVELOUS JOB COPING WITH THE LATEST NATURAL DISASTERS!
WELL, IT'S BEEN NO PICNIC, I'LL TELL YOU THAT! YOU HAVE NO IDEA WHAT THE EMERGENCY RELIEF BUREAUCRACY'S LIKE!
I MUST HAVE SPENT A WEEK PLEADING WITH THOSE MORONS IN WASHINGTON BEFORE THEY'D SEND ME AS MUCH AS A BAND-AID! EVERY LAST AGENCY IN TOWN'S ALL TIED UP WITH LOCAL DISASTERS!
DID YOU TRY THE PEACE CORPS?
SURE, I TRIED THE PEACE CORPS— I CABLED THEM SEVERAL TIMES!
AND?
THEY SENT ME A DOZEN MATH TEACHERS!

WHAT IS IT, MACARTHUR?
EXCELLENCY, THESE TWO WOMEN CRAVE AN AUDIENCE WITH YOU. THERE SEEMS TO BE A DISPUTE OVER A BABY..

OKAY, LADIES— WHAT'S ALL THIS ABOUT?
EXCELLENCY, THIS WOMAN CLAIMS MY BABY HERE IS HERS!
IT IS, EXCELLENCY! EVERYONE KNOWS THIS IS MY CHILD!

HE'S MY BABY, I TELL YOU! HE'S GOT MY BLUE EYES!
DON'T LISTEN TO HER, EXCELLENCY! SHE'S A WELFARE MOTHER AND JUST WANTS ANOTHER DEPENDENT!

YOU KNOW, THIS DISPUTE HAS A RING OF FAMILIARITY TO IT... I BELIEVE THERE'S A BIBLICAL PRECEDENT... AND A SOLUTION!
WHAT IS IT, SIRE?

WAIT A MINUTE... IT'S COMING TO ME... IT'S COMING TO ME...

I'VE GOT IT! — CUT THE KID IN HALF!
HMMM... THAT SOUNDS FAIR..
ARE YOU CRAZY?!

HEY, WHAT'S THIS?! – OUR GOVERNOR LOST IN SOBER REFLECTION?
YOUR GOVERNOR, MY BOY, IS ABOUT TO GO BANANAS! THE RESPONSIBILITIES OF HIGH OFFICE ARE REALLY GETTING TO HIM!
WELL, IF YOU WANT TO RESIGN, IT'S OKAY WITH ME. I'VE FULFILLED MY MAJOR PURPOSE HERE!
MAJOR PURPOSE? WHAT MAJOR PURPOSE?
YOU MEAN YOU HAVEN'T NOTICED?!
OF COURSE! THE PERFECT TAN!
I WRAPPED IT UP YESTERDAY!
CONGRATULATIONS, SIR!
YOU KNOW, YOUNG MAN, WE'RE ALL SORRY TO SEE YOU GO – YOU'VE BEEN ONE HELLUVA ADMINISTRATOR.
THANKS, DUKE! I'D LOVE TO STAY ON, BUT MY WORK IS DONE HERE! IT'S TIME TO BE MOVIN' ON!
HAVE YOU SENT WORD OF YOUR ARRIVAL TO YOUR STATE-SIDE LOVED ONES?
SURE HAVE!
"..SEE YA FRIDAY. FONDLY, LT. GOV. HARRIS."
YEA!!
SO LONG, ACE! TAKE CARE OF THAT TAN OF YOURS, NOW, HEAR?
DON'T WORRY, UNCLE DUKE – I'M AN EXPERT AT TAN MAINTENANCE!
HAVE A GOOD FLIGHT, SIR. WE'LL MISS YOU!
THANK YOU, MACARTHUR. AND THANKS AGAIN FOR THAT GREAT TRIBUTE THIS MORNING!
TRIBUTE? WHAT TRIBUTE?
MACARTHUR AND THE ENTIRE STAFF CAME DOWN TO TELL ME THEY THOUGHT I WAS THE BEST LT. GOVERNOR IN THE ISLAND'S HISTORY!
WE'RE EVEN THINKING OF RETIRING HIS DECK CHAIR!
HECK, I ONLY DID MY JOB!
PAN AM

MACARTHUR, DO YOU EVER GET THE IMPRESSION THAT WASHINGTON DOESN'T EVEN KNOW WHERE WE ARE?
YES, SIR. I'VE HAD THAT IMPRESSION FOR YEARS!

I CAN'T BELIEVE IT! — IT'S BEEN FOUR MONTHS SINCE I REQUESTED EMERGENCY AID FOR SAMOA! WHAT DO I HAVE TO DO TO GET ACTION — DECLARE WAR!?

HEEY... HEEY! THAT'S IT!
SIR?

MACARTHUR, SEE THAT CRUISE SHIP OUT THERE?..
NO, SIR! I DON'T SEE ANYTHING!

MACARTHUR, IF I'M NOT MISTAKEN, THAT SHIP OUT THERE IS VIOLATING OUR WATERS!
SIR, IT'S A CRUISE SHIP OUT OF LONG BEACH — THAT KIND OF TROUBLE WE DON'T NEED!

I KNOW, MAC, BUT I'VE HAD IT! THE TIME HAS COME TO MAKE THOSE YO-YO'S IN WASHINGTON SIT UP AND NOTICE US! I WANT THAT SHIP SEIZED!

SEIZED?! GOVERNOR, WHO AM I GOING TO SEND TO SEIZE IT?! WE DON'T EVEN HAVE A COAST GUARD!

BY GUM, I WISH I COULD BE GOING WITH YOU!
AW, C'MON, GOVERNOR!

GOLLY! WHAT AN EVENING! — THAT VIEW OF PAGO PAGO IS REALLY SOMETHING, HUH?

HEY, LOOK! — A COLORFUL NATIVE OUTRIGGER!
THEY'RE WAVING, TOO!

AHOY! YOU ARE TRESPASSING IN SAMOAN WATERS! HEAVE TO AND STRIKE YOUR COLORS!

HEE, HEE! — DON'T FALL FOR IT! THEY'RE PROBABLY SELLING BANANAS!
YOU HAVE THE RIGHT TO REMAIN SILENT..

I REPEAT! STRIKE YOUR COLORS!
GO AWAY! YOU'RE BOTHERING THE GUESTS!

OKAY— YOU ASKED FOR IT!
BLAM!

WHAT WAS THAT?

THAT WAS A WARNING SHOT ACROSS YOUR BOW!
HEE, HEE! OKAY-WE SURRENDER! COME ON UP FOR A DRINK!

THE DEED IS DONE?! THE SHIP IS SEIZED?!
YES, SIR. YOU'VE GOT YOURSELF A BONA FIDE INTERNATIONAL INCIDENT!

WELL SPARKED, MacARTHUR!
AND YOU DON'T HAVE TO WORRY ABOUT A POSSIBLE DIPLOMATIC SOLUTION—ALL THE PHONES ARE OUT AGAIN!

DIPLOMATIC SOLUTION?.. HOLY COW...

YOU DON'T THINK THEY'LL TRY DIPLOMACY, DO YOU?!
WELL, I DON'T THINK WE WANT TO TAKE ANY CHANCES.

GOOD EVENING! LATE TODAY, THE U.S. COAST GUARD REPORTED THAT AN AMERICAN CRUISE SHIP HAS BEEN SEIZED BY THE TERRITORIAL GOVERNMENT OF SAMOA.

THE REASON FOR THE SEIZURE IS UNKNOWN, BUT INFORMED PAGO PAGO SOURCES REPORT THAT IN SAMOA, THIS SORT OF BEHAVIOR GOES ON ALL THE TIME!

THERE IS NO RESPONSE YET FROM THE WHITE HOUSE, BUT PRESIDENT FORD WILL BE MEETING MOMENTARILY WITH THE NATIONAL SECURITY COUNCIL TO DISCUSS THE VARIOUS OPTIONS.

STOMP 'EM! STOMP 'EM!!
THANK YOU, HENRY. HOW DO THE REST OF YOU FEEL?

WE STILL CAN'T REACH THE GOVERNOR, MR. PRESIDENT—THE PHONES ARE ALL OUT! AND SO FAR, RADIO SAMOA HAS BEEN SILENT!
WHAP!

HMM... I DON'T LIKE THE SOUND OF THAT!.. COLONEL, DO YOU HAVE ANY NEW INTELLIGENCE ON THE CONDITION OF THE HOSTAGES?
ZIP!!

WELL, SIR, OUR LATEST REPORTS INDICATE THAT MOST OF THE PASSENGERS ARE UP ON THE DECK PLAYING SHUFFLEBOARD.
ZIP!
SPROING!
GBTrudeau

ARE THEY BEING TORTURED?
IN MY OPINION, YES.

MR. PRESIDENT, IN MY VIEW, VE MUST DRAW THE LINE AGAINST AGGRESSION! VE MUST PUT THE VORLD ON NOTICE—NO MORE MR. NICE PAPER TIGER!
WHAP!
ZIP!

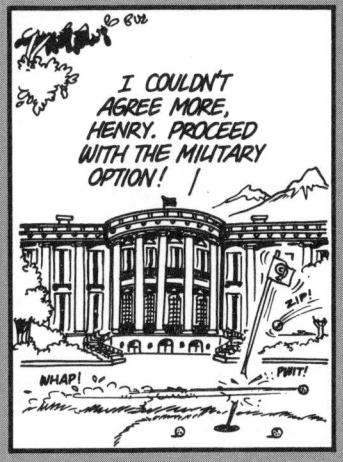
I COULDN'T AGREE MORE, HENRY. PROCEED WITH THE MILITARY OPTION!
ZIP!
WHAP!
PWIT!

YES, SIR!.. HELLO?.. GET ME DEFENSE! ...JIM? THIS IS HENRY!
TALL IN THE SADDLE...
WHAP!
BOP!
BIP!
GBTrudeau

BEGIN OPERATION FREQUENT MANHOOD!!
..WE RIDE AGAIN!
FWIP!
WHAP!
WHAP.
BLIP!
ZIP!

ANY FINAL QUESTIONS?.. YES, WHAT IS IT, MARINE?
SIR, WHEN WE HIT SAMOA, ARE WE EXPECTED TO SUSTAIN HEAVY CASUALTIES?

WELL, I CAN'T SAY FOR SURE, BOY!—BUT IN THE LONG RUN, THAT DOESN'T REALLY CONCERN US! THERE'S A LARGER PRINCIPLE INVOLVED HERE!
WHAT LARGER PRINCIPLE, SIR?

THERE ISN'T TIME TO EXPLAIN, SOLDIER!—WE'VE GOT A BEACHHEAD TO ESTABLISH!
BUT, SIR..

LET'S GO, MARINES!
NOT UNTIL YOU EXPLAIN!
I'M WITH YOU—IT'S GOTTA BE FOR SOMETHING I BELIEVE IN!
WHOMP!
CRUNCH!
GBTrudeau

POW!
BLAM
LET'S GO!!
WHOMP!
CRUNCH!

SERGEANT! TAKE A DETAIL UP THE...
OH, WOW!- MARINES! WELCOME TO FIJI, FELLAHS!

FIJI?
YEAH, FIJI! WHERE'D JA THINK YOU WERE, SAMOA?

FIJI?
HEY! AREN'T YOU GONNA LEAVE A RESIDUAL FORCE?
G B Trudeau

SIR?.. EXCUSE ME!..
MON DIEU! MARINES!

UM..IS THIS SAMOA?!
NON, NON! C'EST TAHITI!

TAHITI?! BOY, ARE WE GONNA BE LATE! WE WERE DUE IN SAMOA AT 1400 HOURS!
YEAH, YEAH, I KNOW, I KNOW!

MONSIEUR? AVEZ-VOUS A TELEPHONE JE COULD USE?!
SORRY.
G B Trudeau

GENERAL? THIS IS THE PRESIDENT! WHAT'S THE LATEST UPDATE ON OPERATION FREQUENT MANHOOD?!

MISSION IS PROCEEDING AS PLANNED, SIR! THE MARINE TASK FORCE WILL BE ESTABLISHING A BEACHHEAD ..UM..ANY MINUTE NOW!

"ANY MINUTE NOW"?
G B Trudeau

YOU CAN'T MISS IT, CHIEF — IT'S JUST PAST THE EQUATOR!

YOU GUYS WAIT HERE— I'LL CHECK IT OUT.
ZIP!

-SIGH-

EXCUSE ME, SIR— THIS ISN'T BY ANY CHANCE SAMOA, IS IT?!
YOU BET YOUR SWEET BOOTS IT IS!

PRAISE THE LORD!!
WHAT TOOK YOU CLOWNS SO LONG?
©BTrudeau

WHAT DO YOU MEAN, YOU JUST LET THEM GO?!
WELL, WE WAITED A WHOLE WEEK, MAN! THE HOSTAGES WERE BECOMING UNRULY..

YOU'RE BLUFFING! YOU COULDN'T HAVE LET THEM GO!
TAKE A LOOK BEHIND YOU. THE SHIP'S A COUPLE MILES OUT TO SEA!

WHA..? HEY.. NO.. NO!
'FRAID SO! DESPITE YOUR BEST EFFORTS, AN INTERNATIONAL INCIDENT HAS BEEN AVERTED!

COME BACK! COME BACK!
'COURSE, YOU COULD ALWAYS CALL IN AN AIR STRIKE...
©BTrudeau

YES, SIR, YOUR NAME'S DEFINITELY GONE. YOU'VE BEEN DROPPED FROM THE MASTHEAD!
IMPOSSIBLE! I'M THE ROLLING STONE NATIONAL AFFAIRS EDITOR! I'M INDISPENSABLE!

I WOULD HAVE THOUGHT SO, SIR.
WENNER WILL PAY FOR THIS! WHEN THAT HITS THE STANDS, HE'S GOING TO HAVE AN ANGRY MOB OF MY FANS TO ANSWER TO!

I THINK HE ANTICIPATED YOU, SIR. YOU'VE BEEN LISTED IN THE OBIT COLUMN.
WHAT?!

"HACK WRITER, PRESUMED DEAD AT 45..."
CALL THE AIRPORT.
©BTrudeau

DID YOU CONFIRM MY RESERVATION, MAC?
YES, SIR. YOUR FLIGHT LEAVES AT 8:30.
AND YOU'VE NOTIFIED ZONKER?
YES, SIR. HE'S ALREADY IN SAN FRANCISCO. HE AWAITS YOUR WORD TO BEGIN ORGANIZING A PROTEST RALLY!
PROTEST RALLY? ON MY BEHALF?
YES, SIR. MR. HARRIS BELIEVES THAT IN A FEW DAYS YOUR EDITOR WILL BE ON BENDED KNEES, BEGGING YOU TO RETURN!
MR. HARRIS ALSO BELIEVES IN THE EASTER BUNNY.
WELL, HE SEEMED PRETTY SURE..
..AND REMIND THE ASSISTANT ATTORNEY-GENERAL HE'S TO SCRUB DOWN MY ROWING SCULL BEFORE I RETURN!
YES, EXCELLENCY.
GOT ALL THAT?
YES, SIR. HERE'S YOUR THERMOS OF FROZEN BANANA DAIQUIRIS FOR THE FLIGHT, SIR.
THANKS.. WELL, GUESS THAT ABOUT DOES IT...
YES, SIR.
SEE YA SOON, MAC— KEEP THE NATIVES OFF MY LTD!
I'LL TRY, SIR. HAVE A GOOD TIME.
AHEM!
IS THAT YOU, DUKE?
YES, I THOUGHT SO. I MUST SAY YOU MADE VERY GOOD TIME, DUKE— THE ISSUE'S ONLY BEEN OUT FOR A WEEK..
TELL ME, DUKE, WHAT WAS IT THAT GALLED YOU THE MOST? WAS IT BEING CUT FROM THE STAFF? LOSING YOUR SALARY? OR WAS IT JUST THE PUBLIC DISGRACE? WAS THAT IT, DUKE, WAS THAT IT?
I'VE COME TO KILL YOU.
YOU POOR, DESPERATE FOOL.

LOOK, BOY WONDER, YOU CAN'T TAKE ME OFF THE MASTHEAD!—MY READERS WILL HAVE YOUR HEAD!
WHAT READERS?! YOU HAVEN'T PRODUCED AN ARTICLE IN YEARS!

DUKE, IF YOU WANT TO STAY WITH THIS ORGANIZATION, YOU'RE GOING TO HAVE TO START PAYING SOME DUES AGAIN! I'M REASSIGNING YOU TO THE ROCK 'N' ROLL BEAT!

ROCK 'N' ROLL BEAT?! ARE YOU MAD!
YOUR FIRST PROJECT WILL BE AN UPDATE REPORT ON CHER.

A WRITER OF MY STATURE?!
CHER'S COOL—SHE WON'T MIND.
GBTrudeau

YOU'RE QUITE MAD, YOU KNOW. NO WAY I'M GOING TO COVER CHER!
YES, YOU ARE, DUKE! OR YOU DISAPPEAR FROM THE MASTHEAD FOR GOOD!

YOU PUP! YOU CAN'T DO THIS TO ME!
WHY? WHERE YOU GOING TO GO, DUKE—"LADIES HOME JOURNAL"?

DO YOU HAVE ANY IDEA WHAT EVEN A TEMPORARY GREGG AND CHER GIG COULD DO TO MY REP?
TEMPORARY? WHO SAID ANYTHING ABOUT TEMPORARY? I'M MAKING YOU BUREAU CHIEF!

GREGG AND CHER BUREAU CHIEF?!
AND I'M ONLY DOING IT BECAUSE WE'RE OLD FRIENDS.
GBTrudeau

WELL, DUKE, I'M SURE YOU'RE ANXIOUS TO MEET THE REST OF OUR CHER TASK FORCE!
CHER WHAT?!
Ch

MICHELLE HERE IS IN CHARGE OF THE MOBILE SURVEILLANCE UNITS... AND THAT'S ANNIE, WHO'S AN EXPERT ON CHER'S MEN. SHE ALSO CO-ORDINATES PAPARAZZI ACTIVITIES.
HI.

LESTER OVER THERE IS OUR INSIDE MAN..
INSIDE MAN?
YEAH—I'M A CLOSE PERSONAL FRIEND OF CHER'S DERMATOLOGIST.

WELL, I'M SURE YOU'VE GOT A LOT TO TALK ABOUT!
I'LL GET YOU FOR THIS..
WE GREW UP TOGETHER!
GBTrudeau

HEY, OLD MAN, WHAT'S HAPPENING?
ZONKER! MAN, AM I GLAD TO SEE YOU!
WHAT'S GOING ON? I UNDERSTAND FROM YAWN YOU'RE HEADING UP A SPECIAL CHER TASK FORCE!
TREMENDOUS HONOR, JUST TREMENDOUS! I'M IN CHARGE OF AN ELITE CORPS OF RAVING IDIOTS!
OH, DEAR.
AND THEY'RE NOTHING COMPARED TO MR. AND MRS. ALLMAN THEMSELVES! CHECK OUT THIS RECENT CHER INTERVIEW!
"GREGG WAS SO THOUGHTFUL AT OUR WEDDING— HE STAYED OFF DRUGS THE WHOLE AFTERNOON."
NOW, YOU KNOW HOW I FEEL ABOUT SICKIES..
GB Trudeau
HER SECRETARY'S GETTING HER..
GOOD. NOW, IF YOU JUST TAKE IT EASY, YOU'LL GET A GOOD INTER-VIEW!
HELLO?
OH..UH..GOOD MORNING, MRS. ALLMAN. ROLLING STONE MAGAZINE HERE. I'D LIKE TO ASK YOU A FEW QUESTIONS IF THAT'S OKAY..
YEAH... ..SURE.. WHAT DO YOU WANT TO KNOW?
OKAY, NOW, DON'T SCARE HER, DUKE. START OFF EASY...
WHAT'S YOUR FAVORITE COLOR?
GOLD.
GOOD! NOW PICK UP THE PACE!
GB Trudeau
MAC! GOOD TO HEAR FROM YOU, MY MAN! HOW'S EVERYTHING ON MY FAVORITE ARCHIPELAGO?
Che
WELL, GOVERNOR, THERE'S BEEN AN INTERESTING DEVELOP-MENT! THE MINISTER OF ECOLOGY WAS OUT TAKING CORE SAMPLES FROM THE OCEAN FLOOR TODAY WHEN HE RUPTURED WHAT HE BELIEVES IS A LARGE DEPOSIT OF OIL!
OIL?! IN SAMOA?! BUT THAT'S CRAZY, MACARTHUR!
Che
GB Trudeau
WELL, HE SEEMS PRETTY SURE, SIR.

OIL?! IN PAGO PAGO BAY?!
THAT'S RIGHT— PERHAPS BILLIONS OF BARRELS WORTH!

DO YOU REALIZE WHAT THIS MEANS FOR OUR LITTLE CLUSTER OF ISLANDS? WHY, SAMOA WILL PROBABLY BE ABLE TO JOIN OPEC!

YES, BOY, MY PEOPLE HAVE A BRIGHT, NEW FUTURE AHEAD OF THEM! BEFORE THE YEAR IS OUT, THERE'LL BE A 21" SCREEN COLOR TELEVISION IN EVERY POT!

AND FOR YOU?
ONLY A MODEST GOVERNMENT PENSION, OF COURSE!

..AND I WANT THAT EFFICIENCY STUDY ON THE ART DEPARTMENT TYPED UP TODAY, OKAY?!.. GOOD, NOW IS THERE ANYTHING ELSE?

YES—DUKE'S OUT HERE. HE SAYS HE'S ABDICATING THE GREGG AND CHER BUREAU CHIEFTAINCY.

HE MOST CERTAINLY IS NOT! TELL HIM TO GET HIS TAIL BACK ON THAT STORY OR HE'S GOING TO FIND HIMSELF COLLECTING UNEMPLOYMENT CHECKS NEXT WEEK!

DON'T BET ON IT!
DUKE, I HAVEN'T THE TIME FOR THIS!

SO, BOY WONDER—WE FINALLY PART WAYS!
YES, DUKE, BUT IT CONSOLES ME TO KNOW THAT MY LOSS IS THE OIL INDUSTRY'S GAIN.

LOOK, KID, I KNOW YOUR CIRCULATION IS GOING TO TAKE A BEATING WITH MY LEAVING, AND I WANT YOU TO KNOW I'M REAL SORRY!
NO HARD FEELINGS, DUKE, I ASSURE YOU!

YOU'RE ANGRY, THOUGH, I CAN TELL! THE BITTER TRUTH IS THAT I'M THE MAINSTAY OF THIS RAG! SURE, YOU'RE ANGRY— WHO COULD BLAME YOU?
DUKE, I AM NOT ANGRY! BUT I AM BUSY!

IT'S NO USE PLEADING WITH ME TO STAY...
DUKE, WILL YOU GET THE HELL OUT OF HERE?!

GO
MR. HARRIS COULDN'T COME, SIR?
NOPE. HE HAD TO BE GETTING BACK TO WALDEN..
THAT'S TOO BAD—WE COULD USE A COOL HEAD IN THE DAYS AHEAD..
ARE WE TALKING ABOUT THE SAME PERSON?
GOVERNOR, WHEN THE BIG OIL MONEY REALLY HITS SAMOA, WE'RE GOING TO NEED ALL THE HELP WE CAN GET!
ANY VISIBLE SIGNS OF CHANGE YET, MAC?
PAGO PAGO AIRPORT
WELL, SIR, THE FIRST HOOKER'S ARRIVED..
PROGRESS! THERE'S NO STOPPING IT!
10-18
©BTrudeau
THE BIG OIL MEN IN TOWN YET, MAC?
OH YES, SIR—THEY'RE ALL STAYING AT THE AMERICANA. THEY CAN'T WAIT TO SEE YOU!
HEE, HEE! I'LL BET!—WE'VE GOT A HOT LITTLE CONCESSION ON OUR HANDS!
I HAVE TO SAY, THOUGH, SIR, THEY'VE BEEN BEHAVING RATHER BADLY! THE MANAGER'S GOING OUT OF HIS MIND!
WELL, MAC, YOU HAVE TO UNDERSTAND..
HIS COMPLAINT SAYS THEY'VE BEEN SINGING AT ALL HOURS, BREAKING GLASSES, SWIMMING IN THE NUDE...
MAC, THEY'VE JUST HAD A WHOLE SEASON OF PRICE CONTROLS!
..OGLING VOLCANO VIRGINS..
©BTrudeau
GOVERNOR, A MR. ANDREWS FROM UNIVERSAL PETROLEUM WAS IN TO SEE YOU. HE SAID HIS COMPANY WAS PREPARED TO SHOW ITS "GRATITUDE" FOR ANY CONSIDERATION YOU MIGHT GIVE HIS OFFER!
ITS GRATITUDE, HUH?..
YES, SIR. SOUNDED LIKE A BRIBE TO ME, SO I THREW HIM OUT.
YOU WHAT?!
ON HIS EAR, SIR! I KNEW YOU WOULDN'T STAND FOR IT.
IT'S THOSE DAMN MISSIONARIES!
AND I RESPECT YOU FOR IT, SIR!
©BTrudeau

WELL, ANDREWS, YOUR COMPANY'S OFFER SEEMS QUITE SINCERE, BUT I MUST WARN YOU BEFORE WE CONTINUE.

I HAPPEN TO THINK THE WORLD OF THE SAMOAN PEOPLE, AND I MUST PUT THEIR INTERESTS ABOVE EVERYTHING ELSE IN MY DELIBERATIONS!
I UNDERSTAND, SIR..

SUBSTANTIVE FINANCIAL BENEFITS, EMPLOYMENT OPPORTUNITIES, ASSURANCES THAT THE FRAGILE ECO-SYSTEM OF THE REEF WILL BE PRESERVED..
THEIRS FOR THE ASKING, SIR!

FINE. NOW ABOUT MY FEE...
GOVERNOR, THINK OF ME AS SANTA!
GBTrudeau

SIR, MR. ANDREWS TOLD ME THAT YOU ALL REACHED AN AGREEMENT WHICH... INCLUDED CERTAIN "BENEFITS" FOR YOU!
WHAT OF IT, MAC?

WELL, SIR, I FEEL IT'S MY PAINFUL DUTY TO REPORT IT TO THE AUTHORITIES.
MAC, WHO'S THE HIGHEST AUTHORITY ON THIS ISLAND?

YOU ARE, SIR.
SO REPORT IT TO ME.

SIR, I SUSPECT YOU OF ACCEPTING A BRIBE.
I'LL LOOK INTO IT.
GBTrudeau

MAC?
ALL RIGHT, BOYS — THE GOVERNOR WILL TAKE YOUR FIRST QUESTION!

GOVERNOR, HOW MUCH WILL UNIVERSAL PETROLEUM BE PAYING SAMOA FOR ITS OIL CONCESSION?
IT WAS MY PRIVILEGE TO BE ABLE TO NEGOTIATE A DEAL IN EXCESS OF $500 MILLION!

SIR, IS IT TRUE THAT YOU FAVORED UNIVERSAL PETROLEUM BECAUSE...
I FAVORED NO ONE! AS A SIMPLE, CIVIL SERVANT, I HAD NO VESTED INTEREST.

OF COURSE, SIR, BUT WE CHECKED YOUR BANK ACCOUNT AND...
MAC?
THAT'S IT, BOYS. WE APPRECIATE YOUR COMING!
GBTrudeau

GOVERNOR, I PICKED UP THAT EXTRA THREE GALLONS OF VODKA YOU WANTED, SO IT LOOKS LIKE WE'VE GOT EVERYTHING FOR YOUR NEW YEAR'S PARTY!
WHAT ABOUT THE COORS?
WELL, SIR, THEIR WEST COAST DISTRIBUTOR HAS ASSURED ME THAT TEN CASES WILL GET HERE ON TIME..
AND THE COKE?
SHOULD BE ARRIVING IN TOMORROW'S DIPLOMATIC POUCH!
GOOD! THEN EVERY-THING'S SET! YOU CALL THE MINISTER OF MARIJUANA YET?
YES, SIR—HE'LL BE HERE AT EIGHT O'CLOCK TO SET UP. THE GUESTS WILL START ARRIVING AT NINE-THIRTY!
GUESTS?! WHAT GUESTS?!
UM.. YOU KNOW, GUESTS.. PEOPLE
YOU INVITED GUESTS?!
I THOUGHT IT'D BE MORE FUN, SIR..

CHINA, MAC! HENRY'S ASKING ME TO GO TO CHINA!
REALLY?! WHAT A WONDERFUL OPPORTUNITY FOR YOU, SIR!

BUSH HAS BEEN RECALLED, AND THE PRESIDENT WANTS ME TO TAKE OVER AS TOP ENVOY!
CHINA'S GOOD FORTUNE IS SAMOA'S MISFORTUNE, SIR. YOU WILL BE SORELY MISSED BY ALL OF US!

I'VE BEEN DIRECTED TO APPEAR AT A SENATE CONFIRMATION HEARING NEXT MONTH..
YOURS HAS BEEN A CAREER OF PUBLIC SERVICE WHICH SAMOANS WILL NOT SOON FORGET!

DO YOU THINK I SHOULD ACCEPT, MAC?
LET US NOT SAY ALOHA, SIR — BUT RATHER, AU REVOIR!
GBTrudeau

MAC, I THINK I'VE FIGURED OUT WHY THE PRESIDENT'S SENDING ME TO CHINA...

FORD'S TOUGHENING UP, SEE, PLAYING TO THE CONSERVATIVES! TO SHOW THAT HE'S NOT BEING DUPED BY THE REDS, HE'S SENDING A NO-NONSENSE CAREER DIPLOMAT TO PEKING TO INSURE THAT DETENTE IS A TWO-WAY STREET!

SOUNDS REASONABLE. BUT WHY YOU?
MY RECORD HERE, MAC — I'VE SHOWN I KNOW HOW TO WORK WITH MINORITIES!

"MINORITIES"?
AND THAT'S IMPORTANT, MAC — THOSE CHINESE ARE AN ESPECIALLY TRICKY PEOPLE!
GBTrudeau

THE IMPORTANT THING TO REMEMBER ABOUT THE CHINESE, MAC, IS THAT THEIR PRIMARY CONCERN IS USSR HEGEMONY.

THE CHINESE BELIEVE IN THE INEVITABILITY OF WAR WITH THE RUSKIES. BUT THEY ALSO HAVE AN ABIDING CONVICTION THAT THEY WILL PREVAIL!

THEIR POSITION IS SUMMED UP IN A POPULAR MAOIST SAYING: "THERE IS GREAT DISORDER UNDER HEAVEN AND THE SITUATION IS EXCELLENT."

SOUNDS LIKE ONE OF YOUR PARTIES, SIR.
YEAH, THAT'S WHY I THINK WE'RE GOING TO HIT IT OFF.
GBTrudeau

A FARE-WELL GIFT? FOR ME?!
YES, SIR – I TOOK UP A COLLECTION FROM ALL 7,652 SAMOAN GOVERNMENT EMPLOYEES!
AW.. MAC, YOU SHOULDN'T HAVE..
THE RESPONSE WAS TERRIFIC, SO WE GOT YOU SOMETHING REALLY SPECIAL– AND APPROPRIATE!
MAC... I'M.. I'M.. OVER-WHELMED!
CHOPSTICKS!
NO, I'M NOT.
THEY'RE SOLID WOOD, SIR!
G B Trudeau

MAC, BEFORE WE GO, I'D LIKE YOU TO TYPE UP A LIST OF MY MAJOR ACHIEVEMENTS – TO SHOW THE COMMITTEE.
ACHIEVE-MENTS, SIR?
RIGHT. A MODEST INVENTORY OF THE MANY SIGNIFICANT CONTRIBUTIONS MADE DURING MY TENURE IN SAMOA!
UM..
OH, C'MON, MAC, DON'T LOOK SO PUT OUT. IT WON'T TAKE YOU THAT LONG!
I WAS JUST THINKING THAT, SIR..
GOD, I PITY THE POOR SUCKER WHO'S GOTTA FOLLOW MY ACT!
G B Trudeau

HOW'S THAT LIST OF MY MAJOR ACHIEVEMENTS SHAPING UP, MACARTHUR?
WELL, SIR, I'M MAKING PROGRESS..
WHY DON'T YOU READ IT BACK TO ME – I PROBABLY SHOULD CHECK IT FOR ACCURACY.
"A COMPREHENSIVE LIST OF THE MANY ACHIEVEMENTS IN-FLICTED ON SAMOA BY HIS EXCELLENCY, GOVERNOR DUKE.."
"INFLICTED"?! MAC, YOU LUNKHEAD – YOU DON'T MEAN "IN-FLICTED"!
WHAT – IS THE TENSE WRONG?
AND YOU CALL YOURSELF FLUENT IN ENGLISH!
G B Trudeau

LISTEN, GEORGE, I'LL TELL YOU WHY I CALLED— I'M TRYING TO CRANK UP FOR THOSE HEARINGS. ANY IDEA WHAT I CAN EXPECT?
"MAJOR ACHIEVEMENTS OF GOVERNOR DUKE:"

WELL, YES, DUKE, I DID TALK TO SOME OF THE COMMITTEE MEMBERS YESTERDAY. THEY'RE GOING TO WANT TO HEAR ABOUT RECENT ALLEGATIONS OF EXTORTION AND OIL KICK-BACKS..
UH-HUH.
TAP! TAP!

IN ADDITION, YOU'LL PROBABLY BE ASKED ABOUT TAX EVASION, MISAPPROPRIATION OF FEDERAL FUNDS, YOUR USE OF MARTIAL LAW, AND REPORTS OF PERSONAL DRUG TRAFFICKING.
I SEE.
TAP! TAP! TAP!

SO THESE ARE THE KINDS OF THINGS I'D BE ON THE LOOK-OUT FOR..
RIGHT. WELL, THANKS, GEORGE.
"1. COMPLETE RESTORATION OF THE EXECUTIVE MANSION PATIO BAR.."
GBTrudeau

GOVERNOR, IF YOU HAVE NO OBJECTIONS, I'D LIKE TO START WITH A FEW INQUIRIES ABOUT THE DISPOSITION OF YOUR PERSONAL FINANCES.

THERE HAVE BEEN SOME ALLEGATIONS—UNGROUNDED, I'M SURE—CONCERNING OIL LEASE KICK-BACKS IN SAMOA. I'D JUST LIKE TO CLEAR THOSE UP...

GULP!
CERTAINLY, SENATOR.
GBTrudeau

HE KNOWS!
SSSHH!
WHAT WAS THAT, YOUNG MAN?

SENATOR, I DON'T KNOW WHAT YOU'RE GETTING AT WITH THIS LINE OF QUESTIONING! MY PERSONAL FINANCES ARE A MATTER OF PUBLIC RECORD!

YOU'RE QUITE CERTAIN, GOVERNOR? NO SECRET ACCOUNTS? A SWISS BANK ACCOUNT, PERHAPS?

A SWISS BANK ACCOUNT?! ARE YOU CRAZY, SENATOR?!
HELVETIAN SAVINGS AND LOAN, ACCOUNT NUMBER 51830.

OH, MAC...
WE'RE UNDER OATH, SIR.
GBTrudeau

GOVERNOR, I HAVE TO SAY, YOUR ACCOUNTING OF RECENT CAPITAL GAINS HAS BEEN HIGHLY IMAGINATIVE. HOWEVER, THE SUDDEN INFLUX OF INCOME SUGGESTS AN EXPLANATION OTHER THAN THAT PROVIDED.
SOMETHING STINKS HERE, GOVERNOR—YOU KNOW IT AND I KNOW IT, BUT THE REAL TRAGEDY OF IT ALL IS THAT NEITHER OF US CARES.
IT'S PART OF THE GAME, GOVERNOR. THERE'S SOMETHING ABOUT PUBLIC SERVICE THAT SEEMS TO BREED CONTEMPT FOR INTEGRITY, AND I CAN'T EXPECT YOU TO BE THE EXCEPTION. SO GO ON, TAKE THE POST IN CHINA—YOU AND WE COULD BOTH DO WORSE.
YOU'RE A VERY CYNICAL MAN, SENATOR.
TELL ME ABOUT IT.
GBTrudeau
MACARTHUR, THE CONDUCT OF THAT COMMITTEE CHAIRMAN ABSOLUTELY SICKENED ME!
HE JUST ASSUMED THERE WAS SOMETHING IRREGULAR ABOUT MY FINANCES, ACCUSED ME OF BEING ON THE TAKE, AND THEN JUST SHRUGGED IT OFF!
I TELL YOU, MACARTHUR, THINGS ARE DETERIORATING FAST IN THIS TOWN—THAT WAS A CHILLING EXPERIENCE!
NOT TO MENTION A CLOSE CALL!
I HAVEN'T THE FAINTEST IDEA WHAT YOU'RE TALKING ABOUT.
GBTrudeau
THANK YOU, MR. SECRETARY, THANK YOU VERY MUCH!
GOOD NEWS, MAC?
YES, SIR—I'M TO BE THE NEW GOVERNOR! IT SEEMS THEY HAD A LITTLE TROUBLE SCARING UP A REPLACEMENT, SO I'VE BEEN APPOINTED!
THAT'S GREAT, MAC—REALLY GREAT!
OF COURSE, IT WON'T BE EASY FOR YOU—NOT BY A LONG SHOT! SAMOANS WILL QUITE UNDERSTANDABLY BE LOOKING FOR A BIG LET-DOWN AFTER MY PERFORMANCE!
YES, SIR—YOURS WILL BE LARGE TENNIS SNEAKERS TO FILL.
NOW, DON'T BE AFRAID TO CABLE, MAC.. IN A JAM, I MEAN..
GBTrudeau

2 PEKING

1976-1977

AS FAR AS DETENTE IS CONCERNED, WE'LL JUST HAVE TO SEE WHAT DEVELOPS. I'M SURE MY CHINESE HOSTS WOULD BE AS SADDENED TO SEE U.S. GUNBOATS STEAMING UP THE YANGTZE AS I WOULD BE.
SIR, DO YOU EXPECT TO CONTINUE INGESTING RECREATIONAL DRUGS DURING YOUR STAY IN CHINA?
ABSOLUTELY— I INTEND TO STRESS CONTINUITY IN MY PERSONAL HABITS!
I HAVE ALSO BEEN ASSURED BY MY ATTENDING MEDICAL OFFICER THAT HE'LL BE ABLE TO FILL THE PHARMACEUTICAL REQUIREMENTS OF THE LIAISON OFFICE SOCIAL FUNCTIONS.
BUT, SIR, AS YOU MUST KNOW, YOUR CHINESE HOSTS FROWN ON ALL FORMS OF EXCESS.
MY CHINESE HOSTS CAN GO SUCK EGGS.
©BTrudeau

A LIGHT DRIZZLE GREETED THE NEW CHIEF OF THE U.S. MISSION AS HIS PLANE TOUCHED DOWN HERE AT PEKING INTERNATIONAL AIRPORT..
THE PASSENGER DOOR OF THE AIRCRAFT HAS BEEN OPENED, AND CHINESE OFFICIALS ARE NOW GATHERING ON THE RUNWAY TO MEET THE NEW TOP ENVOY.
THE GREETING IS EXPECTED TO BE STRAINED, AS AMBASSADOR DUKE IS KNOWN TO BE OPENLY SUSPICIOUS OF HIS CHINESE HOSTS.
COVER ME— I THINK I CAN MAKE THE LIMO!
BUT, SIR— IT'S ONLY AN HONOR GUARD..
©BTrudeau

A FURTHER GOAL OF MINE IS THE SPEEDY IMPLEMENTATION OF NORMALIZATION.
(A FURTHER GOAL OF HIS IS THE SPEEDY IMPLEMENTATION OF NORMALIZATION.)
LASTLY, I COME TO CHINA IN THE HOPE OF FULFILLING A LIFE-LONG AMBITION — DROPPING ACID ON THE GREAT WALL.
(LASTLY, HE WISHES YOU GOOD HEALTH AND LONG LIFE.)
IN CONCLUSION, LET ME JUST SAY THAT I LOOK FORWARD TO A NEW SPIRIT OF CO-OPERATION FROM OUR CHINESE FRIENDS. I SINCERELY HOPE IT WON'T BE NECESSARY TO SHELL ANY PAGODAS.
(HE ALSO WISHES YOUR WIFE GOOD HEALTH.)
(THANK HIM, AND ASK HIM IF HE'D LIKE TO SEE THE GREAT WALL.)
©BTrudeau

P'ING! WHAT ARE YOU DOING HERE?! YOU'RE SUPPOSED TO HAVE DRIVEN AMBASSADOR DUKE OVER TO THE WELCOMING BANQUET!

HE HASN'T COME DOWN YET, SIR.
HASN'T COME DOWN YET?! THE BANQUET STARTED AN HOUR AGO!

YES, SIR. WE THINK HE MIGHT HAVE FORGOTTEN. HIS TRANSLATOR JUST WENT UP TO GET HIM.
GBTrudeau

YOU'RE OFF TO A BAD START, MR. AMBASSADOR.
HOW'S THAT, HONEY?

HI. SORRY I'M LATE.
GOOD EVENING, MR. DUKE. I'M MR. LI, DEPUTY MINISTER OF PROTOCOL.

DELIGHTED, MR. LI. SAY, DO YOU KNOW ANYTHING ABOUT THIS SPEECH I'M SUPPOSED TO BE GIVING?..
YES, SIR— YOU WILL BE EXPECTED TO PARTICIPATE IN AN EXCHANGE OF TOASTS.

OKAY, WELL, WHOSE HEALTH SHOULD I BE TOASTING? SEEMS LIKE THEY'RE ALL SICK..
VICE PREMIER TENG.

I MEAN, THEY'VE REALLY BEEN DROPPING LIKE FLIES, HAVEN'T THEY?
WELL, IT'S MOSTLY THE LONG MARCH VETS..
GBTrudeau

(AND HE BRINGS THE BEST WISHES OF THE AMERICAN PEOPLE.)
YOU KNOW, WHEN I FIRST ARRIVED HERE, I WAS GIVEN MAO'S LITTLE RED BOOK..

(I THINK HE'S ABOUT TO MAKE A JOKE..)
WHEN I ASKED WHY IT WAS SO POPULAR, I WAS TOLD, "BETTER READ THAN DEAD!"

(THE JOKE HAS BEEN MADE, AND HE WILL BE EXPECTING YOU TO LAUGH AT IT. GO WILD.)

HA, HA HA, HA! HA! HEE HEE! HA! HO, HO!
BUT SERIOUSLY, FOLKS, I'M TICKLED PINKO TO BE HERE TONIGHT...
GBTrudeau

(A FINAL WORD OF CAUTION TO OUR AMERICAN FRIEND..)
THE VICE PREMIER RESPECTFULLY CAUTIONS THE U.S. ENVOY..
(THE WIND SWEEPING THROUGH THE TOWER HERALDS A RISING STORM IN THE MOUNTAINS.)
RE: THE SOVIETS, HE PROPOSES A STORM METAPHOR.
(IN CHINA, WE BASE OURSELVES ON INDEPENDENCE, SELF-RELIANCE, AND MILLET..)
OUR BASIC GOAL IS PEACE.
(PLUS RIFLES.)
OF COURSE, WE'RE NOBODY'S FOOLS. ENJOY YOUR DINNER.
GB Trudeau

YOU KNOW, MR. LI, MR. TENG'S SPEECH LEFT ME BAFFLED. WHAT EXACTLY WAS HE GETTING AT?
"THERE IS GREAT DISORDER UNDER HEAVEN, AND THE SITUATION IS EXCELLENT."
I SEE.. WELL, I'D HEARD THAT...
ARE YOU ENJOYING YOUR DINNER?
HUH?..OH, YEAH, ABSOLUTELY! ESPECIALLY THE VEGETABLES— I LOVE YOUR VEGETABLES.
AH, YES—THE VEGETABLES.
SPEAKING OF WHICH, HOW'S THE CHAIRMAN DOING?
"THERE IS CHAOS ON EARTH, AND HIS PULSE IS NORMAL."
GBTrudeau

TELL ME, MR. LI, HOW DOES THE FOREIGN MINISTRY VIEW NORMALIZATION NOW?
THE CHAIRMAN HAS A SAYING PERTINENT TO YOUR QUESTION.
WELL, I THOUGHT HE MIGHT..
IT IS THIS: "IN A SUITABLE TEMPERATURE, AN EGG BECOMES A CHICKEN, AND THERE ARE NO CHICKENS BORN OF STONES."
FASCINATING.. REALLY VERY FASCINATING..
GBTrudeau
YOU REALIZE, OF COURSE, THAT IT MAKES NO SENSE WHATSOEVER.
WELL, YOU KNOW, I'VE WONDERED ABOUT THAT..

BUILT IN THE THIRD CENTURY B.C. TO FEND OFF INVADING HUNS, THE GREAT WALL IS 1,500 MILES LONG..
1,500 MILES?!

YES, SIR.
THAT'S INCREDIBLE— SIMPLY INCREDIBLE!

MAN, THIS BABY MUST HAVE REALLY KICKED HELL OUT OF THE BALANCE OF POWER IN EASTERN ASIA!

HOW DO YOU MEAN, MR. DUKE?
WELL, SAY YOU'RE A HUN— LOOK AT IT FROM HIS POINT OF VIEW...

THERE YOU ARE, SWEEPING DOWN FROM THE NORTH— YOU'RE HOT, YOU'RE 10-0, YOU'RE SO CLOSE TO PEKING YOU CAN TASTE IT! SUDDENLY... THIS! INSTANT RETIREMENT.

YOU MAKE IT SOUND UNFAIR.
NO, NO, MY HAT'S OFF TO YOU— I CAN SEE NOW WHY WE HIRED YOU GUYS TO DO OUR RAILROADS.
G Brandon

"..AND BECAUSE MY CHINESE HOSTS WERE SO EAGER TO ORIENT ME, ENDLESS SIGHTSEEING BECAME MY MAJOR ACTIVITY."
"UNFORTUNATELY, THE GREATEST SIGHT OF ALL, THE CHAIRMAN HIMSELF, ELUDED ME FOR A SOLID MONTH. I BEGAN TO WONDER IF HE'D EVER SURFACE."
"THEN FINALLY LAST WEDNESDAY, AT 3:30 A.M., THE CALL CAME.."
HURRY, SIR—NO TIME TO WASTE!
ALRIGHT, ALRIGHT—JUST LET ME PUT MY PANTS ON, OKAY?!
GBTrudeau

TELL ME, HONEY—IS IT HARD TO CONVERSE WITH THE CHAIRMAN? I WAS TOLD HIS STROKE LEFT HIM WITH A SPEECH IMPAIRMENT..

YES, SIR. CHAIRMAN MAO HAS ALWAYS BEEN HARD TO UNDERSTAND BECAUSE HE SPEAKS AN OBSCURE RURAL DIALECT. AND NOW WITH THE STROKE, I SEEM TO BE THE ONLY TRANSLATOR WHO CAN STILL UNDERSTAND HIM.

NO KIDDING?.. MAN, THAT CERTAINLY LEAVES YOU WITH A HELL OF A RESPONSIBILITY, DOESN'T IT?

YES, SIR. IN A WAY, I'M SORT OF RUNNING THE COUNTRY.
I'LL KEEP THAT IN MIND.
GBTrudeau

..AND I BRING HIM GREETINGS FROM THE AMERICAN PEOPLE.
(AND HE BRINGS YOU GREETINGS FROM THE AMERICAN PEOPLE.)
(MMPHPH SPMUP LI MXZPQU!)

WHAT'D HE SAY?
THE CHAIRMAN SAYS IT GIVES HIM GREAT PLEASURE TO SEE HIS OLD FRIEND DAVID EISENHOWER AGAIN.

YOU MADE THAT UP, RIGHT? THINKING IT FUNNY?
I CALL THEM AS I HEAR THEM, SIR.
GBTrudeau

THE CHAIRMAN SAYS HE'S DELIGHTED TO SEE HIS OLD FRIEND DAVID EISENHOWER AGAIN.

I'D APPRECIATE IT GREATLY IF YOU'D EXPLAIN TO THE CHAIRMAN THAT I'M **NOT** DAVID EISENHOWER!
THE CHAIRMAN SAYS HE CAN'T GET OVER THE RESEMBLANCE.

NOW HOW DO YOU KNOW THAT?! THE MAN DIDN'T SAY A **WORD!**
THE CHAIRMAN'S EYES SPEAK VOLUMES.
(PHLPK SCHPZP!)

OH, YEAH? WHAT'S HE SAYING NOW?
HE WANTS TO KNOW WHY YOU DIDN'T BRING JULIE.

MR. CHAIRMAN, LET'S GET RIGHT TO THE POINT, SHALL WE? AS FAR AS OUR RELATIONS GO, THE NAME OF THE GAME HERE IS CONTINUITY, AND REAFFIRMATION OF SAME!

THE RECENT INSTABILITY IN YOUR TOP ECHELONS IS THUS A LITTLE ALARMING. QUITE FRANKLY, IT'S **DAMN** HARD TO TELL WHO'S IN CHARGE! TAKE TENG, FOR INSTANCE—WHAT'S BECOMING OF HIM?

(HE IS MAKING INQUIRIES ABOUT VICE PREMIER TENG.)

(GLXP?)
WHO?
OH, NO.. ALREADY?!

IS SOMETHING WRONG WITH THE SOUP, MR. DUKE?
YEAH, IT TASTES WEIRD.. WHAT IS IT?

IT'S THE SPECIALTY OF THE HOUSE, SIR—BIRD'S NEST SOUP!
BIRD'S NEST?! THAT'S REVOLTING!

WELL, IT'S SORT OF A MISNOMER, SIR. IT'S NOT REALLY MADE FROM BIRDS' NESTS..
GOOD LORD, I SHOULD HOPE NOT!..

IT'S ACTUALLY MUCUS FROM THE SALIVARY GLANDS OF..
DID I ASK?! DID I ASK?!

IS SOMETHING THE MATTER, SIR? YOU DON'T LOOK VERY WELL..
I KNEW I SHOULDN'T HAVE EATEN THIS SLOP! IT'S PACKED FULL OF TOXINS!

OH, NO, SIR— THAT'S JUST NOT POSSIBLE! THE FINEST CHEFS IN CHINA HAVE..
..POISONED ME! WITH RANCID CHINK CHOW! WHAT IS THIS! THE MINUTE I LET DOWN MY GUARD, YOU PEOPLE...

AAARRGGH!!
CRASH!

WAITER!
PEKING WILL BURN FOR THIS!! I SWEAR IT!
GBTrudeau

(ASK MR. DUKE TO ROLL UP HIS SHIRT SLEEVES!)
THE DOCTOR WOULD LIKE YOU TO ROLL UP YOUR SLEEVES, SIR.
HONEY, IT'S MY GUT THAT'S KICKING UP KING HELL, NOT MY DAMN ARMS!

SIR, HE WANTS TO TAKE YOUR PULSE! IN TRADITIONAL CHINESE MEDICINE, THE STUDY OF PULSES IS A PRIMARY DIAGNOSTIC PROCEDURE!
ALL RIGHT, BUT TELL HIM NOT TO GET ANY IDEAS ABOUT MY CUFF LINKS!

(HMMM..)
OKAY, DOC, WHAT HAVE I GOT?!

(ACUTE APPENDICITIS.)
SIR, YOU'LL BE GLAD TO HEAR IT'S NOT FOOD POISONING.
LUCKY THING FOR YOU, HONEY!
GBTrudeau

APPENDICITIS?!.. OH, LORD, WHY ME?!
TRY TO RELAX, SIR! THE DOCTOR HAS GONE TO CALL FOR AN AMBULANCE!

LISTEN, HONEY.. IF I'M GOING INTO SURGERY, I'M GOING TO NEED HELP! I WANT YOU TO CALL A FRIEND OF MINE!
CERTAINLY, SIR!

HE'S MY CONNECTION, MAURICE LeNEZ! HE CAN BE REACHED AT THE FRENCH EMBASSY! HAVE HIM COME TO THE HOSPITAL WITH HIS BEST STUFF!
STUFF? WHAT STUFF?

WHATEVER'S ON SPECIAL! HURRY! HERE'S A DIME!
I'M NOT GOING TO GET IN TROUBLE, AM I, SIR?
GBTrudeau

HONEY! WHERE'S MAURICE?! I THOUGHT I TOLD YOU TO HAVE HIM GET HIS TAIL DOWN HERE!
SIR, I CALLED MONSIEUR LeNEZ AT THE EMBASSY. HE SAID HE'D NEVER HEARD OF YOU!

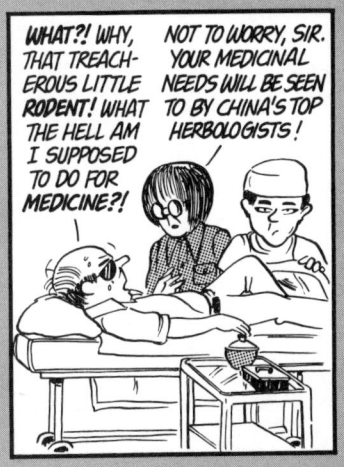
WHAT?! WHY, THAT TREACHEROUS LITTLE RODENT! WHAT THE HELL AM I SUPPOSED TO DO FOR MEDICINE?!
NOT TO WORRY, SIR. YOUR MEDICINAL NEEDS WILL BE SEEN TO BY CHINA'S TOP HERBOLOGISTS!

HERBOLOGISTS! MY GOD, THIS IS NO TIME FOR DILL WEED AND SAGE! I'M IN SERIOUS PAIN! I GOTTA HAVE SOME COKE!
SORRY, SIR— YOU'RE NOT PERMITTED SNACKS.

LET ME SEE IF I CAN EXPLAIN THIS TO YOU..
(HE'S HOT AS A PISTON, DOCTOR!)
(NURSE! PREP THE BALD ONE FOR SURGERY!)
GBTrudeau

I HAVE TO GO NOW, SIR. I'M NOT PERMITTED IN THE OPERATING ROOM!
LISTEN, BEFORE YOU GO, TELL THEM I WANT GENERAL ANAESTHESIA!

YOU WON'T NEED IT SIR. THEY'LL JUST OPERATE WITH LOCAL ACUPUNCTURE ANAESTHESIA!
ACUPUNCTURE?!

GOD HELP ME! CHINESE NEEDLE TORTURE!
DON'T BE SCARED, SIR. THEY USE VERY SLIM NEEDLES!

DIPPED IN WHAT?!!
TRUST YOUR SURGEON, SIR! HE CARES!
GBTrudeau

WE'RE GOING TO ADMINISTER THE ACUPUNCTURE ANAETHESIA NOW, SIR.
I DON'T SUPPOSE THERE'S ANY POINT DISCUSSING IT..

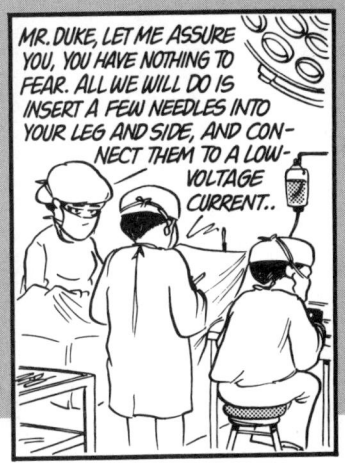
MR. DUKE, LET ME ASSURE YOU, YOU HAVE NOTHING TO FEAR. ALL WE WILL DO IS INSERT A FEW NEEDLES INTO YOUR LEG AND SIDE, AND CONNECT THEM TO A LOW-VOLTAGE CURRENT..

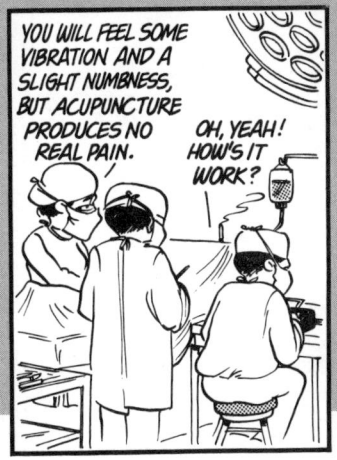
YOU WILL FEEL SOME VIBRATION AND A SLIGHT NUMBNESS, BUT ACUPUNCTURE PRODUCES NO REAL PAIN.
OH, YEAH! HOW'S IT WORK?

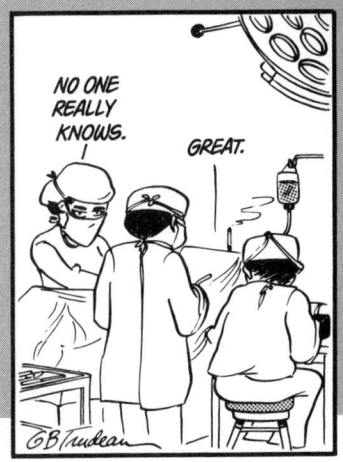
NO ONE REALLY KNOWS.
GREAT.
GBTrudeau

NO, I TELL YOU! NO VICIOUS LITTLE NEEDLES! MY GOD, YOU PEOPLE CALL THIS COUNTRY A CIVILIZATION?!
LOOK, I PROBABLY DON'T EVEN HAVE APPENDICITIS! THAT LITTLE QUACK IN THE RESTAURANT ONLY TOOK MY PULSE!
AS IT TURNS OUT, SIR, HE WAS RIGHT.
YOU...YOU.. MEAN, YOU'VE ALREADY GOT ME OPEN!?
YES, SIR. YOU SMOKE A LOT, DON'T YOU?
HEY! YOU LEAVE MY LUNGS ALONE!!
GBTrudeau

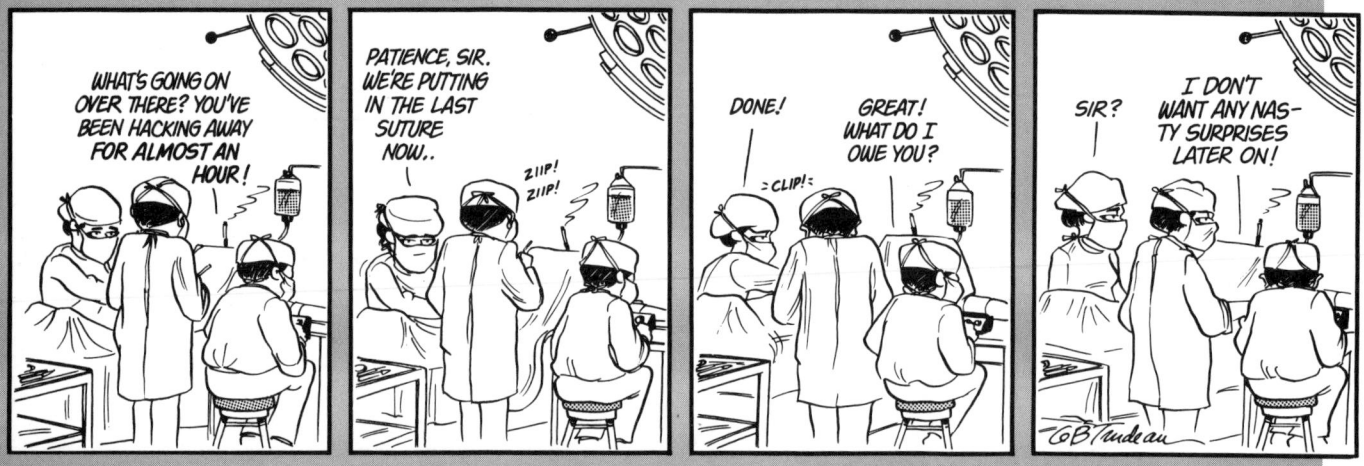
WHAT'S GOING ON OVER THERE? YOU'VE BEEN HACKING AWAY FOR ALMOST AN HOUR!
PATIENCE, SIR. WE'RE PUTTING IN THE LAST SUTURE NOW..
ZIIP! ZIIP!
DONE!
CLIP!
GREAT! WHAT DO I OWE YOU?
SIR?
I DON'T WANT ANY NASTY SURPRISES LATER ON!
GBTrudeau

HELLO?
AMBASSADOR DUKE?
YEAH, SPEAKING.
GOOD EVENING, SIR. THIS IS THE HOSPITAL FRONT DESK..
UH-HUH..
SIR, I JUST THOUGHT YOU'D LIKE TO KNOW THAT YOUR GIRLFRIEND IS ON HER WAY UP TO VISIT YOU!
MY WHAT?!
IT WAS THE ONLY WAY I COULD GET CLEARANCE, SIR.
GBTrudeau

TELL ME, HONEY—SINCE YOU'RE THE ONLY TRANSLATOR IN CHINA WHO CAN STILL UNDERSTAND THE CHAIRMAN, HOW FAITHFULLY DO YOU ACTUALLY CARRY OUT HIS WISHES?
WELL, SIR, HE CHANGES HIS MIND A LOT, AND ALTHOUGH HIS WORD IS ABSOLUTE LAW, I HAVE TO ACCOUNT FOR THAT.
FOR INSTANCE, LAST MONDAY, HE TOLD ME TO HAVE THE GREAT WALL TORN DOWN, SINCE IT'S A SYMBOL OF ANCIENT TYRANNY. ON TUESDAY, I REPORTED THAT ALL 1,500 MILES HAD BEEN DISMANTLED.
THEN ON THURSDAY, HE TOLD ME HE HAD HAD SECOND THOUGHTS, AND THAT HE WANTED THE WALL REBUILT AT ONCE.
FRIDAY NIGHT, I TOLD HIM THAT I HAD PERSONALLY DIRECTED THE MOBILIZATION OF 20 MILLION WORKERS, AND THAT THE ENTIRE WALL HAD BEEN RESTORED TO ITS FORMER CONDITION.
ACTUALLY, I SPENT THE WHOLE WEEK WATCHING T.V., BUT HE THINKS I'M A GENIUS.
IN A WAY, YOU ARE, HONEY..
GBTrudeau

MR. DUKE, I UNDERSTAND FROM YOUR TRANSLATOR THAT YOU ARE BAFFLED BY THE EBB AND FLOW OF OUR INTERNAL AFFAIRS!

IF I MAY SAY SO, MY FRIEND, I THINK YOUR CONFUSION STEMS FROM A FAILURE TO APPRECIATE THE NECESSITY FOR A SUSTAINED STRUGGLE AGAINST REACTIONARYISM!

THE CHAIRMAN, AS USUAL, PUT IT BEST: "IF YOU DON'T HIT REACTIONARYISM, IT WON'T FALL! THIS IS ALSO LIKE SWEEPING THE FLOOR; AS A RULE, WHERE THE BROOM DOES NOT REACH, THE DUST WILL NOT VANISH OF ITSELF!"

HEE, HEE! THERE'S AN OLD JOKE WE TELL DOWN AT THE FOREIGN OFFICE: "THE CHAIRMAN CARRIES A BIG BROOM, BUT SWEEPS SOFTLY!" HA, HA! ISN'T THAT HUMOROUS?!

HA, HA, HA! HA, HA, HA! HEE, HEE, HEE, HEE! HEE!

CAN'T HANDLE IT, HUH?
HEE... WELL, WHAT IS IT, ANYWAY? IT MAKES ME FEEL LIKE I SHOULD BE TOASTING SOMEBODY!
G B Trudeau

WELL, THAT SHOULD DO IT, HONEY! IT'S READY TO TEST-DRIVE! DID YOU PICK UP AN ALBUM FOR ME?
THIS SIDE

YES, SIR. I BOUGHT THE PEKING CHORAL GROUP'S LATEST!
SOUNDS GRIM. WHAT'S IT CALLED?
THIS SIDE

IT'S ENTITLED "INDIGNANTLY CONDEMN THE WANG-CHAN-CHIANG-YAO GANG OF FOUR."
REMAINDERED, WAS IT?
THIS SIDE

OH, NO, SIR! IT'S THE FASTEST-SELLING RECORD IN CHINA! 25 MILLION COPIES TO DATE!
25 MILLION?! WHY.. WHY.. THAT'S AMAZING! ARE YOU SURE, HONEY?
THIS SIDE

OH, YES, SIR! IT'S BEEN THE NUMBER ONE RECORD SINCE JANUARY!
INCREDIBLE.. JUST INCREDIBLE! WHAT'S IT SAY ON THE STICKER HERE?
THIS SIDE

CONTAINS HIT SINGLE, "EVERYONE IS REJOICING OVER THE WIPING OUT OF THE FOUR PESTS!"
OH, WELL, NO WONDER!
THIS SIDE
G B Trudeau

MR. DUKE, HAVE YOU STARTED YOUR SPEECH FOR TONIGHT'S BANQUET YET?
YEAH, HONEY, I GOT A FEW IDEAS DOWN. I'LL PROBABLY JUST WING IT, THOUGH.
IS THAT WISE, SIR? THE WHOLE CENTRAL COMMITTEE WILL BE IN ATTENDANCE.
LOOK, DON'T WORRY! IT'S JUST ANOTHER BANQUET GIG, HONEY!
I MEAN, I ACED THAT UNIVERSITY BANQUET DIDN'T I? YOU KNOW, WITH MY ADDRESS ON AMERICAN HUMOR?
I THOUGHT THOSE WERE POLISH JOKES, SIR.
YEAH, BUT THEY ORIGINATED IN THE STATES!
GBTrudeau
..AND I THANK MY CHINESE HOSTS FOR THEIR RELENTLESS HOSPITALITY!
(HE THANKS YOU FOR BEING HOSPITABLE.)
THE LAST YEAR HAS PASSED WITHOUT ANY MAJOR PROVOCATION AND I APPRECIATE THAT.
(HE THANKS YOU FOR BEING SO TOLERANT.)
I LOOK FORWARD TO MANY MORE YEARS OF WORKING WITH PEKING!
(HE DOESN'T KNOW YET HE'S BEING REPLACED BY LEONARD WOODCOCK.)
YOU'RE NOT PROJECTING, HONEY.
(HE DOESN'T KNOW YET HE'S BEING REPLACED BY LEONARD WOODCOCK!)
GBTrudeau
THERE'S BEEN A LOT OF TALK LATELY THAT JIMMY CARTER HAS BEEN IGNORING CHINA!
(HE BRINGS YOU GREETINGS FROM PRESIDENT CARTER!)
WELL, THERE'S A REASON FOR THAT! THE HUMAN RIGHTS SITUATION HERE IS SO BAD IT BOGGLES THE MIND!
(HE BRINGS GREETINGS FROM VICE-PRESIDENT MONDALE!)
CLAP! CLAP! CLAP! CLAP! CLAP! CLAP! CLAP!
WHY ARE THEY APPLAUDING, HONEY?
THEY LOVE YOU, SIR.
GBTrudeau

HONEY, WHY IS IT I GOT THE DISTINCT IMPRESSION YOU WERE TAKING LIBERTIES IN TRANSLATING MY SPEECH?
UM.. WELL, SIR, I MIGHT HAVE SOFTENED A WORD HERE AND THERE..

SOFTENED? WHO SAID YOU COULD SOFTEN?
MY JOB IS TO LOOK AFTER YOU, SIR. I KNEW YOU'D WANT ME TO MODIFY ANY POTENTIALLY EMBARRASSING REMARKS!

I DON'T BELIEVE THIS! HONEY, TELL ME—WHAT DID MY SPEECH END UP BEING ABOUT?
YOUR ADMIRATION FOR LAST YEAR'S BALL BEARING OUTPUT.

I SPOKE FOR 45 MINUTES ON BALL BEARINGS?!
YES, SIR. AND YOU WERE SPELL-BINDING!
GB Trudeau

HONEY, WHAT'S ALL THIS TALK ABOUT LEONARD WOODCOCK I KEEP PICKING UP AROUND THE EMBASSY?

UM.. WELL, AS I UNDERSTAND IT, SIR, HE'S BEEN NAMED TO THE U.S. MISSION.

HMM.. THAT'S CURIOUS..

HE MUST BE MY NEW AIDE-DE-CAMP OR SOMETHING.
OR SOMETHING, YES.
GB Trudeau

I'M SORRY TO BE THE ONE TO TELL YOU, SIR, I..
WOODCOCK?! LEONARD WOODCOCK IS REPLACING ME?!

I KNEW IT! I KNEW CARTER WAS A FRAUD! ONCE AGAIN, THE POLS PLAY PORK BARREL, AND A TOP FLIGHT CAREER DIPLOMAT IS OUT ON THE STREET!

WELL, THEY WON'T GET AWAY WITH IT, DO YOU HEAR ME?! THEY WON'T GET AWAY WITH IT!

YOU HAVE A PLAN, SIR?
A PLAN.. YOU'RE RIGHT! I'LL NEED A PLAN!
GB Trudeau

I'M TELLING YOU, CY, WOODCOCK'S SLOW FREIGHT! HE'LL NEVER CUT IT HERE! THEY'LL HAVE HIM FOR BREAKFAST HIS FIRST DAY!

SORRY, DUKE. HE'S THE PRESIDENT'S CHOICE. WE'VE GOT ENOUGH TROUBLE WITH LABOR AS IT IS..

BUT, CY, THEY'LL BURY HIM! I KNOW THE CHINESE! THESE PEOPLE ARE VICIOUS, CAPRICIOUS, AND EXTREMELY CUNNING!
BUT POLITE.

OKAY, GRANTED, THEY'RE POLITE..
WE LIKE TO THINK THAT STILL COUNTS FOR SOMETHING.
GBTrudeau

LEONARD WOODCOCK! I JUST CAN'T GET OVER IT! WHAT EVER COULD HAVE POSSESSED CARTER TO PICK WOODCOCK FOR CHINA?

WELL, SIR, MAYBE IT'S BECAUSE MR. WOODCOCK'S CAREER HAS BEEN ONE OF GREAT SENSITIVITY TO THE PLIGHT OF THE WORKING CLASS!

HONEY, ALL LABOR LEADERS ARE SENSITIVE TO THE WORKING CLASS! THAT'S HOW THEY AVOID BELONGING TO IT!

BUT DIDN'T HE TAKE ON THE GANG OF THREE, SIR?
THAT'S THE BIG THREE! AND NEXT TO YOU PEOPLE, THOSE GUYS ARE PUSSY-CATS!
GBTrudeau

CHECKING OUT ALREADY, SIR?
YEAH, I DON'T WANT TO BE HERE WHEN WOODCOCK ARRIVES! IT'S TOO GALLING!

IT'S ALL SUCH A MISTAKE, HONEY! I MEAN, I KNOW THIS COUNTRY! I KNOW THE PEOPLE, THE POLITICS, THE CULTURE, EVEN SOME OF THE LANGUAGE!

SOME OF THE LANGUAGE, SIR?
YOU BET, HONEY! LISTEN TO THIS: (ASK THE BOY TO BRING ME SOME MORE EGG ROLLS!)

IT'S HARD TO BELIEVE YOU WERE ONLY HERE FOR A YEAR, SIR.
AND YOU THINK WOODCOCK WOULD MAKE THE SAME EFFORT? NO WAY, HONEY!
GBTrudeau

3

CARMEL

1977-1978

IT'S A SWEET LITTLE DEAL, NEPHEW! ABOUT AS TASTY A BUSINESS OPPORTUNITY AS I'VE EVER COME ACROSS!

100 ACRES OF THE RICHEST FARM LAND IN THE WHOLE SAN FERNANDO VALLEY! AND EACH ACRE JUST THICK WITH APRICOT TREES!

UH.. DUKE, I'M SURE IT'S A GREAT DEAL, BUT FRANKLY, I CAN'T SEE YOU PURVEYING FRUIT!
FRUIT? WHO SAID ANYTHING ABOUT FRUIT? THE REAL PROFITS ARE IN THE PITS!

PITS?.. OH, DUKE, NOT LAETRILE..
OF COURSE NOT. THAT WOULD BE ILLEGAL.
GB Trudeau

LAETRILE? YOU'RE GOING INTO THE LAETRILE BUSINESS?
BITE YOUR TONGUE, NEPHEW! OF COURSE NOT! LAETRILE'S STILL ILLEGAL IN THIS STATE!

ALL I'M DOING IS BUYING INTO A LITTLE APRICOT FARM! AND IF I JUST HAPPEN TO FIND A MARKET FOR MY PITS IN TIJUANA, WHO COULD BLAME ME FOR SELLING THEM?

UNCLE DUKE, THAT'S JUST AWFUL! HOW COULD YOU EVEN CONSIDER SUCH A SCHEME!
I SUPPOSE I WOULD BE REMISS IF I FAILED TO MENTION THE 600% PROFIT MARGIN.

DUKE, THE STUFF DOESN'T EVEN WORK ON RATS!
THEY'RE NOT BUYING. WHY DO YOU ALWAYS GET SO TICKED WHEN I THINK OF SOMETHING FIRST?
GB Trudeau

LOOK, I DON'T SEE WHAT YOU'RE GETTING SO WORKED UP ABOUT! IT'S NOT LIKE I'M GOING TO BE EXTRACTING THE LAETRILE MYSELF!

BESIDES, THIS APRICOT PLANTATION'S TOO GOOD A DEAL TO PASS UP! THE WHOLE SPREAD'S BEING LET GO FOR LESS THAN 300 BUCKS AN ACRE!

DUKE, WHO EXACTLY IS DOING THE LETTING GO?
FRIEND OF A FRIEND WHO'S FALLEN ON HARD TIMES! NAME'S TONY PLACEBO.

"PLACEBO"?
GUY'S HEARTBROKEN, OF COURSE, BUT BETTER ME THAN THE BANKS, YOU KNOW?
GB Trudeau

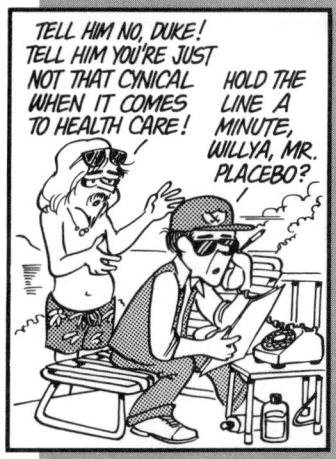
TELL HIM NO, DUKE! TELL HIM YOU'RE JUST NOT THAT CYNICAL WHEN IT COMES TO HEALTH CARE!
HOLD THE LINE A MINUTE, WILLYA, MR. PLACEBO?

LISTEN, NEPHEW! I'M A BUSINESSMAN! I CAN'T AFFORD TO GET EMOTIONAL ABOUT THESE THINGS! WE'RE TALKING SUPPLY AND DEMAND HERE, NOT ETHICS!
IT'S AS AMERICAN AS TWINKIES!

UNCLE DUKE, I..
SORRY, MR. PLACEBO, ONE OF MY BACKERS WAS GETTING COLD FEET.

ONE OF YOUR WHAT?!
SSHH! I'LL EXPLAIN LATER!
GB Trudeau

DUKE, YOU CAN JUST FORGET IT! I'M NOT INVESTING! FIRST, I THINK THE WHOLE SCHEME IS IMMORAL! SECONDLY, I DON'T HAVE A NICKEL TO PUT UP ANYWAY!

WHAT DO YOU MEAN, BOY? I THOUGHT AUNT HATSY LEFT YOU A TRUST FUND!
DUKE, THAT MONEY WAS ALL INVESTED IN PLOUGH YEARS AGO!

WHAT THE HELL IS PLOUGH?
PLOUGH IS THE PARENT COMPANY OF COPPERTONE.

WELL, THAT EXPLAINS YOUR PRECANCEROUS COLORING.
GO AHEAD, LAUGH. BUT MY PICTURE'S MADE THE ANNUAL REPORT THREE TIMES!
GB Trudeau

THANKS, JULIO! I KNEW I COULD COUNT ON YOU! BYE!

WHO WAS THAT, DUKE?
JULIO COROLLA! HE'S GOING TO SOLVE ALL MY FINANCING PROBLEMS ON MY FARM!

JULIO COROLLA? WHO WORKS AT THE POOL HALL?
JULIO'S LATINO, RIGHT? WELL, HE'S AGREED TO HEAD UP MY APRICOT COMPANY, THEREBY QUALIFYING IT FOR A MINORITY SMALL BUSINESS LOAN!

DUKE, WHY DON'T YOU JUST STEAL THE MONEY?
POINT OF PRIDE. I'VE ALWAYS WORKED WITHIN THE SYSTEM.
GB Trudeau

BACK ALREADY?
YUP! THE CLOSING WAS A PIECE OF CAKE!

WITH JULIO ACTING AS PRESIDENT, THE MINORITY SMALL BUSINESS LOAN CAME THROUGH! THE "SHADY GROVES" APRICOT FARM IS MINE!

AND JUST WHAT DOES OL' JULIO GET OUT OF ALL THIS?
2% AND A GREEN CARD.

OH, DUKE...
HEY, I HAD TO DO SOMETHING! HE'S GOT EIGHT LITTLE WETBACKS TO FEED!
GB Trudeau

SORRY, CORNELL, ZONKER'S NOT HOME. HE AND DUKE TOOK OFF TO CHECK OUT DUKE'S NEW APRICOT FARM!

DUKE BOUGHT AN APRICOT FARM?
YEAH, ABOUT TWO HOURS' DRIVE WEST OF HERE.

DUKE SAYS IT'S SUPPOSED TO BE SOME OF THE LUSHEST REAL ESTATE IN ALL OF CALIFORNIA!

MAYBE THE TREES ARE ON THE MESA, DUKE..
WHAT IS THIS?! GIMME THAT MAP!
GB Trudeau

BUT IT'S PLACEBO'S MAP WE USED, DUKE..
YEAH, BUT WHAT THE HELL IS THIS?! WHERE'S "SHADY GROVES"? WHERE'S THE FARM? WHERE ARE THE DAMN APRICOTS?!

UNCLE DUKE, I'M AFRAID YOU..
IT'S A MISTAKE! THAT'S IT! IT'S JUST A MISTAKE! WRONG MAP! A SIMPLE SCREW-UP!

MAYBE YOU COULD IRRIGATE IT, DUKE..
PERHAPS. BUT FIRST, I GOTTA GO REMOVE PLACEBO'S LUNGS..
GB Trudeau

SORRY, BOYS, AIN'T NO "SHADY GROVES" APRICOT FARM OUT HERE! HELL, IT AIN'T NOTHIN' BUT DESERT FOR FIFTY MILES!
ARE YOU SURE?

SURE I'M SURE! LIVED IN THIS TOWN ALL MY LIFE! WHO SENT YOU OUT HERE?
PLACEBO. TONY PLACEBO.

PLACEBO? WHY, I AIN'T SEEN HIM AROUND HERE SINCE THAT LAND FRAUD BUSINESS IN '69!
LAND FRAUD?!

I DIDN'T EVEN KNOW HE'D BEEN PAROLED.
GOSH, NEITHER DID WE!
GB Trudeau

NEPHEW, CAN YOU BELIEVE HOW LOW I'LL SINK FOR A LOUSY GRAND?
BEATS DESTITUTION, DUKE. THE LECTURE FINISHED?

I GUESS. I MEAN, WHAT CAN ONE SAY TO 300 YOUNG REPUBLICANS?
I'M SURE YOU'LL THINK OF SOMETHING..

BUT I SO WANT TO MAKE A GOOD IMPRESSION..
WELL, YOU COULD START BY BEING ON TIME. WE BETTER GET GOING!

IN A MINUTE. I CAN'T DECIDE WHAT HALLUCINOGEN TO TAKE..
DUKE, YOU'RE LATE, MAN! JUST GRAB ANYTHING!
GB Trudeau

DUKE, YOU SURE YOU WANT TO BE TAKING THOSE JUST BEFORE YOUR SPEECH?
BEST TIME! IT'S GOING TO BE A LONG EVENING!

WHAT'S IN THEM, DUKE?
SOMETHING VERY SPECIAL. AN EXTRACT MADE FROM THE PINEAL GLANDS OF MALE ADOLESCENT IGUANAS.
TOP

WHATEVER HAPPENED TO GRASS?
BEATS ME! YOU CAN'T EVEN GET ARRESTED FOR IT ANY MORE!
GB Trudeau

..AND NOW, WITHOUT FURTHER ADO, THE "GONZ" HIMSELF — AMBASSADOR DUKE!
I DON'T GET IT.. YOU'D THINK 75 MICROGRAMS WOULD DO THE JOB!
CLAP! CLAP! CLAP! CLAP! CLAP! CLAP!
NOTHING'S HAPPENING! NOTHING! THIS IS THE WORST STUFF I'VE EVER HAD IN MY LIFE!
UH.. MR. DUKE?.. MR. DUKE?
I'LL KILL HIM! I'LL KILL THAT SON OF A..
MR. DUKE? ARE YOU ALL RIGHT?
AH! THERE WE GO!
GB Trudeau
..AND ONLY ONE YEAR LATER, HE WAS APPOINTED TO OUR MISSION IN CHINA!
HEY! WHAT'S HE TRYING TO PULL HERE?!
AS OUR TOP ENVOY IN PEKING, MR. DUKE WAS..
HOLD IT RIGHT THERE, TWEETY! I CAME HERE TO SPEAK TO PEOPLE, NOT A ROOM FULL OF SAVAGE, WINGED LIZARDS!
WINGED LIZARDS? MR. DUKE..
OOPS.. MY MISTAKE! THEY'RE SHEEP, NOT LIZARDS. SORRY... THEY LOOKED LIKE LIZARDS AT FIRST.
MR. DUKE, ARE YOU..
CARRY ON! SHEEP I CAN HANDLE.
GB Trudeau
GOOD EVENING, FELLOW REPUBLICANS!
I'VE GOT TO THINK THIS THROUGH! WHY AM I TALKING TO AN AUDITORIUM FULL OF MUTANT SHEEP?
I BRING YOU GREETINGS FROM THE PEOPLE'S REPUBLIC OF CHINA!
WHAT ARE YOU SAYING?! THESE PEOPLE ARE LIFELONG REACTIONARIES!
MY SUBJECT FOR TONIGHT IS "OUR FRIEND, THE AMPHETAMINE."
YOU TWISTED MANIAC! NOW YOU'VE DONE IT! THEY'LL TEAR YOU LIMB FROM LIMB!
ER.. I MEAN, "WHY CAN'T JOHNNY BLINK?"
TOO LATE! HERE THEY COME!
GB Trudeau

IN CONCLUSION, A WORD OF CAUTION TO ALL THOSE YOUNGSTERS WHO LOOK TO ME AS A ROLE MODEL..

STAY OFF THE HARD STUFF! UNLESS YOU KNOW WHAT YOU'RE DOING, IT CAN ONLY COME TO GRIEF! THERE IS NO ROOM IN THE DRUG CULTURE FOR AMATEURS! THANK YOU!

BAA! BAA!
BAAA! BAA!
BAA!

BAD CRAZINESS..
BLEAT! THAT WAS JUST BLEAT!
GBTrudeau

YOU HAVE NO IDEA WHERE HE WENT?
HE DIDN'T SAY. HE JUST TOOK OFF!

IT WAS ALL VERY PECULIAR! RIGHT IN THE MIDDLE OF THE QUESTION AND ANSWER PERIOD, HE SUDDENLY STARTED TO SHAKE VIOLENTLY!

THEN HE LURCHED OUT THE BACK DOOR, SCREAMING THAT THE AUDIENCE WAS ABOUT TO ATTACK HIM, AND THAT HE HAD TO GET TO HIGH GROUND!

OKAY, BUDDY, COME ON DOWN..
I'M WARNING, YOU, MAN! I'VE GOT A BOMB!
GBTrudeau

DUKE, YOU'RE LUCKY THAT COP HAD A SENSE OF HUMOR! WHAT WERE YOU DOING UP IN THAT TREE?
HIDING FROM THE KILLER SHEEP! WHAT DO YOU THINK?!

KILLER SHEEP? I THOUGHT YOU WERE TALKING TO THE YOUNG REPUBLICANS!
I HAD 'EM UNDER CONTROL RIGHT UP TO THE END! BUT WHEN I OPENED THE FLOOR UP TO QUESTIONS, THEY ALL STARTED BLEATING, "WE WANT GOLDWATER! WE WANT GOLDWATER!"

AND?..
WELL, NATURALLY, I PANICKED.
GBTrudeau

DUKE, TRY TO GET SOME SLEEP. BEST WAY TO TURN OFF THE HORROR SHOW..
NONSENSE! I DON'T NEED ANY MORE SLEEP! I'M GOING TO THE DODGERS GAME TONIGHT!
YOU ARE NOT, DUKE! YOU'RE NOT GOING ANYWHERE UNTIL I GET YOU DE-TOXIFIED!
DAMMIT, BOY, IT'S OVER, I TELL YOU! NO COLORS. RUSHES, NOTHING! I'M STRAIGHT!
AND I.. ERP!
AHA! I CUT OUT ON YOU, DIDN'T I?
NO.. I'M ALRIGHT.. IF I COULD JUST HAVE A BEER..
GBTrudeau

WHAT DO YOU THINK, CORNELL?
WELL, I DON'T THINK IT'S ANYTHING TOO SERIOUS, MAN. JUST YOUR BASIC BURN-OUT.
ALL HE REALLY NEEDS IS SLEEP, Z. ALSO, LET HIM WATCH A LOT OF TELEVISION. T.V. HELPS EASE THE TRANSITION BACK TO REALITY.
WHAT SORT OF TELE-VISION?
WELL, TAKE IT EASY AT FIRST. I'D START HIM ON TEST PATTERNS OR "DINAH." AND MAKE SURE YOU REMOVE ALL THE CONTROL KNOBS.
EVEN THE TINT AND HUE KNOBS?
NO, LEAVE THEM. HIS COLOR CHOICES WILL GIVE YOU SOME IDEA AS TO HIS PROGRESS.
GBTrudeau

SURE, Z, I'D BE HAPPY TO LOOK AFTER DUKE! WHERE ARE YOU GOING?
BACK TO SCHOOL, MAN. I GOTTA FINISH UP MY TAN AND REPORT TO FOOTBALL PRACTICE.
OH. WELL, IS THERE ANYTHING SPECIAL I SHOULD KNOW ABOUT DUKE?
NOT REALLY. EXCEPT THAT HE BECOMES CATATONIC AT THE SOUND OF JOHN DENVER MUSIC.
O.K., NOW, WHAT DO I FEED HIM?
ONLY BRAND NAME FOODS. AT LEAST UNTIL HE BEGINS TO TRUST YOU.
GBTrudeau

BRENNER, YOU CALL YOURSELF A CARETAKER? LOOK AT THIS PLACE!
NOW, DUKE, HOLD ON! CONSIDERING THE STATE YOU LEFT IT IN, IT LOOKS PRETTY GOOD!
Owl Farm
U.S. MAIL
POSTED

GOOD? GOOD LORD, MAN, IT LOOKS LIKE A TRAINING CAMP FOR VANDALS!
DUKE, I PROMISE YOU, I HAVEN'T TOUCHED A THING!
Owl Farm
U.S. MAIL
POSTED

YOU KNOW, BRENNER, YOU ARE INCREDIBLE! I LEAVE THE COUNTRY FOR A FEW MONTHS..
MONTHS? DUKE, YOU'VE BEEN GONE NEARLY THREE YEARS! I'D GIVEN YOU UP FOR DEAD LONG AGO! YOU..
Owl Farm
U.S. MAIL
POSTED

MY DOBERMANS! BRENNER, WHAT HAPPENED TO MY DOBERMANS!
OH, I'M SORRY, DUKE. GOEBBELS GOT RABIES, AND GOERING WAS SHOT BY A DEER HUNTER.
Owl Farm
U.S. MAIL
POSTED

I DON'T BELIEVE THIS! I JUST DON'T BELIEVE THIS! I TRUST YOU WITH MY HOME! I TRUST YOU WITH... HEY!
WHAT?
Owl Farm
U.S. MAIL
POSTED

MY WIFE! WHERE'S MY WIFE?
OH, C'MON, DUKE – SHE LEFT YEARS AGO!
Owl Farm
U.S. MAIL
POSTED
GBTrudeau

..AND ART BUCHWALD'S NOT AVAILABLE EITHER, WHICH MEANS WE'VE GOT ONLY ONE WEEK LEFT TO FIND SOMEONE TO GIVE THIS YEAR'S JOURNALISM LECTURE!
ABE, I'VE GOT A SUGGESTION! HOW ABOUT FORMER AMBASSADOR DUKE, THE EX-GONZO STRINGER FOR "ROLLING STONE"?
HIS IS A UNIQUE PERSPECTIVE ON THE DARK UNDERSIDE OF OUTLAW JOURNALISM. AND HIS IMMENSE POPULARITY AMONG US KIDS WOULD LEND A CACHET TO THE LECTURE!
ACCORDING TO WHOM?
ZONKER. I'VE NEVER HEARD OF HIM MYSELF.
TRUST ME, GUYS. HE'D BE PERFECT! REALLY!
GB Trudeau
GOOD LORD, KID, IT'S ONLY SEVEN O'CLOCK! HAVEN'T YOU EVER HEARD OF TIME ZONES?
YES, SIR, I'M SORRY, SIR, BUT WE'RE KIND OF PRESSED. YOUR NEPHEW SAID IT WOULD BE OKAY TO CALL..
Duke
MY NEPHEW? ZONKER?
YES, SIR. HE'S ON THE SPEAKER'S COMMITTEE WITH ME..
Duke
LOOK, CHIEF, I DON'T GIVE A DAMN IF HE'S ON THE SAME..
AND HE SAID TO BE SURE TO MENTION THE $3,000. HONORARIUM TO YOU!
Duke
THAT RASCAL. HE REALLY SAID THAT?
YES, SIR. HE SEEMS TO THINK THE WORLD OF YOU.
Duke
GB Trudeau
E8
MR. DUKE! MR. DUKE! OVER HERE, SIR!
TWA
E8
HELLO?
I'M RONNIE, SIR! DID YOU HAVE A GOOD FLIGHT?
TWA
YEAH, IT WAS OKAY.
LET ME JUST SAY, SIR, HOW VERY HONORED WE ALL ARE THAT YOU WERE ABLE TO TAKE TIME FROM YOUR BUSY SCHEDULE TO COME SPEAK TO US!
TWA
UH-HUH. GOT MY FEE WITH YOU?
OH, YES, OF COURSE, SIR. IN TENS AND TWENTIES, AS REQUESTED.
TWA
GB Trudeau

WELL, SIR, I'LL BE BY IN A FEW HOURS TO TAKE YOU TO YOUR LECTURE. IF YOU NEED ANYTHING, JUST..
WELL, KID, AS A MATTER OF FACT, I WILL BE NEEDING A FEW THINGS.

UM.. EVERYTHING ON THIS LIST, SIR?
YES. IT'S VERY IMPORTANT. I'M GOING TO BE DOING A LITTLE WRITING TONIGHT, AND I'LL NEED SUPPLIES!

"ONE IBM SELECTRIC TYPEWRITER, ONE CRATE OF FRESH GRAPEFRUIT, THREE CASES OF WILD TURKEY.."
IF I HAVE TO GO OUT FOR ALL THAT MYSELF, IT'LL BREAK MY CONCENTRATION!

"TWO ALBINO TYPISTS, ONE TRAMPOLINE.."
SAY, YOU DON'T KNOW IF THESE ROOMS HAVE SPRINKLERS, DO YOU?
GB Trudeau

YOU'RE SURE ABOUT THIS PHARMACY, BOY?
OH, YES, SIR. I MAKE IT MY BUSINESS TO BE SURE!

UH..YES, THIS IS DR. DUKE CALLING! I'M FROM OUT OF TOWN, AND I'VE LOST MY PRESCRIPTION PAD, BUT I WONDER IF I COULD ORDER A FEW THINGS TO BE SENT OVER TO MY MOTEL ROOM?

SURE, DOC! NO PROBLEM! WHAT DO YOU NEED?

YOU HAVE AN EXCITING TALENT, LAD. NEVER ABUSE IT.
NO, SIR. THANK YOU, SIR.
GB Trudeau

I DON'T KNOW WHAT TO DO, ZONKER! THE LECTURE STARTS IN AN HOUR, AND YOUR UNCLE IS IN A TOTAL STUPOR!

WHAT DO YOU MEAN, A STUPOR, RONNIE?
WELL, HE'S JUST LYING IN HIS BED WITH A SILLY GRIN ON HIS FACE! AND THE PLACE IS JUST LITTERED WITH LITTLE PLASTIC VIALS!

HMM.. SOUNDS LIKE HE'S BEEN OUT SHOPPING.. NOW, WHERE DO YOU SUPPOSE HE GOT THE MONEY TO BUY..

SAY, RONNIE, I DON'T SUPPOSE YOU PAID HIM IN ADVANCE?
I HAD TO, ZONK! HIS MOTHER NEEDED AN OPERATION RIGHT AWAY!
GB Trudeau

UNCLE DUKE? CAN YOU HEAR ME? UNCLE DUKE?
I DON'T KNOW WHAT HAPPENED, ZONKER. HE WAS FINE WHEN I LEFT HERE A FEW HOURS AGO..

ZONKER? IS THAT YOU, BOY?
YES, IT'S ME, UNCLE DUKE. WHAT IS IT? WHAT'S GOING ON, MAN?

WELL.. I.. I.. I'M..
YOU'RE WHAT, UNCLE DUKE?.. TAKE IT EASY... TELL ME WHAT'S HAPPENING..

I'M TRAPPED IN A SWISS GIRLS' BOARDING SCHOOL, ZONKER..
NOT TO WORRY. I KNOW THIS ONE.
OH, GOOD.
GB Trudeau

WHA.. WHAT HAPPENED?
AH.. HERE HE COMES! BACK FROM THE SWISS GIRLS' BOARDING SCHOOL, UNCLE?

ZONKER!
WELCOME HOME, UNCLE DUKE! YOU FEEL OKAY NOW?

FINE! NEVER BETTER! WHERE'S HELGA!
HELGA?

THE HEADMISTRESS! I WANT YOU TO MEET HER!
I'M GOING TO NEED A LITTLE MORE TIME, MAN..
GB Trudeau

MAY I HAVE YOUR ATTENTION, PLEASE?

THROUGH AN UNFORTUNATE SET OF CIRCUMSTANCES, OUR SPEAKER TONIGHT, FORMER AMBASSADOR DUKE, HAS BEEN DELAYED!

IF YOU'LL ALL JUST BEAR WITH US, I'M SURE MR. DUKE WILL BE ARRIVING HERE JUST AS SOON AS HE IS ABLE!

OKAY, HOW MANY FINGERS?
NINE.
GB Trudeau

..AND NOW, WITHOUT FURTHER ADO, THE PRINCE OF GONZO — AMBASSADOR DUKE!
YEAA!
CLAP! CLAP! CLAP!

HE LOOKS A LITTLE SHAKY STILL, ZONKER..
THAT'S NORMAL. I JUST HOPE HE'S REASONABLY COHERENT!

GOOD EVENING. FEW OF NATURE'S WONDERS HAVE BEEN MORE WIDELY MISUNDERSTOOD THAN THE PLAYFUL PEYOTE BUTTON.

I THINK HE'S GOING TO BE OKAY..
MAY I HAVE THE FIRST SLIDE, PLEASE?
GBTrudeau

MR. DUKE, I'M THINKING OF BECOMING A REPORTER. WHAT ADVICE WOULD YOU GIVE SOMEONE WHO IS JUST STARTING OUT?

LOOK, JUNIOR, JOURNALISM IS A JUNGLE! NEVER FORGET THAT! IN JOURNALISM, THERE ARE NO WINNERS, JUST SURVIVORS! WE ARE TALKING SNAKE PIT CITY, SLIM!

SO DIG IT! I BEEN THERE! IF YOU FALTER FOR A SECOND, YOUR COLLEAGUES WILL WASTE YOU, WILL SAVAGE YOUR REP, YOUR NAME, YOUR.. YOUR..

WHAT WAS THE QUESTION AGAIN?
UM.. HOW DO YOU LIKE OUR CAMPUS?
GBTrudeau

ANY FURTHER QUERIES?
YES, MR. AMBASSADOR, WE MEMBERS OF THE AUDIENCE COULDN'T HELP NOTICING THAT YOU'RE STONED TO THE GILLS!

CONSIDERING YOUR SIZABLE LECTURE FEE, PAID IN PART BY CLASS DUES, CAN YOU THINK OF ANY REASON WHY WE SHOULDN'T BE GROSSLY INSULTED?

PSST! DUKE! YOUR MOM!
LOOK, I WAS HOPING TO AVOID THE SUBJECT OF MOTHER'S TUMOR, BUT..
GBTrudeau

4 WASHINGTON, D.C.

1978-1979

SO WHAT YOU BEEN UP TO, UNCLE DUKE? FOUND A NEW JOB YET?
NO, NOT YET..
BAR

BUT I'VE GOT ALL MY RESUMES OUT. I EXPECT I SHOULD BE HEARING SOMETHING PRETTY SOON...
BAR

WHAT SORT OF JOBS YOU APPLYING FOR?
OH, THE PRESIDENT OF YALE, HEAD OF ABC NEWS, MANAGER FOR THE REDSKINS, SOMETHING OF THIS NATURE...

SOMETHING OF WHAT NATURE?
YOU KNOW, SHOW BUSINESS. QUITE FRANKLY, NEPHEW, I'VE GOT THE BUG!
GBTrudeau

HEY, DUKE, THERE'S SOME ATTORNEY ON THE PHONE FOR YOU! AN EDWARDS WILLIAMS..
NEVER HEARD OF HIM! I'M NOT HOME!
WANT

HE SAYS HE'S WITH THE WASHINGTON REDSKINS!
OH, THAT WILLIAMS! HOT DAMN! HE MUST HAVE GOTTEN MY JOB APPLICATION!
WANT

WHAT JOB APPLICATION?
FOR GENERAL MANAGER! I FINALLY DECIDED IT WAS TIME TO CASH IN ON MY BACKGROUND IN SPORTS MEDICINE!

YOUR WHAT?
NEPHEW, DID YOU KNOW THREE OUT OF FOUR NFL LINEBACKERS REGULARLY USE AMPHETAMINES?
GBTrudeau

MR. DUKE?
YEAH. THIS MR. WILLIAMS?

YES, IT IS.
MR. EDWARD B. WILLIAMS, PRESIDENT OF THE REDSKINS?

WELL, YES.
SORRY TO BE SO SUSPICIOUS. BUT WHEN AN ATTORNEY CALLS, YOU CAN'T BE TOO CAREFUL, Y'KNOW?

ANY PARTICULAR REASON?
NO, NO, I JUST THOUGHT YOU MIGHT BE REPRESENTING THIS LITTLE CO-ED. NO BIG DEAL. WHAT'S UP?
GBTrudeau

GOOD NEWS, UNCLE DUKE?
YOU BET IT IS, NEPHEW! OL' MAN WILLIAMS WANTS TO INTERVIEW ME FOR THE REDSKINS MANAGER POSITION!

YOU? HOW COME?
WELL, HE CHECKED OUT MY RESUME AND CLIPPINGS FROM MY SPORTS WRITING DAYS..

AMONG OTHER THINGS, IT SEEMS HE WAS QUITE IMPRESSED WITH MY DETAILED KNOWLEDGE OF THE NEW WORK THAT'S BEING DONE WITH HIGH-PERFORMANCE STEROIDS!

A MANAGER NEEDS TO KNOW THAT?
OH, ABSOLUTELY! WHY DO YOU THINK HE HAD TO LET GEORGE ALLEN GO?
GB Trudeau

MR. DUKE, I THINK YOU'RE QUITE MISTAKEN ABOUT THE EXTENT OF THE PILL PROBLEM. WHY, NFL OFFICIALS GIVE ANTI-DRUG LECTURES EVERY MONTH..
YEAH, AND 90% OF YOUR PLAYERS ARE LAUGHING THEIR JOCKS OFF THE WHOLE TIME!

MR. WILLIAMS, YOUR PLAYERS AREN'T PILLHEADS BECAUSE THEY WANT TO BE. HELL, NOBODY LIKES TAKING PILLS! THEY TAKE 'EM BECAUSE THEY'RE CONCERNED ABOUT WHAT THE NEXT ATHLETE MIGHT BE DOING!

OH.. OH, I SEE.
IT'S A REAL PROBLEM, SIR! AND I'LL TELL YOU, SOMETIMES IT JUST BREAKS MY HEART TO SEE IT!

BUT YOU SAY YOU'VE HAD SOME EXPERIENCE IN THIS AREA?
I'VE BEEN AROUND THE TRACK A FEW TIMES, YES.
GB Trudeau

MR. WILLIAMS, I HOPE I'M NOT BEING OUT OF LINE IN TELLING YOU THAT I THINK I UNDERSTAND YOUR PROBLEM. BASICALLY, YOU'RE HOT FOR THE SUPER BOWL!

CAN YOU GET ME THERE, MR. DUKE?
WITH TIME? WITHOUT QUESTION, SIR! BUT I'D BE REMISS IF I FAILED TO MENTION THAT MY TALENTS ARE IN CONSIDERABLE DEMAND NOW!

WELL, DO YOU THINK YOU COULD LIVE WITH $100,000 A YEAR?
HMM.. I'D LIKE TO, SIR, I REALLY WOULD. BUT WITH MY MOTHER IN THE HOSPITAL NOW..

PITY. COULD YOU SUGGEST ANYONE ELSE WHO..
OH, THE HECK WITH MOM! THIS IS TOO IMPORTANT!
GB Trudeau

"..AND WE IN THE FRONT OFFICE OFFER MR. DUKE OUR WARMEST WELCOME TO THE REDSKINS ORGANIZATION!"..OKAY, WE'LL TAKE QUESTIONS NOW..

MR. DUKE, AS FAR AS WE CAN TELL, YOU BRING NO RELEVANT EXPERIENCE TO YOUR JOB. COULD YOU COMMENT?
YEAH. THAT'S A COMPLETE BUNCH OF GARBAGE.

BESIDES MY RECORD IN ADMINISTRATION, I BRING TO MY JOB AN AWESOME EXPERTISE IN SPORTS MEDICINE. IT WILL BE MY DUTY TO SEE THAT EACH AND EVERY MAN IS SAFELY WIRED BEFORE HE GOES OUT ON THAT BALL FIELD!

WHAT? YOU MEAN YOU'LL ACTUALLY BE DISPENSING PILLS?
YES. MY CONTRACT EXPLICITLY..
THANKS FOR COMING, BOYS!
GBTrudeau

DUKE, THERE'S NO WAY WE'RE GONNA GET ANY OF THESE KIDS! THE BEST OF THEM WILL BE ALL GONE BY ROUND SEVEN.
SEVEN? WE CAN'T MAKE A PICK UNTIL ROUND SEVEN?

THAT'S RIGHT. OUR TOP DRAFT CHOICES HAVE BEEN LONG SINCE TRADED AWAY..
A POX ON GEORGE ALLEN! NO WONDER THE TALENTLESS TOAD BOLTED TOWN WHEN HE DID!

TELL ME ABOUT IT. THIS IS THE THIRD YEAR I'VE HAD TO JUNK MY SCOUTING REPORTS!
I JUST DON'T SEE HOW HE GOT AWAY WITH THAT "THE FUTURE IS NOW" GARBAGE AS LONG AS HE DID!

I GUESS BECAUSE NOBODY ELSE HERE UNDERSTOOD POETRY.
YEAH, WELL, THINGS ARE GOING TO CHANGE AROUND HERE!
GBTrudeau

WELL, DUKE, IF WE CAN'T DRAFT, WE MIGHT AS WELL GO SHOPPING. GOT ANY FREE AGENTS YOU LIKE?
YEAH, HOW ABOUT "LAVA-LAVA" LENNY? YOU FAMILIAR WITH "LAVA-LAVA'S" WORK?

NOPE. WHO IS HE?
A KID I DISCOVERED SLINGING COCONUTS DURING MY TENURE IN PAGO PAGO. HE'S NOW PLAYING FRONT FOUR FOR THE LIONS.

ALL FRONT FOUR? SOUNDS LIKE A BIG BOY..
BIG? BOBBY, THE OPPOSITION'S LUCKY IF IT EVEN GETS A GLIMPSE OF THE QUARTERBACK!

UH-HUH..
I'M NOT KIDDING! WHEN I FIRST SAW HIM IN SAMOA, I THOUGHT HE WAS AN OFFSHORE ISLAND!
GBTrudeau

DUKE, IF THIS SAMOAN BOY IS AS GOOD AS YOU SAY, THERE'S NO WAY WE COULD AFFORD HIM.
WRONG, BOBBY. IN FACT, HE COULD SAVE THE 'SKINS A BUNDLE.
WITH "LAVA-LAVA" OUT THERE, WE CAN CUT BACK ON OTHER LINEMEN. THEY'D JUST GET IN THE WAY, ANYWAY. AND THAT GOES FOR OFFENSE AS WELL AS DEFENSE.
WHAT'RE YOU TALKING ABOUT?
SEE, BEFORE EACH GAME, THE BOY WORKS HIMSELF UP INTO SUCH A FEVER PITCH THAT YOU HAVE TO LET HIM PLAY ON BOTH SQUADS!
HOW DO YOU GET HIM OFF AT HALF-TIME?
DART GUN. ALSO, THE REFS USUALLY HELP.
GB Tuckow
THAT'S RIGHT, MIKE, IN THE EIGHTH AND NINTH ROUNDS, DRAFT THEM BOTH! WE'RE STILL WEAK IN THE MIDDLE!
THE HELL WE ARE!
HUH?
YOUR PRAYERS HAVE BEEN ANSWERED, BOBBY BOY! GUESS WHO JUST SIGNED WITH YOURS TRULY?
NOT "LAVA-LAVA"?
390 LBS. OF STEAMING SAMOAN! OUR FRONT FOUR PROBLEMS ARE OVER!
MIKE? CANCEL THAT ORDER OF BUCKEYES!
BARTENDER! CHAMPAGNE FOR EVERYONE ON MR. WILLIAMS!
GB Tuckow
I CAN'T BELIEVE IT, DUKE. YOU REALLY SIGNED "LAVA-LAVA" LENNY?
THAT'S RIGHT, BOBBY! THE POLYNESIAN PANZER IS OURS!
BUT HOW DID YOU DO IT? I THOUGHT WE COULDN'T AFFORD HIM.
LET'S JUST SAY HIS ATTORNEY AND I WENT TO THE MATS!
UH.. WAIT A MINUTE, DUKE. JUST HOW MUCH DID YOU GIVE HIM?
NOT A PENNY MORE THAN HE'S WORTH! I SWEAR IT! BESIDES, THE PENSION FUND WAS JUST SITTING THERE!
OH, NO..
SO WE CHARGE A LITTLE MORE FOR HOT DOGS THIS YEAR. BIG DEAL!
GB Tuckow

.. AND ON BEHALF OF THE ENTIRE FRONT OFFICE, I'D LIKE TO WELCOME "LAVA-LAVA" LENNY TO THE REDSKINS FAMILY OF STARS! OKAY, WE'LL TAKE YOUR QUESTIONS NOW..

DUKE, THERE ARE REPORTS THAT YOU SPENT A FORTUNE IN REDSKIN MONEY TO BRING "LAVA-LAVA" TO WASHINGTON. WHAT'S THE FINAL FIGURE ON HIS CONTRACT?

WELL, THE SCHEDULE OF PAYMENTS IS VERY, VERY COMPLICATED, SO IT'D BE DIFFICULT FOR ME TO SAY EXACTLY WHAT LENNY WILL RECEIVE ON A PER ANNUM BASIS..

TWO MILLION BIG ONES.
OKAY, BUT PART OF THAT GOES TO YOUR PAROLE OFFICER.
GB Trudeau

MR. DUKE, I HAVE A QUESTION FOR "LAVA-LAVA.."
YEAH, WELL, MAKE IT QUICK.

LENNY, ARE YOU AWARE OF THE RUMORS THAT MR. DUKE DIPPED INTO THE PLAYERS' PENSION FUND TO MEET YOUR SALARY DEMANDS?

UH.. I DON'T KNOW NOTHIN' 'BOUT NO PENSION FUND. I JUST GOT INTO TOWN..

YES, LENNY, BUT..
HE'S CALLING YOU A LIAR, LENNY.
OH, YEAH?
GB Trudeau

DUKE? CALL FOR YOU ON TWO!
EXCUSE ME A MINUTE, WILL YOU, COACH?

DUKE? HI, IT'S THE DUTCHMAN.
WHO?

LISTEN, I HEARD THE TEAM'S REPORTING SOON, AND I WONDERED IF YOU'RE INTERESTED IN A LITTLE ACTION?
ACTION? LISTEN, I DON'T KNOW WHO YOU ARE, CREEP, BUT WE IN THE NFL DON'T LOOK KINDLY ON GAMBLING!

CATCH YOU AT A BAD TIME, DUKE?
YOU'RE DAMN RIGHT, FELLAH!
GB Trudeau

SEE, THE WAY I FIGURE IT, WITH YOUR INSIDE DOPE, WE COULD CLEAN UP, DUKE..
WHAT SORT OF INSIDE DOPE, DUTCHMAN?
YOU KNOW, PLAYER ANALYSIS. WHO'S UP, WHO'S NOT, WHO'S PLAYING HURT, WHO'S PLAYING HIGH, THAT SORT OF THING..
I DUNNO, DUTCH, YOU'RE TALKING ABOUT SOME PRETTY HEAVY DUTY SCAM. IT COULD COST, TOO. HOW'S YOUR SEED MONEY SITUATION?
NEVER BETTER. I'M IN THE MOB NOW.
OH, THAT'S RIGHT. NICE PICTURE IN "NEWSWEEK," BY THE WAY.
GBTrudeau

YOU KNOW, "LAVA-LAVA," I WAS TALKING TO AN ASSOCIATE THE OTHER DAY, AND HE SAID HE WAS SURE THAT YOU'D BE BREAKING THE SOLO TACKLE RECORD THIS YEAR..
WHAT DO YOU THINK OF THAT, BIG FELLAH? WHAT DO YOU FIGURE YOUR CHANCES ARE OF TAKING ALL THE MARBLES THIS SEASON?
EXCELLENT.
THAT SO?
YOU CAN BET ON IT.
WELL, NOW, I'M GLAD TO HEAR THAT..
GBTrudeau

SIR, I UNDERSTAND YOU'RE DEVELOPING A NEW SPORTS MEDICINE PROGRAM..
THAT'S RIGHT, RILEY. THE WAY I SEE IT, THE REDSKINS DESERVE THE BEST.
WHEN A PLAYER GOES OUT ONTO THAT FIELD, I BELIEVE HE HAS EVERY RIGHT TO EXPECT CHEMICAL PARITY WITH THE OPPOSING TEAM!
WOW.. WHAT A RESPONSIBILITY!
YOU BETTER BELIEVE IT.
WHAT CAN I DO TO HELP, BOSS?
WELL, I SUPPOSE YOU COULD STAND LOOKOUT.
GBTrudeau

WHAT ARE YOU PUTTING IN THE GATOR-ADE, SIR?
I'M JUST GOOSING THE JUICE WITH A FEW STEROIDS, BOY. I'M DOING A STUDY..
igloo

WITHOUT THE PLAYERS' KNOWLEDGE, SIR?
LOOK, THOSE GUYS HAVE ENOUGH ON THEIR MINDS WITHOUT HAVING TO FUSS WITH ADDITIVES.
igloo

DON'T WORRY, KID, IT'S ALREADY BEEN TESTED. THERE'S NO WAY I'D GIVE MY BOYS ANY DRUG OR DRUGS I HADN'T TRIED MYSELF IN EVERY CONCEIVABLE COMBINATION!
igloo

WHY DON'T I FIND THAT REASSURING, SIR?
BECAUSE YOU MISSED THE '60'S, BOY. YOU KIDS TODAY LIVE IN A DREAM WORLD!
igloo
GBTrudeau

GOOD WORK-OUT, "LAVA-LAVA".
WELL, I'M JUST TRYIN' TO FIT IN, KNOW WHAT I MEAN?
igloo

HEY.. WHAT'S IN THE GATOR-ADE? TASTES FUNNY..
YOU'RE RIGHT, IT DOES.
igloo

WHATEVER IT IS, I CAN FEEL IT PROMOTING MUSCLE DENSITY.
MUST BE SOME SORT OF ANABOLIC STEROID.
igloo

HMM.. THEY'RE MORE SOPHISTICATED THAN I THOUGHT..
SIR, ARE YOU SURE THE COACH KNOWS ABOUT YOUR STUDY?
GBTrudeau

WHAT IS IT, RILEY?
SIR, JOE THE TRAINER WANTS TO SEE YOU..
KILMER 17
THOMAS 22

WHAT ABOUT?
EDDIE JUST GOT WIPED OUT ON A BLINDSIDE BLOCK. HE LOOKS PRETTY HURT.
KILMER 17
THOMAS 22

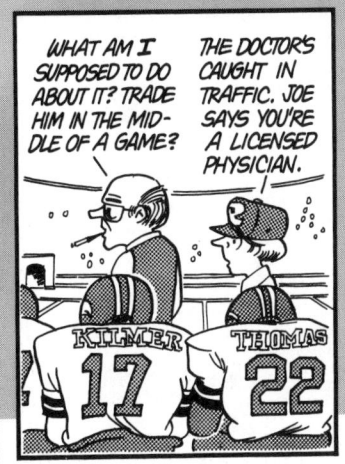
WHAT AM I SUPPOSED TO DO ABOUT IT? TRADE HIM IN THE MIDDLE OF A GAME?
THE DOCTOR'S CAUGHT IN TRAFFIC. JOE SAYS YOU'RE A LICENSED PHYSICIAN.
KILMER 17
THOMAS 22

QUITE RIGHT.
SHOULD I BOIL SOME WATER OR SOMETHING, SIR?
GBTrudeau
THEISMANN 7
RIGGINS 44

RILEY SAID YOU WANTED TO SEE ME, JOE..
YEAH, DUKE, EDDIE HERE JUST GOT HIMSELF SPEARED IN THE RIB CAGE.
BREAKS OF THE GAME, SON..
THE DOCTOR'S CAUGHT IN TRAFFIC. JACK SAYS YOU'RE A LICENSED PHYSICIAN.
MORE LIKE A THERAPIST, REALLY..
WHATEVER. DO YOU THINK YOU COULD GIVE THE KID SOMETHING TO KILL THE PAIN THE REST OF THE GAME?
SURE. DOES HE HAVE TO BE UPRIGHT?
IDEALLY.
WHAT IS THIS STUFF, MAN?
JUST A COUPLE HUNDRED MGS. OF DEX. IT'LL TEMPORARILY MASK THE PAIN IN YOUR RIBS.
ANY SIDE EFFECTS?
OH, A FEW. NOTHING TO GET EXCITED ABOUT.
WHAT ARE YOU TALKIN' ABOUT, MAN?
OKAY, OKAY, SO YOU MAY EXPERIENCE THE ODD VIOLENT FIT OF PSYCHOTIC HYPERACTIVITY.
I MAY?
BUT YOU'RE A LINEBACKER! WHO THE HELL'S GONNA KNOW THE DIFFERENCE?
DUKE, WHERE THE HELL IS EDDIE? WE GOT KICK-OFF IN TWO MINUTES!
GEE, I WOULDN'T KNOW, COACH. I RELEASED HIM ON HIS OWN RECOGNIZANCE RIGHT AFTER TREATMENT.
EXCUSE ME, SIRS..
RILEY, HAVE YOU SEEN EDDIE? WE GOT A HURT PLAYER WANDERING AROUND..
HURT? ARE YOU KIDDING ME?
YOU'VE SEEN HIM?
HE'S RIPPING APART HIS LOCKER!
AMAZING. WHAT DO YOU CALL THAT?
A PRE-PSYCHOTIC RAGE. USE IT WISELY.

TIME OUT!
OH, NO, EDDIE! NOT AGAIN!
KILMER 17
THOMAS 22
THAT'S THE SECOND QUARTERBACK IN A ROW THAT HE'S CLOTHESLINED! HE'S GOING TO KILL US WITH PENALTIES!
KILMER 17
THOMAS 22
DUKE, WHATEVER YOU FED THAT KID WAS WAY THE HELL OUT OF LINE!
I'M SORRY, COACH. I MUST HAVE MISCALCULATED THE DOSAGE..
KILMER 17
THOMAS 22
OH, MY GOD! HE'S GOING AFTER THE REF!
GO FETCH MY DART GUN, BOY.
DOWLING 10
HILL 30
G B Trudeau
SO HOW'S EDDIE DOING, KID?
HE'S OUT FOR THE SEASON. AS ARE BOTH OF THE GUYS HE CLOTHESLINED.
SIR, I MAY BE A LITTLE OLD-FASHIONED, BUT ALL THESE OVER-AMPED PLAYERS BASHING EACH OTHER'S BRAINS OUT.. CAN THAT BE GOOD FOR THE GAME?
IT'S THE OWNERS, SON. THEY'RE BLIND TO THE PROBLEM. WITHOUT URINE TESTS, WHAT CAN I DO?
I DON'T KNOW, SIR, BUT RIGHT NOW YOU'RE PUTTING A LOT OF GUYS IN THE HOSPITAL!
HEY, LOOK, CHOIR BOY..
SIR, I'VE DECIDED TO GO TO THE PAPERS.
G B Trudeau
GO TO THE PAPERS? ARE YOU MAD, KID? YOU WANT TO GET THE WHOLE FRONT OFFICE BUSTED?
WELL, NO, SIR, BUT I JUST CAN'T SIT BY AND WATCH THE GAME RUINED BY HOMICIDAL SPEED-FREAKS!
LOOK, RILEY! THIS IS FOOTBALL! TO QUOTE HARRY TRUMAN, IF YOU CAN'T TAKE THE HEAT, THEN GET THE HELL OUT OF NAGASAKI!
YOU LETTING ME GO, SIR?
WELL, NOW THAT YOU MENTION IT, THAT'S A DAMN GOOD..
"BOY, 15, AXED BY REDSKINS' DRUG DOC."
SIT DOWN, RILEY..
IT'S TOO LATE FOR THAT, SIR..
G B Trudeau

HELLO?
HELLO, IS THIS RICK REDFERN, ACE INVESTIGATIVE REPORTER FOR THE "POST"?
NOT ACCORDING TO MY EDITOR.
I HAVE SOMETHING FOR YOU, SIR. LISTEN CAREFULLY..
THE INJURIES IN LAST SUNDAY'S REDSKINS GAME? THEY WEREN'T JUST BAD LUCK. THE PLAYER RESPONSIBLE WAS STONED OUT OF HIS GOURD AT THE TIME! INTERESTED?
NOT REALLY. HOW OLD ARE YOU, SON?
I'LL BE IN TOUCH. >CLICK!<
GB Trudeau
MR. REDFERN?
YO?
IT'S ME. DON'T TURN AROUND. THEY MIGHT BE WATCHING.
WHO?
THE NFL. I'M HERE AT GREAT PERSONAL RISK. MINE IS A TALE RIFE WITH SCANDAL AND INTRIGUE.
NOT TO MENTION MELODRAMA. MAYBE YOU BETTER ORDER FIRST.
RIGHT. HOW ARE THE CHEESEBURGERS?
THEY CAN BE TRUSTED.
GB Trudeau
.. AND BOTH QUARTERBACKS ARE NOW OUT FOR THE REST OF THE SEASON!
WELL, THAT'S QUITE A STORY, KID. I'LL HAVE TO CHECK IT OUT, OF COURSE..
TAKE YOUR TIME, MR. REDFERN. THE PROBLEM ISN'T GOING AWAY TOMORROW. WHAT TIME HAVE YOU GOT?
OH..IT'S ABOUT ONE.
OKAY, I GOTTA GO. HERE'S WHAT I WANT YOU TO DO. ORDER THE APRICOT FLAMBÉ. WHEN THE WAITER STARTS TO LIGHT IT, KNOCK HIS ARM SO THAT THE BRANDY SPILLS ALL OVER THE TABLE..
AS THE FLAMES SPREAD TO THE TABLECLOTH, I'LL SLIP OUT IN THE CONFUSION.
KID, DO YOU COME HERE OFTEN?
GB Trudeau

CLACKITY!
RUUMMBLE!
CLACKITY!
WHIPPITY! WHIP!

EXTRA! INSIDER, 15, RAPS 'SKINS IN SPEED SCANDAL!
Post

SPORTS
MONDA
Drug Doc Termed 'Menace To Sport'
By Richard Redfern
WASHINGTON- An Int
amphetamine
scandal-
Injuries?
page 43

RING! RING!
GET THAT, WILL YA, KID?
I WONDER IF WE COULD TALK FIRST, SIR..
GB Trudeau

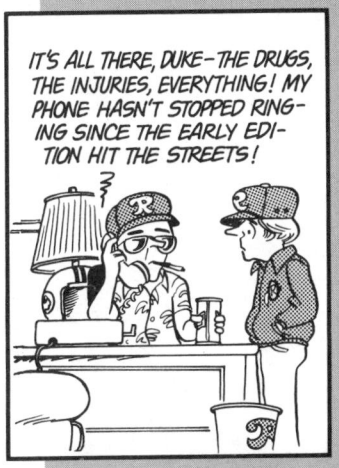
IT'S ALL THERE, DUKE-THE DRUGS, THE INJURIES, EVERYTHING! MY PHONE HASN'T STOPPED RINGING SINCE THE EARLY EDITION HIT THE STREETS!

DAMN! THIS COULD BE WORSE THAN THE STOLEN PLAYBOOK! HOW THE HELL DID THE "POST" FIND OUT, COACH? EDDIE'S THE ONLY ONE BESIDES US WHO KNOWS ABOUT IT, AND HE'S IN A COMA!

I DON'T KNOW, DUKE, BUT IF YOU DON'T TRACK THE LITTLE SNITCH DOWN FAST, YOU MIGHT AS WELL START PACKING!
TROUBLE, SIR?

IT JUST CAME TO ME, COACH.
IT WASN'T MY FAULT, SIR. THEY PLIED ME WITH CHEESEBURGERS.
GB Trudeau

YOUR FOOTBALL ARTICLE SEEMS TO BE CAUSING QUITE A STIR, RICHARD..
YEAH, THAT GUY DUKE SURE DOESN'T TAKE THINGS LYING DOWN.

HE RELEASED A 2,000 WORD REBUTTAL YESTERDAY, AND TODAY HE'S HOLDING A PRESS CONFERENCE IN HIS OFFICE..

HE CLAIMS HE'S EVEN GOING TO PRODUCE THE INJURED PLAYER TO TESTIFY ON HIS BEHALF!

I DUNNO, SIR, HE DOESN'T LOOK SO GOOD..
NURSE! CUT THIS MAN DOWN!
GB Trudeau

..AND DESPITE MY HEATED PROTESTATIONS, EDDIE HAS CRAWLED FROM HIS HOSPITAL BED TO JOIN ME IN OUTRAGED DENIAL OF THIS ALLEGED PIECE OF REPORTING!
THIS ARTICLE REPRESENTS THE SHODDIEST KIND OF JOURNALISM! NAMES, DATES, PLACES ARE ALL INACCURATE! EVEN DOSAGES ARE DISTORTED AND TAKEN TOTALLY OUT OF CONTEXT!
AS EDDIE VIGOROUSLY CONFIRMS, THE "CONTROLLED SUBSTANCES" I GAVE HIM IN LAST SUNDAY'S GAME WERE NOTHING MORE THAN COMMON ASPIRIN TABLETS! RIGHT, EDDIE?
MMPHH.
NOW, I HOPE WE'VE HEARD THE LAST OF THIS SILLY EPISODE!
GB Trudeau

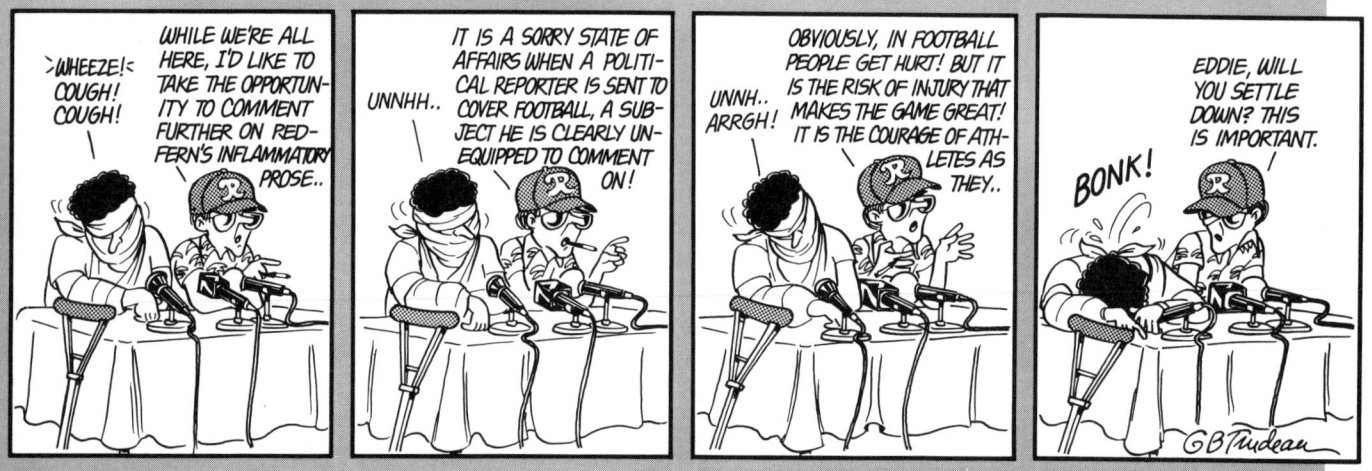
>WHEEZE!< COUGH! COUGH!
WHILE WE'RE ALL HERE, I'D LIKE TO TAKE THE OPPORTUNITY TO COMMENT FURTHER ON REDFERN'S INFLAMMATORY PROSE..
UNNHH..
IT IS A SORRY STATE OF AFFAIRS WHEN A POLITICAL REPORTER IS SENT TO COVER FOOTBALL, A SUBJECT HE IS CLEARLY UNEQUIPPED TO COMMENT ON!
UNNH.. ARRGH!
OBVIOUSLY, IN FOOTBALL PEOPLE GET HURT! BUT IT IS THE RISK OF INJURY THAT MAKES THE GAME GREAT! IT IS THE COURAGE OF ATHLETES AS THEY..
BONK!
EDDIE, WILL YOU SETTLE DOWN? THIS IS IMPORTANT.
GB Trudeau

HEY, BOSS! WHAT ARE YOU DOING? YOU'RE DUE AT A RECEPTION IN TEN MINUTES!
RECEPTION? WHAT RECEPTION?
FOR THE CHINESE FOREIGN EXCHANGE STUDENTS! YOU ACCEPTED WEEKS AGO!
OUT OF THE QUESTION, RILEY! CAN'T YOU SEE I'M BUSY?
BUSY? DOING WHAT?
I FORGET. CHECK MY APPOINTMENT BOOK.
"11:30 TO 4:00, FIELD TRIP TO FRONTAL LOBES.."
THAT'S IT! I LEFT AN HOUR AGO!
GB Trudeau

DR. CAVENDISH?
YES! YOU MUST BE RILEY!

YES, MA'AM. I WAS ASKED TO BRING MR. DUKE OVER HERE TO MEET YOUR CHINESE STUDENTS.
WELL, THEY'RE ALL HERE AND MOST ANXIOUS TO MEET HIM!

I DON'T KNOW IF YOU'RE AWARE OF THE IMPACT YOU MADE IN PEKING, MR. DUKE. APPARENTLY, YOUR TENURE THERE WAS MUCH DISCUSSED!

RILEY, WHY IS THIS WOMAN SHRIEKING AT ME?
IF YOU COULD JUST SIGN HERE, MA'AM..
I'M SORRY, WAS I TALKING TOO LOUD?
GB Trudeau

SIR, IT IS A GREAT HONOR TO MEET THE FORMER AMBASSADOR TO OUR COUNTRY..
WHO IS THIS STRANGE LITTLE MAN?

OUR LEADERS STILL TALK ABOUT YOU WITH AWE..
MAYBE IF I SHOW HIM MY LUGER, HE'LL GO AWAY..

SIR!
WHAT THE.. OH, MY GOD!

SIR! IT'S ME, HONEY!
BRAIN TO EYEBALLS: WILL NOT COMPUTE!
GB Trudeau

THIS ISN'T HAPPENING..
SIR! IT'S ME, HONEY!

I DON'T GET IT. I'M A RESPONSIBLE CONSUMER..
(THIS IS MR. DUKE. I USED TO BE HIS TRANSLATOR!)

I ONLY USE THE BEST PRODUCT. I NEVER MISCALCULATE DOSAGES..
I'M AN EXCHANGE STUDENT NOW! RIGHT HERE AT GEORGETOWN!

SO WHY AM I SURROUNDED BY TINY, PANTING ORIENTALS?
(HE'S REALLY A GREAT GUY. HE'S JUST A LITTLE SHY.)
GB Trudeau

WELL! THE STUDENTS CERTAINLY SEEM TO BE FASCINATED BY YOUR MR. DUKE!
UH-HUH. SAY, WHO'S THE YOUNG LADY WHO HAS BEEN MONOPOLIZING HIM?
THAT'S MS. HUAN. SHE'S FROM PEKING.
ACCORDING TO HER, SHE AND MR. DUKE WERE CLOSE FRIENDS DURING HIS TOUR OF DUTY IN CHINA..
WILL YOU BE SHOWING ME WASHINGTON BY NIGHT, SIR?
CAN'T MAKE ANY SUDDEN MOVES.. HAVE TO STAY CALM..
GBTrudeau

EXCUSE ME, SIRS. I WONDER IF YOU COULD TELL ME WHERE I MIGHT FIND MR. DUKE..
SHOULD BE IN THE CLUB-HOUSE, MISS. FIRST DOOR ON THE RIGHT.
THANK YOU.
NOT AT ALL.
MAY I JUST SAY YOU'RE QUITE A PAIR OF SPECIMENS, SIRS.
PART OF THE JOB, MISS.
YOU SHOULD SEE THE GUYS WHO START.
GBTrudeau

THERE YOU ARE, SIR!
OH, NO..
I'VE BEEN LOOKING ALL OVER FOR YOU! I'VE JUST BEEN TALKING TO YOUR RESERVE QUARTERBACK! WHAT A GREAT GUY!
THIS BETTER BE AN AFTER-EFFECT..
LISTEN, I THINK YOU SHOULD PLAY HIM. HE'S MUCH BETTER LOOKING THAN THE GUY YOU GOT PLAYING NOW.
USED TO BE A TIME WHEN YOU KNEW WHAT WENT INTO THIS STUFF..
UM.. YOU'RE NOT GOING TO CHANGE FOR OUR DATE, SIR?
THAT DOES IT! I'M SWITCHING PHARMACISTS!
GBTrudeau

I'M CERTAINLY LOOKING FORWARD TO OUR DATE TONIGHT, SIR. THE OTHER GIRLS IN MY DORM SAY THE NIGHT LIFE HERE IS REALLY SOMETHING!
REDSKINS

YOU'RE NOT GOING TO TAKE ME TO A DISCO, ARE YOU, SIR? I MEAN, I'M NOT SURE IF THAT'S ALLOWED. I'D HAVE TO CHECK WITH THE EMBASSY FIRST.
REDSKINS

REDSKINS

IT'S REALLY YOU, ISN'T IT?
YES, SIR. I CHANGED MY HAIR A LITTLE. THAT MAY BE THROWING YOU.
GB Trudeau

YOU KNOW, SIR, IT WAS MORE THAN JUST A HAPPY ACCIDENT, US BUMPING INTO EACH OTHER LIKE WE DID..
REDSKINS

IN FACT, THE FIRST THING I DID AFTER CLEARING CUSTOMS WAS CALL THE STATE DEPARTMENT TO FIND OUT WHERE YOU WERE!
REDSKINS

IMAGINE MY SURPRISE WHEN I LEARNED YOU WERE RIGHT HERE IN WASHINGTON, WORKING WITH THE NATIVE AMERICANS!
REDSKINS

REDSKINS.
RIGHT. IT'S SO LIKE YOU TO BE HELPING OUT OTHERS, SIR.
GB Trudeau

I'M SORRY, HONEY, I JUST HAVEN'T THE TIME TO DEAL WITH YOU RIGHT NOW..
WHERE YOU GOING, SIR?
REDSKINS

ZEIBERT'S. I'M GOING TO HAVE A FEW BEERS, AND THEN WATCH THE DALLAS GAME. BY MYSELF!
WHAT IS ZEIBERT'S, SIR? SOME SORT OF "JOINT"?

THIS IS BUSINESS, HONEY. I'M AFRAID I CAN'T ASK YOU TO..
DON'T TELL ME YOU'RE GOING TO SHOW ME THE SOFT UNDERBELLY OF WASHINGTON NIGHTCLUB LIFE?

THE WHAT?
DON'T YOU THINK WE BETTER MAKE RESERVATIONS?
REDSKINS
GB Trudeau

GOOD MORNING, FRONT DESK.
YEAH, THIS IS MR. DUKE. WHERE AM I?
UH.. YOU'RE AT THE RAMADA INN IN MIAMI, SIR.
MIAMI? OH, C'MON, WHAT THE HELL WOULD I BE DOING IN MIAMI?
I WOULDN'T KNOW, SIR. MAYBE THE SUPER BOWL. IS EVERY-THING OKAY?
OKAY? ARE YOU GOING TO PRETEND YOU DON'T KNOW THERE'S AN OVER-TURNED GOLF CART IN MY BATHROOM?
THIS MUST BE ROOM 402.
LISTEN, THIS PLACE IS FILTHY! I WANT TO CHECK OUT!
IT'S THE BELLBOY, SIR. I'VE GOT THE REST OF YOUR ORDER, SIR..
ORDER? WHAT ORDER?
THE CASE OF GIN, SIR. AND THE GRAPEFRUIT AND THE BADMINTON NETS YOU WANTED!
BADMINTON NETS? I ORDERED BADMINTON NETS?
UH.. YES, SIR. YOU SAID YOU WERE CONDUCTING SOME SORT OF EXPERI-MENT!
EXPERIMENT? LOOK, I DON'T KNOW WHAT'S GOING ON HERE. JUST SET EVERY-THING BY THE DOOR, OKAY?
OKAY. YOU THROUGH WITH THE GOLF CART YET?
UH.. I'M NOT SURE. I NEED TIME TO PIECE THIS THING TOGETHER..
MR. DUKE? IT'S RILEY HERE..
RILEY! WHERE ARE YOU, BOY?
DOWNSTAIRS. THE BELLBOY SAID YOU WERE FINALLY UP, SO I..
RILEY, WHAT THE HELL AM I DOING IN MIAMI? WHAT'S GOING ON? I CAN'T REMEMBER A DAMN THING!
WELL, SIR, THERE WAS AN INCIDENT IN YOUR OFFICE AT REDSKIN PARK. A U.S. MARSHAL WAS INVOLVED..
YOU MEAN, I'M.. I'M..
YES, SIR. YOU'RE ON THE LAM.
DAMN! I KNEW IT! GET UP HERE AND GIVE ME A HAND WITH THESE MATTRESSES!

FOR GOD'S SAKE, SIT DOWN, BOY! BEFORE SOMEONE RECOGNIZES US!
OH, DON'T WORRY, SIR. NO ONE COULD POSSIBLY KNOW YOU'RE IN TOWN..

DON'T BE SO SURE. WHAT DID I DO, ANYWAY?
WELL, SIR, IT ALL STARTED WHEN MR. WILLIAMS FIRED YOU LAST FRIDAY. YOU WOULDN'T LEAVE, SO HE GOT A COURT ORDER TO HAVE YOU REMOVED..

YOUR UNCLE SENT THE DAMN FEDS AFTER ME?
YES, SIR. BUT AS USUAL, WHEN THE MARSHALS TURNED UP, YOU ACTED LIKE YOU'D NEVER EVEN HEARD OF THE U.S. CRIMINAL CODE!

GOOD FOR ME! DAMN THING SHOULDA BEEN SCRAPPED YEARS AGO WHEN...
FORTUNATELY, YOU'RE NOT MUCH OF A SHOT.
GB Trudeau

MY GOD! YOU MEAN, I GOT INTO A FIREFIGHT WITH THE HEAT?
WELL, NOT A FIREFIGHT EXACTLY. YOU JUST SHOT OUT ALL THE FRONT WINDOWS AND TOOK OFF..

THAT NIGHT YOU CALLED ME FROM THE AIRPORT IN A RAGE. YOU SAID YOU KNEW THAT WILLIAMS WAS GOING TO BE AT THE SUPER BOWL, AND THAT YOU WERE GOING TO "TRACK HIM DOWN AND GREASE HIM" FOR FIRING YOU.

BEING HIS NEPHEW, I FELT I HAD AN OBLIGATION TO FIND YOU AND NIP THIS SICK, VIOLENT NOTION IN THE BUD! DON'T YOU RECALL ANY OF THIS, SIR?

A PLAN.. I MUST HAVE HAD A PLAN.
THINK, SIR! WAS THERE A GUN? I'VE GOT TO TRY TO STOP YOU!
GB Trudeau

YOU BETTER GET ON THAT PLANE, SIR. THE BLACK AND WHITES COULD TURN UP ANY MINUTE NOW..
YOU AND YOUR UNCLE HAVEN'T HEARD THE LAST OF ME, KID!

I HOPE SO, SIR. GOODBYE.
THE FANS WON'T LET YOU GET AWAY WITH THIS, BOY! WHEN WORD GETS OUT I'M FIRED, THEY'LL TEAR THE STADIUM APART!

YOU'RE A LOSER, RILEY, YOU HEAR ME? YOU'RE A TREACHEROUS LITTLE WORM! THERE'S A SPECIAL PLACE IN HELL FOR SNITCHES LIKE YOU! YOU HEAR ME?

HE'S OVER THERE, OFFICER!
SMOKING! HURRY!
ZIP!

BRENNER! IT'S ME, DUKE!
HI, DUKE. WHERE YOU CALLING FROM?
DENVER AIRPORT! LISTEN, I NEED A RIDE HOME!
SO RENT A CAR. I'M YOUR CARETAKER, MAN, NOT YOUR CHAUFFEUR.
I HAVEN'T GOT TIME TO ARGUE, BRENNER! JUST GO GET MY PICK-UP AND GET THE HELL DOWN HERE!
OKAY, OKAY, KEEP YOUR SHIRT ON! IS SOMETHING WRONG, DUKE?
NO. NOTHING. SMEAR MUD ON THE LICENSE PLATES, OKAY?
ARE YOU KIDDING ME, MAN? THREE APB'S IN UNDER A YEAR?
©B Trudeau
CAN YOU BEAT THAT OL' LADY OF MINE, BRENNER? SHE MUST HAVE CHANGED THE LOCK ON EVERY DAMN DOOR OF THE HOUSE!
DUKE, ABOUT YOUR WIFE..
FORTUNATELY, I ALWAYS KEEP A VIAL OF NITRO IN THE TOOL SHED FOR JUST THIS SORT OF EMERGENCY.. OKAY, STAND CLEAR..
DUKE, YOUR..
KABLOOM!
I'M HOME, HONEY!
I'VE BEEN TRYING TO TELL YOU, MAN, THE DIVORCE IS FINAL.
©B Trudeau
MR. DUKE? YOUR CARETAKER SAID I MIGHT FIND YOU HERE..
MY NAME'S SPRINGFIELD. YOU'RE A HARD MAN TO TRACK DOWN, MR. DUKE. I UNDERSTAND YOU'RE ON THE RUN FROM THE LAW. IS THAT RIGHT?
ISN'T THAT RIGHT, MR. DUKE?
DON'T EVEN BLINK.
WHEE! THIS IS COLORADO! SIT UP, I HAVE AN OFFER.
©B Trudeau

OKAY, MAC, WHO ARE YOU?
TAKE IT EASY, COWBOY. THE NAME'S SPRINGFIELD. I HAVE AN OFFER FOR YOU..

OF COURSE YOU DO. NOW, GET YOUR HANDS OUT OF THAT CASE OR I'LL..
NOW, NOW, MR. DUKE. WE BOTH KNOW THAT THING ISN'T LOADED..

CLICK!
CLICK!

WELL, I'LL BE DAMNED. HOW'D YOU KNOW..
OKAY, FELLAH! THE DEAL'S OFF!
GBTrudeau

OKAY, SPRINGFIELD, IF YOU AREN'T THE HEAT, WHO ARE YOU?
I'M FROM THE NATIONAL RIFLE ASSOCIATION, MR. DUKE! AND I WAS GOING TO MAKE YOU AN OFFER..

THE N.R.A.? NOW, WAIT A MINUTE, PERHAPS I WAS BEING A LITTLE HASTY..
YOU..YOU KNOW OUR WORK?

KNOW IT? HELL, I'VE SUPPORTED IT FOR YEARS! THESE ARE REPRESSIVE TIMES, SPRINGFIELD!
AND HOW! EVEN AS WE SPEAK, NEW GUN CONTROL LAWS ARE BEING PREPARED BY LIBERALS AND THEIR ILK!

WHAT? LIBERALS? THEIR ILK? YOU'VE SEEN THEM?
THE EROSION OF FREEDOM IS NOT A PRETTY SIGHT, MR. DUKE.
GBTrudeau

OKAY, SPRINGFIELD, WHERE EXACTLY DO I FIT INTO ALL OF THIS?
MR. DUKE, THE N.R.A. KNOWS YOU TO BE AN ARTICULATE DEFENDER OF THE HANDGUN OWNER..

IF YOU'LL COME TESTIFY BEFORE THE JUDICIARY COMMITTEE HEARINGS ON GUN CONTROL, OUR LAWYERS WILL TAKE CARE OF YOUR LITTLE PROBLEM WITH THE D.A.'S OFFICE.

REALLY? THEY COULD DO THAT?
A TRIAL WOULD ONLY EMBARRASS YOUR FORMER BOSS. WE THINK WE CAN CONVINCE HIM TO DROP THE CHARGES.

GREAT! CAN YOU SUE HIM FOR ME, TOO?
WELL..OKAY, BUT THAT'S MY FINAL OFFER!
GBTrudeau

I'LL BE PACKED IN A MINUTE, SPRINGFIELD. JUST MAKE YOURSELF COMFORTABLE.
QUITE A PLACE YOU HAVE HERE, MR. DUKE..

THANKS. I BUILT THIS CABIN MYSELF, BACK IN 1963. DID THE DECORATING AND EVERYTHING.

VERY NICE. MAY I ASK WHY YOU KEEP LAND MINES ON ALL THE SOFAS?

YEAH, I WAS TRYING TO TEACH THE DOGS TO STAY OFF THE FURNITURE.
WHAT DOGS?
GBTrudeau

OKAY, MR. DUKE, YOU'VE BEEN HERE BEFORE, SO I DON'T HAVE TO TELL YOU THAT THIS CONGRESS IS EVERY BIT AS SPINELESS AS ITS PREDECESSORS!
SENAT
JUDIC
IN SES

REMEMBER, THE LEGISLATORS WE DON'T OWN OUTRIGHT ARE SCARED TO DEATH OF MAIL! THEY'RE IN YOUR POCKET, MR. DUKE, SO WHEN YOU WALK THROUGH THAT DOOR, WALK TALL!
SEN
JUD
IN S

GOTCHA. I DON'T REALLY HAVE TO READ ALL OF THESE CRIME-STOPPER STORIES, DO I?
NO, NO, OF COURSE NOT. YOU JUST BE YOURSELF. YOU'RE OUR ACE IN THE HOLE, MR. DUKE!
SEN
JUD
IN S

I AM? WHAT HAPPENED TO THE WIDOW WHO WASTED NINE MUGGERS?
SHE FOLLOWS YOU. YOU'RE OUR NUMBER ONE GUN!
GBTrudeau
SENAT
JUDIC
IN SES

..AND IT IS THE POSITION OF THE NATIONAL RIFLE ASSOCIATION THAT WHEN IT COMES TO ARBITRARY SOCIAL CONTROLS, MORE IS LESS!"

"WHAT IS NEEDED INSTEAD IS A SENSE OF RESTRAINT AND FAIR PLAY. IF OUR ONCE PROUD SCHOOLS WERE TO RESUME THE TEACHING OF.."
EXCUSE ME, MR. DUKE..

YES?
I WANT TO GET THIS STRAIGHT. IS IT ACTUALLY YOUR VIEW THAT THE ANSWER TO RISING HANDGUN VIOLENCE IS A RENEWED EMPHASIS ON SPORTSMANSHIP?

EXACTLY. WE ADVOCATE A RETURN TO RESPONSIBLE GUNPLAY.
IN OUR ONCE PROUD SCHOOLS?
GBTrudeau

"THE NATIONAL RIFLE ASSOCIATION THEREFORE OPPOSES ANY AND ALL LEGISLATIVE ATTEMPTS TO CONTROL OUR CONSTITUTIONAL RIGHT TO BEAR ARMS!"

THAT'S THE END OF OUR PREPARED STATEMENT, MR. CHAIRMAN. I'D BE HAPPY TO ENTERTAIN ANY QUESTIONS.

MR. DUKE, DOES YOUR GROUP'S OPPOSITION EXTEND TO A SIMPLE REQUIREMENT OF SERIAL NUMBERS TO AID POLICE IN IDENTIFICATION?

WHAT'S WRONG WITH DENTAL RECORDS?
I WAS REFERRING TO THE GUNS.
GB Trudeau

SENATOR, THE POINT IS THAT ONCE YOU HAVE GUN CONTROL, THE ONLY PEOPLE LEFT WITH GUNS ARE CRIMINALS!
WHICH WOULD PREVENT A GREAT MANY MURDERS, MR. DUKE!

AS YOU WELL KNOW, ALMOST 70% OF ALL MURDERS ARE COMMITTED AMONG FAMILY MEMBERS OR FRIENDS. AND OVER HALF OF THEM INVOLVE HANDGUNS!

EXACTLY! SO LOOK AT IT FROM THE POINT OF VIEW OF THE VICTIM! WHAT IF YOUR WIFE WERE ATTACKING YOU WITH A HANDGUN?
I DON'T FOLLOW, MR. DUKE.

WELL, WOULDN'T YOU WANT TO BE IN A POSITION TO RETURN THE FIRE?
WELL, I..UH..
YOU DON'T HAVE TO ANSWER THAT, JIM.
GB Trudeau

THE QUESTION WE ARE FACING, THEN, MR. DUKE, IS WHETHER THE WISHES OF 80% OF THE AMERICAN PEOPLE WILL AGAIN GO UNHEEDED..

I CANNOT SPEAK FOR MY COLLEAGUES, BUT I FOR ONE AM FED UP WITH YOUR DEADLY LOBBY AND ITS FANATICAL DEFENSE OF A TRAGIC AND UNCONSCIONABLE PUBLIC POLICY!

I SEE.
GB Trudeau

SHALL I PUT YOU DOWN FOR A MILLION POST CARDS, THEN, SENATOR?
DON'T TRY TO INTIMIDATE ME, MR. DUKE!

5 TEHERAN

1979-1981

DUKE! HOLD YOUR FIRE! I'M A FRIEND!
I'LL BE THE JUDGE OF THAT, STRANGER! PUT YOUR HANDS UP WHERE I CAN SEE 'EM!

DUKE, IT'S ME! YOUR OL' BUSINESS ASSOCIATE FROM SAMOA - JIM ANDREWS!
ANDREWS? YOU MEAN, UNIVERSAL PETROLEUM ANDREWS?

THEN YOU HAVEN'T FORGOTTEN!
FORGOTTEN? HOW DOES ONE FORGET A GUTLESS, GOUGING OIL PUSHER WHO'D TRADE HIS OWN GRANDMOTHER TO THE ARABS!

HEY, C'MON, AT LEAST HER SINUSES CLEARED UP..
STILL BANKING AT GENEVA SAVINGS AND LOAN, ARE YOU?
GBTrudeau

SO, DUKE! HOW'S TRICKS?
HOW'S "TRICKS"?

ANDREWS, A MAN CAPABLE OF CREATING A MASSIVE OIL SHORTAGE BY MAKING A SINGLE PHONE CALL DOES NOT FLY HALF WAY ACROSS THE COUNTRY TO ASK ABOUT "TRICKS"!

QUITE RIGHT. I'LL BE DIRECT: WHAT'S YOUR GOING RATE FOR COMMITTING AN UNSPEAKABLY DEPRAVED BUT HIGHLY PATRIOTIC ACT?
$100,000, PLUS 10% OF THE GROSS.

I RESPECT YOU TOO MUCH TO HAGGLE.
BUT I DON'T WORK WITH ALBANIANS! AND CHILDREN AND PETS ARE EXTRA.
GBTrudeau

ONLY ONE THING MISSING FROM THIS CONTRACT, ANDREWS: ANY MENTION OF THE JOB!
ALL IN GOOD TIME, DUKE. THE STAKES ARE HIGH IN THIS BUSINESS. I'M SURE YOU APPRECIATE THE NEED FOR SECURITY.

YEAH, ESPECIALLY MY OWN! YOU'LL HAVE TO DO BETTER THAN THAT, ANDREWS!
I ASSURE YOU, DUKE, YOUR MISSION FOR THE COMPANY IS QUITE WITHIN THE SCOPE OF YOUR CONSIDERABLE TALENTS.

DAMMIT, MAN! I HAVE TO KNOW WHAT I'M GETTING INTO!
DUKE, LET'S JUST SAY THAT IF YOU SUCCEED, YOU MAY WELL ALTER THE ENTIRE COURSE OF AMERICAN ECONOMIC HISTORY!

ME? THE COURSE OF HISTORY? HOW LONG WOULD THAT TAKE?
TWO WEEKS, TOPS. AND WE HANDLE ALL THE PAPERWORK.
GBTrudeau

DUKE, MAY I JUST SAY ON BEHALF OF THE BOARD OF UNIVERSAL PETROLEUM HOW GLAD WE ARE TO HAVE YOU ABOARD!
TELL ME, ANDREWS, DO YOU EVER TIRE OF PLAYING GOD?

ON OCCASION. SOMETIMES IT CAN BE AN AWESOME RESPONSIBILITY. REMEMBER THE 1974. RECESSION?
YEAH?

I CAUSED IT.
YOU WHAT?

I JUST GOT BEHIND IN MY MAIL. PURE CARELESSNESS.
YOU KNOW, I THOUGHT THAT HAD YOUR FINGERPRINTS ON IT!
GBTrudeau

DUKE? DUKE, ARE YOU OKAY? IT'S ME, BRENNER!
BRENNER? BRENNER, MY MANSERVANT?

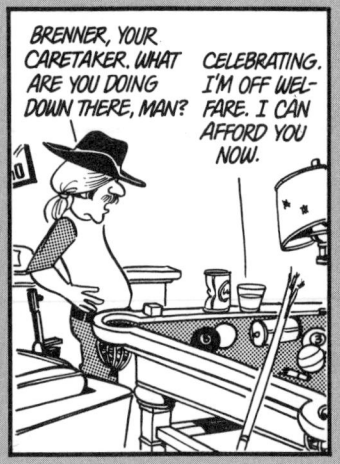
BRENNER, YOUR CARETAKER. WHAT ARE YOU DOING DOWN THERE, MAN?
CELEBRATING. I'M OFF WELFARE. I CAN AFFORD YOU NOW.

THAT'S GOOD NEWS, MAN. WHAT'S THE JOB?
IT'S CONFIDENTIAL, BRENNER. IN FACT, IT'S SO SENSITIVE, SO CRITICAL, EVEN I DON'T KNOW WHAT IT IS! AS OF TODAY YOU'RE WORKING FOR A MAN ON THE CUTTING EDGE OF HISTORY!

SOUNDS DICEY, MAN. I'LL NEED A DEPOSIT.
BRENNER, YOU JUST WROTE YOURSELF OUT OF MY MEMOIRS.
GBTrudeau

LOOK, DUKE, BEFORE YOU GO, WE HAVE TO TALK ABOUT FINANCES. I HAVEN'T BEEN PAID IN A YEAR!
NEITHER HAVE I, BRENNER. WE ALL HAVE OUR CROSSES TO BEAR.

DUKE, I'M SERIOUS! IF YOU DON'T PAY ME NOW, I DON'T SEE HOW I'LL BE ABLE TO KEEP..
PAY YOU? PAY YOU FOR WHAT? YOU CALL YOURSELF A CARETAKER? LOOK AT THIS PLACE!

YOU DON'T UNDERSTAND, MAN. SEE, MY OL' LADY IS EXPECTING, AND..
DAMMIT, BRENNER! DON'T DRAG YOUR PERSONAL LIFE INTO THIS! IT'S UNPROFESSIONAL!

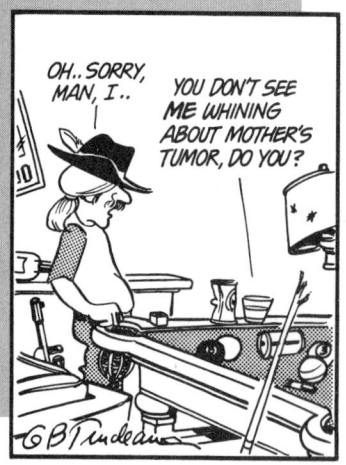
OH.. SORRY, MAN, I..
YOU DON'T SEE ME WHINING ABOUT MOTHER'S TUMOR, DO YOU?
GBTrudeau

YEAH?
DUKE? ANDREWS HERE. LISTEN VERY CAREFULLY. YOU'RE LEAVING TONIGHT FOR THE DENVER AIRPORT..
POT O'G

AT EXACTLY 11:30 P.M., GO TO THE PAY PHONE BEHIND THE AVIS COUNTER. ON THE THIRD RING, PICK UP THE RECEIVER AND ASK FOR "MOTHER"..
POT O'G

NOT SO FAST, BIG FELLAH! I'M NOT GOING **ANYWHERE** UNTIL I SEE AN ADVANCE! WHERE THE HELL ARE MY KRUGERRANDS?
NICE TRY, DUKE. YOUR GOLD WAS DELIVERED YESTERDAY. WE'VE GOT YOUR CARETAKER'S SIGNATURE.
POT O'G

WHOSE SIGNATURE?
LOOK, DUKE, IF YOU CAN'T KEEP YOUR OWN PEOPLE IN LINE, DON'T BLAME ME!
POT O'G
GB Trudeau

OKAY, BRENNER, DON'T EVEN BLINK.
DUKE! WHAT ARE YOU **DOING**, MAN? PUT THAT THING DOWN!
22

I'M ONLY GOING TO ASK YOU ONCE, BRENNER! WHERE THE HELL ARE MY KRUGERRANDS?
YOUR WHAT? I DON'T KNOW WHAT YOU'RE TALKING ABOUT, MAN!
38

DON'T GIVE ME **THAT**, FUZZ-FACE! WHERE'S THE BOX YOU SIGNED FOR YESTERDAY?
THE BOX? I PUT IT IN THE REFRIGERATOR.
45

THE REFRIGERATOR?
IT SAID "RUSH," MAN. I THOUGHT IT WAS YOUR FRUIT-OF-THE-MONTH CLUB.
MEX
GB Trudeau

$5,000! BRENNER, ARE YOU OUT OF YOUR **SKULL**?
I'LL ACCEPT GOLD, DUKE. EITHER PAY UP NOW OR I LEAVE YOUR HOUSE TO THE WOLVES.

YOU SNIVELING **PUP!** THIS IS MY **SEED** MONEY! I NEED IT FOR EXPENSES!
YOU SHOULD KNOW I'M ALREADY GETTING INQUIRIES FROM THE LOCAL VANDALS.

ALL **RIGHT**, DAMN YOU, I'LL GIVE YOU A CHECK! MY **LAST** HUNDRED BUCKS! MOTHER'S CHEMOTHERAPY MONEY!

SATISFIED?
I'LL NEED SOME IDENTIFICATION.
RRRIP!
GB Trudeau

"MOTHER," I PRESUME?
DUKE! WELCOME TO MIAMI!
107

I WANT SOME ANSWERS, ANDREWS! FIRST OF ALL, WHAT THE HELL AM I DOING HERE?
ALL IN GOOD TIME, MY MAN. COME ON IN. HOW WAS YOUR FLIGHT FROM DENVER?

NEVER MIND THAT! WHY IS AN ALLEGEDLY CLASSY OPERATION BEING RUN OUT OF A GRUBBY, LITTLE MOTEL ROOM?
IT WAS GOOD ENOUGH FOR GORDON LIDDY, DUKE. THIS IS OUR COMMUNICATIONS BASE.

I SEE. YOU GOT A PHONE AND EVERYTHING.
RIGHT. THIS PLACE IS LIKE A NERVE CENTER. WANT A DRINK?
GB Trudeau

OKAY, ANDREWS, LET'S CUT OUT THE BROMIDES AND GET DOWN TO BRASS TACKS!
DON'T WORRY, DUKE, WE WILL. FIRST, LET ME FILL YOU IN ON THE BIG PICTURE..

AS YOU KNOW, DUKE, UNIVERSAL PETROLEUM IS VERY CONCERNED ABOUT OIL SHORTAGES. IT IS ESPECIALLY ALARMED AT PRODUCTION CUTBACKS BY THE MADCAP MULLAHS OF TEHERAN.

NEEDLESS TO SAY, IF SOMETHING COULD BE DONE TO RESUME THE FLOW OF OIL FROM IRAN, IT WOULD HAVE A PROFOUND IMPACT ON THE MORALE OF OUR BOARD OF DIRECTORS!

NOT TO MENTION THE AMERICAN PUBLIC.
WELL, ACTUALLY, WE'LL PROBABLY SELL IT TO JAPAN.
GB Trudeau

LISTEN, ANDREWS, I STILL DON'T SEE WHERE I FIT IN!
THEN LET ME COME TO THE POINT. YOUR MISSION, DUKE, IS TO GET TO "DIPSTICK," OUR OPERATIVE AT THE AHVAZ OILFIELDS!

IT'S A VITAL MISSION, DUKE. WITH THE COOPERATION OF AN INSIDER LIKE HIM, WE'LL BE ABLE TO GET THE OIL MOVING OUT OF IRAN AGAIN!

LET ME GET THIS STRAIGHT. ALL I HAVE TO DO IS FLY TO AHVAZ AND MAKE A PAY-OFF? THAT'S THE WHOLE GIG?
AT THE COMPLETION OF WHICH, YOU WILL BE $100,000 THE WEALTHIER, AS PER OUR AGREEMENT.

I LIKE IT. SIMPLE, SAFE..
GOOD. NOW, I HAVE HERE SOME COLOR SWATCHES FOR YOUR PARACHUTE..
GB Trudeau

PARACHUTE? ME? ARE YOU MAD, ANDREWS?
A SMALL RISK CONSIDERING THE STAKES, DUKE..

MAY I JUST REMIND YOU THAT AT THIS POINT, THE ONLY THING STANDING BETWEEN OUR WHOLE WAY OF LIFE AND ARMAGEDDON IS ONE 42-YEAR-OLD BALDING BAGMAN—YOU!

ANDREWS, HAVE YOU EVER HURLED YOURSELF OUT OF AN AIRPLANE AT 30,000 FEET?
IT'S PERFECTLY SAFE, DUKE. BESIDES, THE IRANIAN AIR FORCE ALMOST NEVER PATROLS AT NIGHT.

NIGHT? HOW AM I SUPPOSED TO FIND THE DAMN TARGET AT NIGHT?
YOU JUST FOLLOW THE TRACERS. LOOK, DUKE, I'D DO IT MYSELF IF IT WEREN'T FOR MY BACK.
GB Trudeau

WELL?
THEY LEFT ANKARA ON TIME, "MOTHER." "EAGLE" SHOULD HAVE LANDED IN IRAN NEARLY TWO HOURS AGO.
CINZANO

DAMN HIM! DUKE KNOWS HE'S SUPPOSED TO CONTACT US ON TOUCHDOWN!
MAYBE HIS PARACHUTE DIDN'T OPEN, SIR.
CINZANO

NOT A CHANCE. I PACKED IT MYSELF.
WELL, MAYBE HE DECIDED TO KEEP THE PAYOFF MONEY FOR HIMSELF.
CINZANO

PERHAPS. I WAS HOPING HIS MOTHER WOULD DISCOURAGE THAT.
THAT REMINDS ME. I BETTER CHECK ON HER AIR SUPPLY.
GB Trudeau

SORRY, "MOTHER," NO WORD FROM "EAGLE" YET.
DAMN! THERE'S GOING TO BE HELL TO PAY AT THE NEXT BOARD MEETING FOR THIS!
CINZANO

IF THEY'VE GOT "EAGLE," WE'VE LOST "DIPSTICK," COMPROMISED OUR LIBYAN SPOT MARKET OPERATIVES, AND PROBABLY EXPOSED THE KUWAIT PAYOFFS!
WE'RE STARING AT A MILLION BARREL SHORTFALL!
CINZANO

OH.
CINZANO

WHATEVER HAPPENED TO EXPLORATORY DRILLING?
TOO RISKY. YOU DON'T SUPPOSE "EAGLE" WAS TOO STONED TO PULL HIS CORD, DO YOU?
CINZANO
GB Trudeau

"MOTHER"! A CABLE FROM TEHERAN!
FINALLY! GIVE IT HERE!
CINZANO
"REGRET TO INFORM YOU EAGLE HAS BOMBED. DIPSTICK."
CINZANO
MOTHER OF ALLAH! THEY CAUGHT HIM ALREADY?
GOD HELP US ALL.
CINZANO
A TOURIST? WITH OVER $200,000 IN CASH?
SO I'M NOT KARL MALDEN. SUE ME.
GBTrudeau
GOOD EVENING. TODAY FORMER UNITED STATES AMBASSADOR DUKE WAS CAPTURED WHILE PARACHUTING INTO THE AHVAZ OIL FIELDS IN IRAN. ROLAND HEDLEY HAS DETAILS.
THE REVOLUTIONARY GOVERNMENT OF THE AYATOLLAH KHOMEINI ANNOUNCED TONIGHT THAT THE ONETIME WASHINGTON REDSKINS FIELD GENERAL WOULD BE TRIED AND CONVICTED OF HIGH CRIMES AGAINST GOD.
ALTHOUGH DUE PROCESS AS PRACTICED IN THE WEST IS VIRTUALLY UNKNOWN HERE, ABC NEWS HAS LEARNED THAT AMBASSADOR DUKE WAS PERMITTED THE CUSTOMARY PHONE CALL..
HEY, MAN, THOSE ARE THE BREAKS.
DAMMIT, BRENNER! I NEED THOSE KRUGGERRANDS!
GBTrudeau
THIS IS ROLAND HEDLEY. IT'S A BLEAK, DARK MORNING HERE IN TEHERAN AS THE ESPIONAGE TRIAL OF FORMER AMBASSADOR DUKE GETS UNDER WAY!
IN THE NEW IRAN, THE ISLAMIC KANGAROO COURTS ARE CUSTOMARILY GAVELED TO ORDER AT AN UNGODLY 4:00 A.M.! TODAY SHOULD BE NO EXCEPTION.
TENSION HAS BEEN MOUNTING HERE ALL WEEK AS..
THE WHOLE WORLD IS WATCHING! THE WHOLE WORLD IS WATCHING!
AH, HERE COMES THE DEFENDANT NOW!
THE WHOLE..
THUD!
UNH!
GBTrudeau

THE REVOLUTIONARY TRIBUNAL WILL NOW COME TO ORDER! THE COURT WILL HEAR THE ISLAMIC REPUBLIC OF IRAN VS. AMBASSADOR DUKE!
BAM! BAM!
HAS THE STATE PREPARED ITS CASE?
WE HAVE, EXCELLENCY.
LOOKS IRONCLAD TO ME.
THANKS. SORRY ABOUT THE TYPOS.
NOW, WAIT A MINUTE!
GBTrudeau
"THE PEOPLE FURTHER CHARGE THAT MR. DUKE ENTERED THIS COUNTRY FOR THE EXPRESS PURPOSE OF ESPIONAGE AND BRIBERY."
WHAT IS THE DEFENSE OF THE ACCUSED?
HE MAINTAINS HE'S AN INNOCENT TOURIST.
IS THAT CORRECT, MR. DUKE?
MR. DUKE?
OH, SORRY, YOUR HONOR, I WAS JUST WRITING A FEW POSTCARDS.
GBTrudeau
THE DEFENDANT, AMBASSADOR DUKE, IS CHARGED HERE WITH HIGH CRIMES AGAINST GOD AND THE ISLAMIC REPUBLIC OF IRAN.
HE IS FURTHER ACCUSED OF ESPIONAGE, BRIBERY, ILLEGAL ENTRY AND POSSESSION OF DRUGS. THE PENALTY IN ALL CASES IS DEATH.
THE EVIDENCE IS OVERWHELMING. I FIND THE DEFENDANT GUILTY AS CHARGED!
WHAT? THE HELL I AM!
THE BAILIFF MAY FIRE WHEN READY.
OKAY, OKAY! I'M WILLING TO DEAL!
GBTrudeau

MR. DUKE WAS THEN DRAGGED SCREAMING AND KICKING TO THE GRAVEL ROOFTOP OF THE COURTHOUSE, A POPULAR SPOT IN RECENT MONTHS FOR DISCIPLINING FORMER SAVAK AGENTS.

AS YET, HOWEVER, THERE HAS BEEN NO OFFICIAL INDICATION THAT THE SENTENCE HAS BEEN CARRIED OUT. CERTAINLY THIS REPORTER HAS HEARD NO SHOTS, AND HE HAS KEPT HIS EARS PRICKED.

MOREOVER, THERE ARE NOW REPORTS THAT SENSITIVE NEGOTIATIONS MAY BE UNDER WAY IN A LAST-DITCH ATTEMPT TO SAVE THE FORMER AMBASSADOR'S LIFE.

$500,000! IN GOLD!
$250,000! AND THAT'S MY FINAL OFFER!
GB Trudeau

WHAT'S IT SAY, ZONK?
"REGRET TO INFORM YOU YOUR UNCLE DUKE HAS BEEN DECLARED LEGALLY DEAD."

"READING OF WILL SCHEDULED FOR MONDAY. PLEASE COME SOONEST TO HELP ORGANIZE PERSONAL EFFECTS. CONDOLENCES. T. BANNON, ATTORNEY-AT-LAW."

GEE.. WHO DO YOU SUPPOSE MOVED TO HAVE HIM DECLARED LEGALLY DEAD?
I'M NOT SURE, BUT I'VE GOT A PRETTY GOOD IDEA!

YOU WANT THE STEREO PACKED TOO, BUDDY?
NO, NO, JUST PUT IT IN THE BACK OF MY VAN.
THIS SIDE UP
FRAGILE
GB Trudeau

IS THAT YOU, BRENNER?
HEY, ZONK! GOOD TO SEE YOU AGAIN, MAN!
DUKE

BRENNER, WHAT THE HELL IS GOING ON? WHO HAD DUKE DECLARED DEAD?
IT HAD TO BE DONE SOONER OR LATER, MAN. LIFE GOES ON, YOU KNOW?
DUKE

SO YOU WROTE HIM OFF? JUST LIKE THAT?
WELL, WE WERE THINKING OF A MEMORIAL SERVICE, BUT HIS ATTORNEY AND I FIGURED WE OUGHTA TRY TO KEEP EXPENSES DOWN.
DUKE

AS A COURTESY TO HIS HEIRS, NO DOUBT.
RIGHT. BESIDES, I COULDN'T REMEMBER WHICH CULT HE BELONGED TO.
DUKE
GB Trudeau

GLAD YOU GOT HERE SO FAST, ZONK. THERE'S A LOT OF STUFF TO SORT THROUGH BEFORE THE WILL READING!
FRAGILE

WHO'S COMING TO THE READING, BRENNER?
A PRETTY HEAVY CROWD, MAN. A GANG OF CREDITORS, A COUPLE IRS GUYS, AND A U.S. MARSHAL.
FRAGILE

A U.S. MARSHAL?
NOT TO WORRY, MAN. I CHECKED IT OUT, AND MOST OF DUKE'S ESTATE IS INADMISSIBLE.
FRAGILE

IMAGINE MY RELIEF.
ALL WE GOTTA DO IS GET THE SERIAL NUMBERS OFF.
FRAGILE
GB Trudeau

FIND ANYTHING INTERESTING YET, MAN?
ARE YOU KIDDING? JUST LOOK AT ALL THIS STUFF!

PARKING TICKETS, EVICTION NOTICES, BETTING STUBS, FOOD STAMPS, BOUNCED CHECKS, REJECTION SLIPS, UNFINISHED MANUSCRIPTS, OVERDUE BILLS..

..PRESCRIPTION BLANKS, FORGED PASSPORTS.. WHY, BRENNER, THERE'S A RECORD OF FAILURE AND MALFEASANCE HERE THAT SPANS OVER TWENTY YEARS!

YOU THINKING OF EDITING HIS PAPERS, MAN?
I DON'T KNOW IF I COULD DO IT JUSTICE!
GB Trudeau

DID YOU KNOW DUKE STARTED KEEPING JOURNALS A FEW YEARS BACK, BRENNER?
NO KIDDING, MAN? DOES HE MENTION ME IN THEM?

SURE, RIGHT AT THE TOP. "JAN. 13, 1975. APPOINTMENT TO SAMOA CAME THROUGH. AM CELEBRATING WITH PART OF BRENNER'S NEW SHIPMENT OF AMYLS.."
OH, WOW..

"I'M ON MY FIFTH TAB AND IT LOOKS LIKE I'VE BEEN RIPPED OFF AGAIN. THIS STUFF IS SO BAD I'M NOT EVEN SLIGHTLY BIFFLE DINKED!"
HEE, HEE!

"IF THAT LEBBLE BIFFDECKER SNIT FIDDLE-GANG, WHIMSICK RIPPIZ LUNGS OUT."
HE ALMOST DID, TOO.
GB Trudeau

"JAN. 16, 1975, PAGO PAGO. ARRIVED TODAY TO SERVE IN MY CAPACITY AS NEWLY APPOINTED GOVERNOR OF AMERICAN SAMOA."

"RECEPTION WAS MAGNIFICENT. GREETED BY 21-GUN SALUTE, AND MY NEW AIDE-DE-CAMP, MACARTHUR, PRESENTED ME WITH A SILVER THERMOS OF DAIQUIRIS."

"HAVE TAKEN INSTANT LIKING TO SAMOAN PEOPLE, ESPECIALLY STAFF AT GOVERNOR'S MANSION. THEY ARE GENTLE, WARM, AND POSSESSED OF AN ALMOST CHILDLIKE INNOCENCE."

"JAN. 17. HONEYMOON OVER. FOUND SEED IN ORANGE JUICE. HAD COOK FLOGGED."
GB Trudeau

"JULY 1, 1975. THIS MORNING AT 3 A.M., PAGO PAGO SLAMMED TWICE BY MASSIVE TIDAL WAVE."

"HAVE EXTENDED STATE OF EMERGENCY DECLARED AFTER TYPHOON. ALSO IMPOSING MARTIAL LAW TO KEEP STREETS FREE OF LOOTERS."

"CURRENTLY SUFFERING FROM SEVERE SHORTAGES OF FOOD, FRESH WATER, MEDICAL SUPPLIES AND ENGLISH TEACHERS. CHOLERA EPIDEMIC ALSO SEEMS IMMINENT."

"JULY 3. SITUATION HOPELESS. OFF FOR WIMBLEDON FINALS."
GB Trudeau

"APRIL 15, 1976. PEKING. INTENSE NEGOTIATIONS ON STATUS OF U.S./CHINA RELATIONS CONTINUE AT GREAT HALL OF THE PEOPLE.."

"TENG IS UNCOMPROMISING ON TAIWAN ISSUE. I MAKE NINE SEPARATE PROPOSALS, INCLUDING GENEROUS CASH SETTLEMENTS, PLUS POINTS. AM REBUKED AT EVERY TURN."

"APRIL 16. TENG REMAINS INTRACTABLE. IN ATTEMPT TO BREAK DEADLOCK, I CALL IN AIR STRIKES ON IMPERIAL PALACE."

"APRIL 17. PENTAGON OVERRULES STRIKES. AM LOSING FACE."
GB Trudeau

OKAY, IF EVERYONE HAS SOMETHING TO DRINK, I'D LIKE TO GET THIS SHOW ON THE ROAD.

I'M T.F. BANNON, COUNSEL FOR THE FIRM OF TORTS, TARTZ AND TORQUE, AND PERSONAL ATTORNEY FOR AMBASSADOR DUKE.

IT IS MY UNHAPPY TASK TO BE HERE TODAY TO READ THE WILL OF MR. DUKE, WHO IS.. UH.. PRESUMED DEAD AT THIS TIME.

STILL NO WORD FROM THE DECEASED YET, RIGHT?
NOT A PEEP, MAN. LET'S DO IT.
GBTrudeau

YOU A FRIEND OF THE FAMILY?
YOU MIGHT SAY THAT I WORK FOR THE INTERNAL REVENUE SERVICE.

REALLY? HAVE YOU KNOWN DUKE LONG?
I WAS FIRST ASSIGNED TO HIS CASE IN 1963.

WOW..

HOW YOU BEARING UP?
NOT SO GOOD. IT'S SORT OF THE END OF AN ERA.
GBTrudeau

.."AND BEING OF ACCEPTABLY SOUND MIND AND WILL, I HEREBY LEAVE MY ENTIRE ESTATE TO.."

..MY BELOVED PROTEGE, MR. ZONKER HARRIS."
HUH?

OH, WOW..

YOU WERE HIS FAVORITE DEALER, I TAKE IT.
NO, NO, I'M AS SURPRISED AS YOU ARE!
GBTrudeau

YOU HEARD ME, PAL. PUT IT ALL IN ESCROW. NO ONE TOUCHES DUKE'S ESTATE UNTIL I SAY SO!
BUT, MR. HARRIS, WE'VE WORKED OUT A WHOLE INVESTMENT PROGRAM FOR YOU..

I'LL JUST BET YOU HAVE! WELL, YOU CAN FORGET IT! NOW, I HAVE A PLANE TO CATCH.
BE REASONABLE, MAN. WE COULD PUT YOUR MONEY TO WORK!

NO! AND THAT'S FINAL!

YOU'LL HAVE HIM DECLARED INSANE, OF COURSE.
CAN'T. THE JUDGE I USE IS ON VACATION.
GBTrudeau

A BOOK? WHAT SORT OF BOOK?
A MEMOIR OF DUKE, MAN. IT'S A NATURAL FOR ME! AND SINCE YOU WERE HIS ATTORNEY, I WANT YOU TO HANDLE THE BIDDING.

WAIT A MINUTE, BRENNER. WHAT DO YOU KNOW ABOUT WRITING BOOKS?
NOTHING. BUT I'VE CONTACTED ONE OF THE BEST GHOST WRITERS IN THE BUSINESS. HE'S COMING BY TOMORROW.

IT CAN'T FAIL, MAN. EVER SINCE THE HOSTAGE SITUATION IN IRAN STARTED, PEOPLE HAVE SEEN DUKE AS A MARTYR, A GENUINE FOLK HERO. WE'D BE FOOLS NOT TO STRIKE WHILE THE IRON'S HOT!

WHAT IF HE TURNS UP ALIVE?
NO PROBLEM, WE JUST GIVE HIM A CUT AND CHANGE THE ENDING.
GBTrudeau

HI. ARE YOU ZEKE BRENNER?
YEAH. YOU MUST BE POPEYE MALONE!

THAT'S RIGHT. MY AGENT SAID YOU'RE IN THE MARKET FOR A GHOST WRITER.
CORRECTO, POPS. THEY TELL ME YOU'RE THE BEST AROUND-AND THE FASTEST!

COULD BE. WHO'S THE BOOK ON?
AMBASSADOR DUKE, THE GUY WHO WAS CAUGHT PARACHUTING INTO IRAN AND SENT BEFORE A FIRING SQUAD.

GOOD ANGLE. IRAN'S HOT RIGHT NOW. HARD COVER OR QUICK-AND-DIRTY?
QUICK-AND-DIRTY. YOU DON'T WASTE ANY TIME, DO YOU?
GBTrudeau

..AND HIS JOURNALS GO CLEAR BACK TO HIS EARLY PORNO DAYS.
PRETTY BIZARRE STUFF. BUT YOU MIGHT JUST HAVE A BOOK HERE, SON.
YOU KIDDING? THIS BOOK WILL WRITE ITSELF!
RIGHT. BUT IN CASE IT DOESN'T, HERE'S MY OFFER: I'LL DELIVER 75,000 WORDS FOR 50% PLUS 25% OF THE MOVIE RIGHTS.
HOMBRE, YOU GOT YOURSELF A DEAL!
OF COURSE, IF YOU WANT IT TO HAVE LITERARY MERIT, I'LL HAVE TO CHARGE YOU EXTRA.
WHAT DO YOU MEAN BY LITERARY MERIT?
ADJECTIVES, ADVERBS, THAT SORT OF THING.
GB Trudeau

TAP! TAP! TAP! TAP!
GOOD NEWS, MAN. WE'VE STARTED THE ACTUAL WRITING. I THINK IT'S TIME YOU PUT OUT THE WORD TO PUBLISHERS.
TAP! TAP! TAP! TAP!
I'LL GET RIGHT ON IT, ZEKE. DO YOU HAVE ANY PREFERENCES IN PAPERBACK HOUSES?
TAP! TAP! TAP!
NO, JUST SO LONG AS IT'S A CLASSY OUTFIT. I MEAN, I'VE GOT AN IMPORTANT STORY TO TELL HERE. WE'RE NOT JUST OUT TO MAKE A FAST BUCK.
FINISHED!
TALK TO YOU LATER, MAN. I GOTTA GO HELP WITH THE FOOTNOTES.
GB Trudeau

J.J.! IT'S HIM.
WHO?.. ZEKE!
HI, DOLL! JUST GOT IN. PACK YOUR BAGS. WE'RE GOING TO BERMUDA.
BERMUDA? ZEKE, WHAT ARE YOU TALKING ABOUT?
I FINISHED MY BOOK ON DUKE. BANTAM IS PUBLISHING IT, AND I'M GETTING AN ADVANCE OF $100,000!
DUKE? YOU WROTE A BOOK ON DUKE? WHAT DO YOU SAY ABOUT HIM?
UM.. I DUNNO. I HAVEN'T HAD A CHANCE TO READ IT YET.
$100,000! IT MUST BE REALLY GOOD!
GB Trudeau

YOU REALLY WROTE A BOOK, ZEKE! I DIDN'T KNOW YOU WERE A WRITER.
I DIDN'T EITHER, MAN. IT WAS SORT OF AN UNTAPPED TALENT.
AND NOW HE'S ON THE WAY TO FAME AND FORTUNE!
THERE'S GOING TO BE A WHOLE BOOK TOUR, MOTHER. ZEKE'S GOING TO DO TALK SHOWS, BOOK SIGNINGS, INTERVIEWS, THE WORKS!
YOU MUST BE VERY EXCITED, ZEKE.
YEAH, I AM, MAN. I JUST HOPE I DON'T OUTGROW MY FAMILY AND FRIENDS.
IT'S GOT US BOTH WORRIED. ZEKE KNOWS PEOPLE THAT'S HAPPENED TO.
G B Trudeau

I THINK THE BOOK CALLS FOR A SMALL CELEBRATION, DON'T YOU, DEAR?
CHAMPAGNE? GEE, THAT'S GREAT OF YOU, MOM.
WHERE'D ZEKE GO?
OH, HE WENT UPSTAIRS TO BREAK THE NEWS TO RICK.
WHAT DO YOU MEAN, BREAK THE NEWS?
WELL, SINCE RICK IS A WRITER, TOO, ZEKE'S WORRIED HE'LL BE A LITTLE JEALOUS.
SAY WHAT?
$100,000. YOU'RE NOT JEALOUS, ARE YOU, MAN?
G B Trudeau

SO YOU THINK YOU'LL BE HITTING THE TALK SHOW CIRCUIT, ZEKE?
OH, FOR SURE, MAN. HELL, THAT'S THE BEST PART OF PUBLISHING A BOOK!
THE ACTUAL AUTHORING, THOUGH, IS SOMETHING ELSE. WRITING A BOOK REQUIRES PATIENCE, CONCENTRATION AND AN INCREDIBLE AMOUNT OF SELF-DISCIPLINE.
WOW..
SO WHAT'D YOU DO, HIRE A GHOST?
RICK! OF COURSE NOT!
MORE LIKE A PROOF-READER REALLY.
G B Trudeau

MY NEXT GUEST IS THE AUTHOR OF A SENSATIONAL NEW BEST-SELLER! PLEASE WELCOME MR. ZEKE BRENNER!
CLAP! CLAP! CLAP! CLAP!
HI, MERV.
GOOD TO SEE YOU, ZEKE! WHAT HAVE YOU BEEN UP TO? WHERE ARE YOU APPEARING? WHAT'S IT LIKE BEING A BIG STAR?
HAVE YOU WORKED WITH ANY OTHER BIG STARS? WHAT ARE THEY REALLY LIKE? I'M A BIG FAN OF ALL OF THEM! AREN'T THE FOLKS HERE IN VEGAS JUST GREAT?
CLAP! CLAP! CLAP!
YEAH, THEY..
MY NEXT GUEST IS ANOTHER BIG STAR..
GBTrudeau
ZEKE, SOMEBODY TOLD ME YOUR BOOK IS ALL ABOUT AMBASSADOR DUKE. DID YOU TELL ME THAT, ED?
THAT'S RIGHT, JOHNNY. IT'S ALL IN THAT BOOK—NAMES, DATES, PLACES, IN FACT, EVERYTHING YOU MIGHT WANT TO KNOW ABOUT DUKE!
YES, IF YOU WANTED INFORMATION ON DUKE, ALL YOU'D NEED IS THAT BOOK, BECAUSE ABSOLUTELY EVERYTHING IS IN THERE, RIGHT THERE IN THAT BOOK!
WRONG, ALPO BREATH.
HA, HA! THAT'S MY LINE! STAY WITH US!
TAPPITY! TAP! TAP!
GBTrudeau
MOM?
WELL, HELLO, DEAR. HOW'S EVERYTHING / GOING?
MOM, GO TURN ON T.V.! CHANNEL TWO! ZEKE'S ON "DINAH" TALKING ABOUT DUKE!
"DINAH"? ZEKE'S ON THE DINAH SHORE SHOW?
THEN HE WOULD ADD TWO TABLESPOONS OF ETHER..
MMM! IT SOUNDS WONDERFUL!
GBTrudeau

WE'RE BACK!
THIS IS "PROFILES ON PARADE", AND TODAY WE'RE TALKING WITH ZEKE BRENNER, AUTHOR OF "DUKE: PORTRAIT OF A MENTOR."
ZEKE, A MOMENT AGO YOU TOLD ME SOMETHING RATHER EXTRAORDINARY. YOU SAID YOU HAVEN'T ACTUALLY READ YOUR OWN BOOK.
THAT'S RIGHT, MARK.
ANY SPECIAL REASON FOR THAT?
WELL, TO BE HONEST, THE REVIEWS HAVEN'T BEEN THAT HOT.
GB Trudeau

ZEKE, AS DUKE'S CARETAKER AND CONFIDANT, YOU MUST HAVE HAD A FEW WEIRD EXPERIENCES..
WELL, WE HAD A LOT OF GOOD TIMES, I'LL TELL YOU THAT..
THERE WERE ALL THE HUNTING EXPEDITIONS, AND THE GREAT PARTIES, AND THE FIELD TRIPS, LIKE THE TIME WE BROKE INTO THAT CATHOLIC GIRLS' SCHOOL IN DENVER AND WE.. AND WE..
FORGIVE ME.. I.. I'M AFRAID I JUST CAN'T TALK ABOUT THAT, MAN..
I'M SORRY.. IT MUST BE PAINFUL TO REMEMBER ALL THE..
NO, NO, IT'S JUST THAT THE CHARGES ARE STILL PENDING.
GB Trudeau

IT'S A GOOD WAY TO HELP, CAMPERS, SO IF YOU DIG DUKE THE WAY I DO, GET ON DOWN TO YOUR BOOKSTORE AND PICK UP "DUKE: PORTRAIT OF A MENTOR"!
REMEMBER, FOR EVERY COPY SOLD, ZEKE BRENNER WILL BE DONATING A SHARE OF HIS ROYALTIES TO FUND AN URGENT INVESTIGATION INTO DUKE'S FATE!
RING!
HELLO, MARVELOUS MARK SHOW!
HOW BIG A SHARE?
MAYBE 2%. THERE'S NOT MUCH HOPE.
GB Trudeau

GOOD EVENING. THERE WAS ANOTHER DRAMATIC BREAKTHROUGH TODAY IN THE CONTINUING SAGA OF THE AMERICAN HOSTAGES.

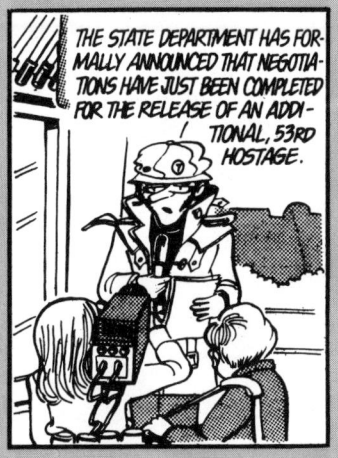
THE STATE DEPARTMENT HAS FORMALLY ANNOUNCED THAT NEGOTIATIONS HAVE JUST BEEN COMPLETED FOR THE RELEASE OF AN ADDITIONAL, 53RD HOSTAGE.

THE HOSTAGE'S IDENTITY IS STILL NOT KNOWN, BUT HE IS BEING REFERRED TO BY IRANIAN SOURCES AS "THE BALD SPY."
G B Trudeau

YOU KNOW A BALD SPY?
THE WHAT?

..AND SOURCES SAY THE 53RD HOSTAGE, KNOWN ONLY AS "THE BALD SPY," WILL BE FREE WITHIN HOURS.

NEGOTIATIONS FOR THE MYSTERY HOSTAGE'S RELEASE WERE SAID TO HAVE BEEN DIFFICULT, INVOLVING SEVERAL HOURS OF HAGGLING OVER EXACT TERMS.

A BREAKTHROUGH WAS FINALLY REACHED LATE LAST NIGHT WHEN U.S. OFFICIALS AGREED TO UNFREEZE ADDITIONAL IRANIAN ASSETS TOTALLING $300.
G B Trudeau

HOW MUCH?
IT WAS THE BEST WE COULD DO, BALD ONE.

GOOD EVENING. TODAY THE IDENTITY OF THE 53RD HOSTAGE WAS MADE KNOWN. HE IS FORMER U.S. AMBASSADOR DUKE..
I KNEW IT! I KNEW IT WAS UNCLE DUKE!

AT THE TEHERAN AIRPORT THIS MORNING, HE SPOKE WITH REPORTERS..
MR. DUKE, HOW DOES IT FEEL TO BE FREE?

GREAT. AND I WANT TO THANK THE THOUSANDS OF PEOPLE AROUND THE WORLD WHO PRESSURED IRAN FOR MY RELEASE. I'M CERTAIN THAT PUBLIC OUTRAGE WAS THE ONLY THING THAT STOOD BETWEEN ME AND A BRUTAL DEATH!

UH.. BUT NOBODY KNEW YOU WERE A HOSTAGE, SIR..
BALONEY. THERE WAS INTERNATIONAL PRESSURE. I COULD FEEL IT.
G B Trudeau

WHERE.. WHERE AM I?
DON'T BE ALARMED, MR. DUKE. YOU'RE IN A SPECIAL ARMY HOSPITAL. IN GERMANY. HOW DO YOU FEEL THIS MORNING?
ARE YOU FEELING ANXIOUS? A LITTLE DISORIENTED? THAT'S QUITE NORMAL. HOW ABOUT DEPRESSION? ANY DEPRESSION?
MR. DUKE, I CAN'T HELP YOU IF YOU WON'T LET ME. YOU'VE GOT TO OPEN UP, YOU'VE GOT TO TALK TO ME, DO YOU UNDERSTAND?
WHERE THE HELL IS MY WALLET?
GOOD. LET IT OUT. WHAT ELSE ARE YOU FEELING?
GBTrudeau
MR. DUKE, I'M AFRAID WE'RE GOING TO HAVE TO KEEP YOU WITH US FOR A FEW DAYS FOR OBSERVATION.
WHAT THE HELL FOR? I'M FINE, DOC!
YOU'RE SUFFERING FROM WHAT WE CALL THE "STOCKHOLM SYNDROME," WHICH IS THE TENDENCY OF A HOSTAGE TO SYMPATHIZE WITH HIS TORMENTORS.
TORMENTORS? ARE YOU CRAZY? HOW DO YOU EXPLAIN ALL THE GOOD TIMES? THE SOCCER GAMES BEHIND THE COMPOUND? THE LATE NIGHTS OF DRINKING?
ALL TYPICAL ELEMENTS OF THE CAPTOR-HOSTAGE RELATIONSHIP.
THE SAILING VACATION IN GREECE?
LESS TYPICAL, BUT NOT UNHEARD OF.
GBTrudeau
LET'S GO BACK TO THE BEGINNING OF YOUR CAPTIVITY, SHALL WE, MR. DUKE? AT LAST REPORT YOU WERE FACING A PRE-DAWN FIRING SQUAD.
RIGHT. AT THAT POINT, NEGOTIATIONS HAD KIND OF BOGGED DOWN. I WAS FORCED TO MAKE A LAST-DITCH OFFER OF $250,000, WHICH IT TURNED OUT WAS THE GOING RATE FOR A STAY OF EXECUTION.
IT WAS AN INCREDIBLE RIP-OFF, BUT I FIGURED, WHAT THE HELL, I'D BE LONG GONE BY THE TIME MY CHECK BOUNCED. UNFORTUNATELY, THEY LOCKED ME UP IN A HOTEL AS INSURANCE.
OKAY, BALD ONE, BACK TO THE ROOF.
I CAN'T UNDERSTAND IT. THEY MUST HAVE FROZEN MY ASSETS.
GBTrudeau

OKAY, BALD ONE, BACK TO THE ROOF.
LOOK, FELLAHS, I REALLY THINK YOU'RE OVERREACTING. WHY RISK WAR WITH THE U.S. OVER ONE LOUSY BAD CHECK?
I MEAN, IF YOU'RE SO BENT ON CREATING AN INTERNATIONAL INCIDENT, WHY DON'T YOU JUST SEIZE THE WHOLE UNITED STATES EMBASSY?
YOU SAID WHAT?
I WAS JUST KIDDING, FOR GOD'S SAKE..
GBTrudeau
THE NEXT DAY ALL HELL BROKE LOOSE..
HUH?
THE EMBASSY'S BEEN SEIZED!
IT'S YOUR LUCKY DAY, BALD ONE. WE'VE BEEN TOLD TO KEEP YOU ALIVE AS A BARGAINING CHIP!
GOOD PLAN. YOU WON'T REGRET IT.
SO WHAT DO YOU WANT TO DO WHILE THEY NEGOTIATE?
I DUNNO. WHY DON'T WE GO GRAB A BEER?
GBTrudeau
ACTUALLY, DOC, LOOKING BACK ON IT NOW, I THINK THE WORST PART OF THE WHOLE ORDEAL WAS THE EXCRUCIATING BOREDOM..
TO KEEP MYSELF ENTERTAINED, I USED TO FEIGN VARIOUS DISEASES DURING THE MEDICAL CHECK-UPS. THE DOCTOR WOULD INVARIABLY PRESCRIBE SOMETHING, AND I'D SAVE IT.
THEN, EVERY SIX WEEKS OR SO, I'D HAVE A PARTY. IT NEVER FAILED TO SCARE THE HELL OUT OF THE GUARDS.
GBTrudeau
IS HE DEAD?
I DON'T THINK SO. HE JUST GIGGLED.

DOCTOR, WHAT SORT OF CONDITION IS THE 53RD HOSTAGE IN?
PHYSICALLY, HE SEEMS TO BE FINE..

PSYCHOLOGICALLY, THERE APPEAR TO BE SOME PROBLEMS. WHAT IS NOT CLEAR, HOWEVER, IS HOW MANY OF THEM EXISTED PRIOR TO HIS CAPTIVITY.

DOC, HAS HE CALLED HIS FAMILY YET?
AS A MATTER OF FACT, I THINK HE WAS PLANNING ON PHONING HIS LOVED ONES THIS MORNING..

$1000 ON OAKLAND, GOT IT?
DUKE, THE GAME WAS TWO WEEKS AGO. WHERE YOU BEEN?
GB Trudeau

BRENNER? IS THAT YOU?
DUKE?.. YOU'RE.. YOU'RE ALIVE!

SORRY TO DISAPPOINT YOU, BRENNER..
HEY, MAN, I KNEW YOU'D COME THROUGH IT. I NEVER GAVE UP HOPE!

LISTEN, BRENNER, I'LL BE HOME BY TOMORROW. IF THAT HOUSE ISN'T EXACTLY THE WAY I LEFT IT, I'LL HAVE YOUR HIDE! YOU HEAR ME?
HEY, NOT TO WORRY, MAN, THE HOUSE IS FINE..

ACTUALLY, I'VE SORT OF IMPROVED IT.
DUKE
zeke Brenner, Esq.
KEEP OUT!
GB Trudeau

WELCOME HOME, DUKE! RAH! RAH! WAY TO GO, DUKE! WHOOPIE!

WHAT'S GOING ON HERE? WHERE THE HELL'S THE BAND, BRENNER?
UH.. YOU DIDN'T TELL ME YOU WANTED A BAND, MAN.

THERE WAS SUPPOSED TO BE A BAND! AND WHERE'S THE PRESS? WHAT HAPPENED TO MY HERO'S WELCOME?
HEY, YOU'RE A HERO TO ME, DUKE! I EVEN GOT A GREEN RIBBON FOR YOU!

IT'S SUPPOSED TO BE YELLOW, PINHEAD.
OH. I COULDN'T REMEMBER. I'M NOT INTO TONY ORLANDO, MAN.
GB Trudeau

6 ON THE LAM

1981

THERE IT IS AGAIN.. SOMEBODY'S DEFINITELY DOWNSTAIRS!
HMM.. I COULD BE WALKING INTO A TRAP.. I BETTER SHOOT FIRST, ASK QUESTIONS LATER..
BLAM! BLAM! BLAM! BLAM! BLAM!
HELLO? ANYONE THERE?
>GURGLE..<
GBTrudeau

ONE MOVE AND YOU'RE A DEAD MAN!
DUKE..DON'T SHOOT.. IT'S ME..>COUGH< BRENNER..
BRENNER! WHAT THE HELL ARE YOU DOING HERE?
YOU.. >GASP< YOU..
WHOA.. I REALLY WINGED YOU GOOD, DIDN'T I? SORRY ABOUT THAT, KID.. ACCIDENTS HAPPEN..
YOU.. YOU TRIED TO KILL ME!
DON'T BE SILLY. I THOUGHT YOU WERE A RACCOON. WANT A BEER?
GBTrudeau

HERE.. USE THIS TOWEL AS A TOURNIQUET.. YOU'RE BLEEDING LIKE A STUCK PIG..
YOU.. >COUGH< YOU.. TRIED TO KILL ME, MAN..
WILL YOU GET OFF THAT, BRENNER? I TOLD YOU, I THOUGHT YOU WERE A RACCOON!
YOU TRIED TO MURDER ME, MAN..
WHY YOU PATHETIC LITTLE PUP! DO YOU REALLY THINK I WOULD JEOPARDIZE MY CAREER BY WASTING A PUNK LIKE YOU? DON'T FLATTER YOURSELF, JACK!
MURDERER.
LOOK, I GOTTA GET SOME SHUT-EYE. YOU WANT AN AMBULANCE OR WHAT?
PLEASE.
GBTrudeau

MUR-DERER!
HEY, HOLD IT DOWN, WILLYA KID? I'M ON THE PHONE!
GOOD EVENING, ASPEN AMBU-LANCE.

HELLO, LES? DUKE HERE. LOOK, WE'VE HAD A LIT-TLE ACCIDENT OUT AT THE HOUSE. BRENNER'S TAKEN A SLUG. HE'S BLEEDING ALL OVER THE PLACE.
OKAY, HOLD ON, DUKE. I'LL SEND A WAGON OUT RIGHT AWAY.

GOOD. LISTEN, LES, THIS IS KIND OF A SENSITIVE MATTER. I'M THINKING ABOUT GETTING BACK INTO POLITICS, SO I'D APPRECIATE YOUR DIS-CRETION.
I HEAR YOU, OL' BUDDY. I'LL HAVE THE GUYS USE THE BACK ROAD.

GREAT. SAY, COULD YOU HAVE THEM SWING BY AND PICK ME UP A PIZZA?
NO PROBLEM. YOU WANT IT WITH EVERY-THING?
G B Trudeau

IT WAS REALLY HIS OWN FAULT. I CAUGHT HIM BREAKING IN..
MAN, WHAT A MESS! WHAT'D YOU USE, DUKE, AN M-60?

ACCIDENTS HAPPEN, LEO. I HOPE I CAN TRUST YOU TO KEEP THIS LITTLE MISHAP TO YOURSELF..
HEY, HAVE WE EVER LET YOU DOWN BE-FORE, DUKE?

REMEMBER THAT TIME I CAME OUT HERE AND PUMPED OUT THAT LADY'S STOMACH? YOU NEVER HEARD ANOTHER WORD ABOUT THAT, DID YOU?

I'M HEARING IT RIGHT NOW, LEO.
HEY, MAN, THIS DUDE'S UNCONSCIOUS. THAT'S GOING TO BE EXTRA.
G B Trudeau

PREP HIM RIGHT AWAY AND GET HIM INTO O.R.!
HOW BAD IS IT, DOC?

I WON'T KNOW UNTIL I OPEN HIM UP. WHAT HAPPENED?
IT WAS JUST SOME FREAK ACCIDENT. WILL HE MAKE IT?

IT COULD GO EITHER WAY. HE'S GOT A HOLE IN HIM THE SIZE OF A GRAPEFRUIT.
THAT'S TERRIBLE.. JUST TER-RIBLE..

I'LL LET YOU KNOW IF IT'S HOMICIDE OR ASSAULT.
THANKS. I'LL BE OUT IN MY CAR, OKAY?
G B Trudeau

MR. DUKE?
YO?
I HAVE SOME GOOD NEWS FOR YOU, MR. DUKE..
BRENNER'S GOING TO MAKE IT?
HE IS INDEED. WE WERE ABLE TO STOP THE BLEEDING AND REMOVE THE BULLET.
OH, THANK GOD! BLESS YOU, DOCTOR!
MOM? GOOD NEWS! HE'S GOING TO BE OKAY!
SWISSAIR. THANK YOU FOR HOLDING.
GB Trudeau

GREAT TO HAVE YOU BACK, BRENNER. I WAS ROOTIN' FOR YOU.
SURE YOU WERE, DUKE..
EXCUSE ME, SON. ARE YOU ZEKE BRENNER?
HOLD IT, BUDDY, DIDN'T YOU SEE THE NO VISITORS SIGN?
DENVER POLICE. THE NAME'S LT. O'MALLEY.
POLICE? SOMEBODY SENT FOR THE POLICE?
YES, IT'S CUSTOMARY FOLLOWING A CRIME.
OH, NO.. DON'T TELL ME HE'S MIXED UP WITH DRUGS AGAIN!
HEY, WAIT A MINUTE..
GB Trudeau

TRY TO KEEP THE QUESTIONS BRIEF, LIEUTENANT. THE BOY'S BEEN THROUGH A TERRIBLE ORDEAL.
MR. BRENNER, WHAT HAPPENED AT MR. DUKE'S HOUSE TONIGHT?
I JUST DROPPED BY TO PICK UP MY STEREO. I WAS WALKING THROUGH THE DEN WHEN SUDDENLY, WITHOUT WARNING, DUKE OPENS FIRE!
I SEE. THEN WHAT?
THEN HE STUMBLES DOWNSTAIRS, TURNS ON THE LIGHT, AND SEES IT'S ME!
I WAS SHOCKED, OF COURSE.
WHAT'D HE SAY?
"GIVE ME ONE GOOD REASON WHY I SHOULDN'T FINISH YOU OFF."
IT WAS THREE O'CLOCK IN THE MORNING, FOR GOD'S SAKE!
GB Trudeau

OKAY, LET ME GET THIS STRAIGHT. YOU WENT TO HIS HOUSE TO PICK UP YOUR HI-FI.
CORRECTO.

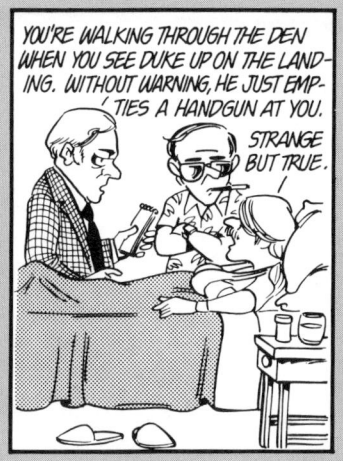
YOU'RE WALKING THROUGH THE DEN WHEN YOU SEE DUKE UP ON THE LANDING. WITHOUT WARNING, HE JUST EMPTIES A HANDGUN AT YOU.
STRANGE BUT TRUE.

MAY I ASK WHY YOU DID THAT?
I'M CAUTIOUS BY NATURE. I DON'T LIKE TO WALK INTO A DARK ROOM UNTIL I'VE SOFTENED IT UP.

DO YOU REALIZE THAT'S COMPLETELY **INSANE?**
IT IS?
DON'T RULE IT OUT, DUKE. IT'S A GOOD DEFENSE.
GBTrudeau

LOOK, I'M TELLING YOU, IT WAS ALL JUST A TERRIBLE ACCIDENT! I THOUGHT HE WAS A **RACCOON,** FOR GOD'S SAKE!

MAYBE. BUT I'M GOING TO HAVE TO TAKE YOU DOWNTOWN ANYWAY.
NOW SEE WHAT YOU'VE DONE!
YOU TRIED TO KILL ME, MAN.

LOOK, O'MALLEY, LET'S BE REASONABLE. DON'T YOU HAVE SOME FAVORITE CHARITY?
NOW HE'S TRYING TO **BRIBE** YOU!

ARE YOU TRYING TO BRIBE ME?
NOT IF YOU'RE GOING TO GET SNITTY ABOUT IT.
OFFICER, DO YOUR **DUTY!**
GBTrudeau

OKAY, LET'S HAVE YOUR HOME ADDRESS FIRST..
LOOK, LIEUTENANT, LET'S BE REASONABLE, OKAY?

A REPUTATION IS AT STAKE HERE! LIKE YOURSELF, I'M A LIFE-LONG PUBLIC SERVANT! IN FACT, I'M JUST ABOUT TO RUN FOR POLITICAL OFFICE..

POLITICAL OFFICE? NO KIDDING?

THAT WOULD EXPLAIN ALL THE CAMERAS OUTSIDE.
OH, NO..
GBTrudeau

WHO'S IT FROM, ZONK?
MY UNCLE DUKE. HE SAYS HE'S THINKING OF GETTING BACK INTO POLITICS.
WALDEN
DUKE? HEY, HE WAS ON THE NEWS LAST NIGHT.
HE WAS? WHAT FOR?
WALDEN
I FORGET.
PROBABLY ACCEPTING ANOTHER AWARD OR SOMETHING.
WALDEN
GBTrudeau
DUKE! OVER HERE!
ANY COMMENT, DUKE?
DUKE!
CLICK!
CLIK! CLIK!
ANY NEW DETAILS, HONEY?
WELL, DUKE WAS ARRAIGNED YESTERDAY. THE JUDGE HAS SET THE BAIL AT $5,000.
"AS THE FORMER AMBASSADOR WAS LED FROM THE COURT-ROOM, HE LOUDLY DENIED ALL RESPONSIBILITY FOR THE SHOOTING OF EX-HANDYMAN ZEKE BRENNER."
I CAN BELIEVE IT. KNOWING ZEKE, HE PROBABLY SHOT HIM-SELF.
WHICH MEANS THE MAN I LOVE MIGHT BE WASTING AWAY IN JAIL FOR A CRIME HE DIDN'T COMMIT!
GOSH.. HOW ROMANTIC!
I KNOW. IT'S LIKE A COUN-TRY-WESTERN SONG OR SOMETHING.
GBTrudeau
I'VE GOT TO GO GET HIM, HONEY. I CAN'T LET DUKE JUST SIT IN JAIL ON SOME SILLY TRUMPED UP CHARGE!
BUT WHERE WILL YOU GET THE $5,000 FOR BAIL, HONEY?
I COULD USE MY TUITION MONEY. DUKE WOULD PAY ME BACK, I'M SURE.
WOW.. GETTING YOUR MAN OUT OF JAIL! THAT WOULD BE ROMANTIC!
DARE I?
YOU MUST! GO TO HIM, HONEY!
BUT MY DRESSY MAO JACKET'S AT THE CLEANERS.
GBTrudeau

OKAY, SUNSHINE, UP AND AT 'EM!
HUH?

MOVING DAY, PAL! YOUR BAIL'S BEEN POSTED!
YOU'RE KIDDING!

NOPE. PAID IN FULL BY YOUR FIANCÉE.
MY WHO?

THE REASON I'M NOT WEARING AN ENGAGEMENT RING IS I HAD TO PAWN IT FOR THE BAIL.
WHATEVER YOU SAY, MISS.
GB Trudeau

THANKS FOR SPRINGING ME, HONEY. I WAS BEGINNING TO GO A LITTLE STIR-CRAZY IN THERE.

JAIL MUST BE ROUGH, SIR.
IT'S A LIVING HELL, HONEY, A STINKING PIT OF INHUMANITY WHICH ONLY THE STRONG SURVIVE.

GOSH.. IT SOUNDS AWFUL..

SO HOW LONG HAVE YOU BEEN WITHOUT A WOMAN, SIR?
SINCE FRIDAY. JUST DROP ME OFF AT THE BUS STATION, BUDDY.
GB Trudeau

YOU KNOW, MIKEY, YOU HEAR ABOUT SCANDAL EVERY DAY IN PLACES LIKE WASHINGTON, BUT YOU NEVER DREAM ANYTHING LIKE THAT COULD HAPPEN TO YOU!

NOT THAT I'M SAYING IT WAS AN ACT OF GOD OR SOMETHIN'! HELL, NO! I'M RESPONSIBLE FOR WHAT I DONE. I'M THE ONE WHO LET DOWN MYSELF AND MY FAMILY.

WELL, UNCLE HENRY, AT LEAST YOU'RE WILLING TO ADMIT IT. THERE ARE A LOT OF FOLKS WHO COMMIT FAR WORSE ACTS OF DEPRAVITY AND DON'T EVEN KNOW IT.

GUESS WHO, FISH-FACE!
NO! WAIT! GUARD!
GB Trudeau

DUKE! WHAT?.. HOW?..
I TOLD YOUR GUARD HE HAD A PHONE CALL. BRIGHT FELLOW.

DUKE.. PLEASE.. LET'S BE REASON-ABLE!
LISTEN VERY CAREFULLY, DOG-BREATH. YOU'RE GO-ING TO PICK UP THAT PHONE AND CALL THE POLICE.

SURE, DUKE. WHAT FOR?
YOU'RE GOING TO TELL THAT DETECTIVE YOU'VE DECIDED TO DROP ALL CHARGES. AND YOU'RE GOING TO TELL IT TO HIM VERY CALMLY.

CALMLY, YOU SAY.
RIGHT. YOU'RE EVEN GOING TO THROW IN A JOKE OR TWO.
GB Trudeau

LIEUTENANT O'MALLEY? HI, IT'S ZEKE BRENNER.

YEAH, ZEKE, WHAT'S UP?
WELL, LIEUTENANT, I'VE BEEN THINKING IT OVER, AND I'VE DECIDED NOT TO PRESS CHARGES AGAINST DUKE.

WHAT?
I JUST CAN'T, LIEUTENANT. DUKE'S BEEN TOO GOOD TO ME, ALMOST LIKE A FATHER. TRY TO UNDERSTAND.

STALL HIM. WE'LL BE RIGHT DOWN.
WHAT CAN I TELL YOU, LIEUTENANT? I JUST LOVE THE GUY.
GB Trudeau

NICELY HANDLED, KID! I APPRECIATE YOUR DROPPING THE CHARGES.
WELL, TO BE HONEST, DUKE, I'M GLAD IT'S BEHIND US. WE'VE BEEN FRIENDS TOO LONG.

WELL?
WELL, WHAT, DUKE?

AREN'T YOU GO-ING TO OFFER ME SOME OF YOUR MEDICATION?
OH, GOSH, WHERE ARE MY MANNERS? WHAT'S YOUR PLEASURE, DUKE?
GB Trudeau

YOU KNOW, BRENNER, IT'S A SHAME WE COULDN'T HAVE WORKED THIS OUT A LITTLE EARLIER. YOUR GETTING SHOT HAS REALLY SET BACK MY PLANS TO..OH, MY GOD!
THE WHOLE PARKING LOT IS LOUSY WITH BLACK AND WHITES! THAT DAMN GUARD MUST HAVE CALLED THEM!
YOU BETTER GET DOWN THERE AND TELL THEM YOU'VE DROPPED THE CHARGES! YOU HEAR ME, BRENNER? BRENNER?
GBTrudeau
I THINK YOUR CLEANEST SHOT IS FROM THE NURSE'S STAND.
THANKS, KID! WE'LL TAKE IT FROM HERE!
IS THAT YOU, HONEY?
SIR! WHERE ARE YOU?
OUT AT THE AIRPORT. I JUST GOT IN..
I HEARD ABOUT YOUR GUN BATTLE, SIR. IT'S IN ALL THE PAPERS.
IT IS?
YES, SIR. ACCORDING TO THE POLICE, YOU SHOT UP AN ENTIRE INTENSIVE CARE WARD, PUTTING FOUR PATIENTS INTO SHOCK.
IT HAPPENS, HONEY. CAN WE MEET?
THAT WOULD BE NICE, SIR. I UNDERSTAND YOU'VE GROWN YOUR HAIR.
GBTrudeau

I'M SORRY, SIR, I JUST DON'T HAVE ANY MORE MONEY. IN FACT, AFTER YOU JUMPED BAIL, I HAD TO TAKE OUT A STUDENT LOAN.
SIGH.. IF I DON'T GET A STAKE SOON, I'M GOING TO HAVE TO PACK IT IN.

SIR, MAY I ASK YOU A QUESTION?
IF YOU KEEP IT SHORT.

WHY DID YOU DO IT, SIR? WHY DID YOU SHOOT ZEKE?
HONEY, HAVE YOU EVER HAD THE PLEASURE OF BRENNER'S COMPANY?

UM.. WELL, YES, AS A MATTER OF FACT. I MET HIM OVER A YEAR AGO.
IF YOU'VE MET HIM, THEN YOU SHOULDN'T HAVE TO ASK.

OH, SIR.. SIR.. IS **THAT** WHAT THIS IS ALL ABOUT?
DAMN STRAIGHT.

YOU BIG LUNK, SIR.. HE MEANS **NOTHING** TO ME!
I'M NOT TOO CRAZY ABOUT HIM MYSELF.
GB Trudeau

7 MIAMI

1981-1982

THE NURSE TELLS ME THEY'RE SPRINGING YOU TOMORROW, SPORT..
THAT'S RIGHT, LIEUTENANT. HOW'S YOUR MANHUNT GOING?

NOT SO GOOD, KID. YOU HAVE ANY IDEAS WHERE DUKE MIGHT BE?
WELL, MY GUESS IS HE'S JUST LAYING LOW, TAKING ODD JOBS UNTIL THE HEAT'S OFF.

KNOW ANY FRIENDS HE MIGHT TRY TO MAKE CONTACT WITH?
HMM.. NONE I CAN THINK OF, EXCEPT MAYBE THAT CRAZY CHINESE CHICK WHO USED TO WORK FOR HIM.

I CAME AS SOON AS I COULD, SIR.
HI, SANTA! I'D LIKE..
TAKE A HIKE, KID.
GB Trudeau

YOU WANTED TO SEE ME, SIR?
YEAH, HONEY, I'VE GOT A SURE-FIRE INVESTMENT I WANT TO DISCUSS WITH YOU.

BUT, SIR, I..
HEY, SANTA!
NOT NOW, KID.

SANTA, YOU'RE NOTHING BUT A BALD, SKINNY FAKE!
YEAH, WELL, YOU'RE NOTHING BUT A SNOTTY-FACED, WHIMPERING LITTLE GREEDHEAD!

WAAH!
YOU HAVE A NICE TOUCH, SIR.
THANKS. WHY DON'T WE GO SOMEPLACE QUIETER?
GB Trudeau

NOT THAT I HAVE ANY MONEY, SIR, BUT WHAT'S YOUR INVESTMENT?
IT'S RIGHT HERE, HONEY. THE OPPORTUNITY OF A LIFETIME!

WHY, IT'S.. IT'S JUST A BOAT!
IT'S NOT JUST A BOAT, HONEY! IT'S A 2000 H.P. CABIN CRUISER! COMPLETELY OUTFITTED FOR FISHING CHARTERS OUT OF MIAMI!

THE DECK LOOKS A LITTLE SMALL, SIR. HOW MANY CAN SHE ACCOMMODATE?
WELL, NOT TOO MANY PASSENGERS, BUT THE CARGO HOLD IS BIG ENOUGH TO TAKE 50 BALES EASY!

BALES, SIR?
I MEAN, FISH. LOTS OF ROOM FOR FISH.
GB Trudeau

ISN'T SHE A BEAUT, HONEY? THE OWNER'S HAVING A FEW LEGAL PROBLEMS RIGHT NOW, SO HE'S WILLING TO LET HER GO FOR ONLY $2,000!

$2,000? WHERE WOULD I GET THAT KIND OF MONEY, SIR?
I'M SURE YOU'LL THINK OF SOMETHING. BESIDES, I'D PAY YOU BACK RIGHT AFTER THE FIRST HAUL!

DEEP-SEA CHARTERS PAY THAT WELL, SIR?
THEY DO ON THESE BIG TWIN-ENGINE JOBS! THEY JUST DON'T BUILD THEM LIKE THIS ANYMORE, HONEY!

AND YOU SAY SHE'S IN GOOD SHAPE?
PERFECT! WELL, THE DECK GUN MAY NEED A LITTLE WORK..
GB Trudeau

CYNTHIA? HI, IT'S J.J. LISTEN, IS HONEY OVER THERE AT THE SORORITY BY ANY CHANCE?

NO? GEE, THAT'S STRANGE. I CAN'T SEEM TO FIND HER ANYWHERE..

LOOK, IF SHE COMES IN, WILL YOU TELL HER THAT HER EMBASSY IS TRYING TO REACH HER ABOUT SOME NEW STUDENT LOAN SHE JUST TOOK OUT?
GB Trudeau

I DECIDED TO FOLLOW MY HEART, SIR.
GREAT. DID YOU BRING THE MONEY?
GIVE!!

AHOY!
SI?

ARE YOU RODRIGUEZ?
SI, AMIGO! YOU MUST BE SENOR DUKE! WHO IS THAT WITH YOU?

MY FAITHFUL ORIENTAL COMPANION. CAN WE COME UP AND SEE THE BOAT?
BY ALL MEANS! YOU ARE MOST WELCOME ABOARD!

EXCUSE ME, SIR. WOULD YOU HAVE SOME PLACE I COULD CHANGE INTO MY BIKINI?
TRY THE CAR, HONEY. THIS IS A BUSINESS MEETING!
GB Trudeau

THIS TUB'S GOT A HELLUVA LIST, PAL..
HEY, AMIGO, WHAT DO YOU WANT FOR TWO GRAND, THE LOVE BOAT? SHE'S FLOATING, ISN'T SHE?
MR. RODRIGUEZ?

SI?
MR. RODRIGUEZ, THERE DON'T SEEM TO BE ANY FISHING CHAIRS.

THEY MUST BE IN FOR REPAIRS, HONEY.
FISHING CHAIRS? WHAT'S SHE TALKING ABOUT?

SHE LIKES TO TROLL WHEN WE'RE OUT ON A RUN.
YOU TROLL AT 60 MPH?
I HAVEN'T YET, BUT I'M LOOKING FORWARD TO IT.
GB Trudeau

OKAY, RODRIGUEZ, WE'LL TAKE HER. GIVE HIM THE MONEY, HONEY.

HERE YOU GO, SIR. $2,000, AS AGREED.
THANKS. WHO IS THIS CHICK, ANYWAY, DUKE?

SHE'S MY ASSOCIATE, MISS HUAN. SHE'S INTERESTED IN MAKING IT IN THE BUSINESS WORLD, SO I AGREED TO TAKE HER ON!
A BUDDING CAPITALIST, EH, SENORITA?

NO, SIR. ACTUALLY, I'M A COMMUNIST.
WHAT?
IT'S OKAY. THEY'RE INTO INCENTIVES NOW.
GB Trudeau

YEAH, IS DUKE THERE?
I'M SORRY, SIR, MR. DUKE IS OUT, BUT THIS IS HIS ASSOCIATE. MAY I HELP YOU?

YEAH, I WANT HIM TO MAKE A RUN TONIGHT. RODRIGUEZ SAYS DUKE'S MY MAIN MAN NOW.
WELL, THAT WAS MOST KIND OF MR. RODRIGUEZ TO REFER YOU TO US, SIR. HOW LONG WOULD YOU BE CHARTERING THE BOAT FOR?

THE FREIGHTER'S IN CLOSE TODAY. SHOULDN'T TAKE MORE THAN 30 MINUTES.
30 MINUTES? WELL, LET'S SEE, SINCE YOU WANT OFF-PEAK HOURS, WE SHOULD BE ABLE TO DO THE JOB FOR ABOUT $35. IS THAT WITHIN YOUR BUDGET?

UH.. YEAH.. I SUPPOSE I COULD SWING THAT..
GOOD! WILL YOU BE BRINGING YOUR OWN BAIT, SIR?
GB Trudeau

ANY MESSAGES FOR ME WHILE I WAS GONE, HONEY?
YES, SIR! WE GOT OUR FIRST JOB!

WE DID?
YES, SIR. A GENTLEMAN BY THE NAME OF DIAZ WANTS YOU TO GO OUT TO SOME FREIGHTER TONIGHT AND PICK UP A SMALL PARCEL HE'S EXPECTING!

HOT DAMN! THIS IS IT, HONEY! WE ARE GOING TO CLEAN UP!
HE FIGURES IT WON'T TAKE MORE THAN A HALF HOUR, SO I QUOTED HIM A PRICE OF $35.

YOU WHAT?
AS AN INTRODUCTORY RATE. HE SEEMED VERY PLEASED!
©B Trudeau

$35? YOU GAVE HIM A QUOTE OF $35?
YOU JUST HAVE TO MEET SOME FREIGHTER, SIR. IT'S ONLY A SMALL JOB.

SMALL JOB? HONEY, WHAT WOULD YOU SAY IF I TOLD YOU THAT THAT SMALL JOB COULD HAVE BEEN WORTH $50,000!

WELL?
I'D SAY THAT WAS A LITTLE HIGH. WE'RE JUST STARTING OUT.
©B Trudeau

I CAN'T BELIEVE I'M RISKING MY TAIL FOR A LOUSY 35 BUCKS!
WE HAVE OUR REPUTATION TO THINK OF, SIR. WE CAN'T RENEGE ON OUR COMMITMENTS.

YOU MEAN, YOUR COMMITMENTS! WHAT'S THE NAME OF THAT FREIGHTER AGAIN?
THE "SAN PEDRO," SIR. IF I MAY ASK, SIR, YOU'RE NOT GOING OUT DRESSED LIKE THAT, ARE YOU?

WHAT'S WRONG WITH HOW I'M DRESSED? I'M ON A MISSION, FOR GOD'S SAKE!
YES, SIR, BUT IT'S OUR FIRST DELIVERY. IT'S IMPORTANT THAT YOU MAKE A VERY GOOD IMPRESSION!

I SEE. WHAT DID YOU HAVE IN MIND, HONEY?
WELL, I THOUGHT MAYBE A NICE BLAZER, SIR. LIKE THE GUYS AT FEDERAL EXPRESS.
©B Trudeau

AND WATCH FOR FLARES, OKAY? I DON'T TRUST THIS ENGINE!
YES, SIR. WHAT ABOUT THE SOUP I MADE YOU? DON'T YOU WANT IT?

WHAT FOR? I'LL ONLY BE GONE FOR 20 MINUTES.
NOT IF THE ENGINE CONKS OUT, YOU WON'T. PLEASE, SIR, I'LL FEEL BETTER IF YOU TAKE IT!
RRUM!

NO TIME, HONEY, I'M LATE! CAST OFF THE LINE!
GIVE MR. DIAZ MY REGARDS, OKAY? AND TRY TO BE COURTEOUS, SIR. HE'S OUR FIRST CLIENT AND WE HAVE TO CULTIVATE HIM!
VAROOM!

THE LINE, DAMMIT, THE LINE!
AND GET A RECEIPT! WE MIGHT NEED IT FOR THE TAX BOYS!
VROOOM!
CRAK!
GB Trudeau

AHOY, UP THERE!
WHO'S THERE?

WHO DO YOU THINK? THROW DOWN THE STUFF. I HAVEN'T GOT ALL NIGHT!
WHAT STUFF?

UH.. ISN'T THIS THE FREIGHTER "SAN PEDRO" OUT OF CARACAS?
NO, IT'S THE U.S. COAST GUARD CUTTER "NEMESIS" OUT OF MIAMI.

OH.. SORRY. MY MISTAKE.
SURE LOOKS THAT WAY. LET'S CUT OUR MOTOR, SHALL WE?
GB Trudeau

SIR! WHAT HAPPENED? DIAZ CALLED AND SAID..
I GOT BUSHWHACKED BY THE COAST GUARD, HONEY. THEY DE-TAINED ME ALL NIGHT!

DID YOU MAKE THE PICK-UP, SIR?
NO, AND IT'S A DAMN GOOD THING! THEY WENT OVER EVERY LAST INCH OF THAT BOAT!

HOO BOY.. $35 DOWN THE TOILET..
FOR THE LOVE OF GOD, HONEY, IS THAT ALL YOU CAN THINK ABOUT? YOUR LOUSY 35 BUCKS?

YOU HAVE TO ADMIT IT'S KIND OF A BLACK EYE FOR OUR BUSI-NESS, SIR.
NOT NECESSARILY. I MANAGED TO LIFT A COAST GUARD CODE BOOK.
GB Trudeau

SIR, IF WE DON'T START GETTING A FEW JOBS SOON, WE'RE GOING TO LOSE THE BOAT.
DON'T WORRY, HONEY, THE BIG HAITIAN DEAL IS GOING TO SOLVE ALL OUR PROBLEMS.

HAITIAN DEAL? WHAT HAITIAN DEAL?
DIDN'T I TELL YOU? A PARTY OF 200 DEEP-SEA FISHERMEN IN HAITI HAS CHARTERED THE BOAT.

200? ALL AT THE SAME TIME?
THE HAITIANS ARE JUST CRAZY ABOUT SPORT FISHING. WHOLE FAMILIES DO IT TOGETHER.

BUT.. BUT THEY'LL SWAMP THE BOAT!
SO? YOU WANT TO TELL ALL THOSE LITTLE KIDS THEY CAN'T GO?
GB Trudeau

GOOD NEWS, SIR! YOUR MAN IN PORT-AU-PRINCE CALLED. THE PICK-UP OF YOUR PARTY OF HAITIAN SPORT FISHERMEN IS ON FOR TONIGHT!
GOOD. IS THE BOAT READY TO GO?

YES, SIR, ALTHOUGH I'M NOT SURE WE'LL HAVE ENOUGH PROVISIONS FOR ALL 200. I TOLD THEM TO BRING THEIR OWN BOX LUNCHES.
GOOD. THE LAST THING WE NEED IS AN ON-BOARD FOOD RIOT.

YOU HAVEN'T SAID A WORD ABOUT MY NEW BIKINI, SIR.
DON'T RUSH ME.
GB Trudeau

WELCOME TO HAITI, MONSIEUR!

HOLD IT RIGHT THERE, PAL! WHO ARE YOU?
ALPHONSE PETIT-POIS. I'M YOUR CONTACT.

WHERE ARE THE OTHERS? YOU PROMISED ME 200 PAYING REFUGEES!
ANOTHER CAPTAIN OFFERED THEM A BETTER DEAL. THEY DIDN'T HAVE MUCH MONEY, SO THEY TOOK IT.

I CAN'T STAND IT.
LISTEN, I'M A LITTLE SHORT MYSELF. COULD I OWE YOU UNTIL I STRIKE IT RICH IN AMERICA?
GB Trudeau

TEN BUCKS? THAT'S ALL YOU HAVE? THREE DAYS ON THE OPEN SEA FOR TEN BUCKS?
IT'S NOT MY FAULT YOUR OTHER PASSENGERS DROPPED OUT, SIR.

LOOK, LET'S FORGET THE WHOLE THING, FELLAH! THIS IS AN INSULT!
NOW, SIR, A DEAL IS A DEAL. WE HAVE OUR REPUTATION TO CONSIDER HERE.

BESIDES, IF MR. PETIT-POIS HAS AN ENJOYABLE CHARTER, I'M SURE HE'LL MAKE IT UP TO US IN THE WORD-OF-MOUTH DEPARTMENT. LET'S JUST THINK OF THIS RUN AS A LOSS LEADER!

LOSS LEADER?
WELCOME ABOARD, SIR. CAN I GET YOU ANYTHING?
YEAH, I'LL TAKE A BEER IF YOU HAVE ONE.
GB Trudeau

THANKS FOR EVERYTHING, MES AMIS. I'LL SEND YOU A POSTCARD FROM LITTLE HAITI!
SORRY YOU DIDN'T CATCH ANY FISH, SIR.

THAT'S OKAY, MISS. I'VE SEEN QUITE ENOUGH FISH TO LAST ME A LIFETIME!
WHAT ARE YOUR PLANS, ALPHONSE? WHAT WILL YOU DO NOW?

I'LL PURSUE THE AMERICAN DREAM, OF COURSE. ISN'T THAT WHAT EVERYONE DOES HERE?
NOT ME. I'M PURSUING THE CHINESE DREAM.

WELL, AS LONG AS YOU'VE GOT ONE.
WHAT THE HELL IS A CHINESE DREAM?
IT'S LIKE YOURS, ONLY WITHOUT THE MORTGAGE PAYMENTS.
GB Trudeau

BAD NEWS, SIR. HE DIDN'T MAKE IT.

WHO DIDN'T MAKE IT?
ALPHONSE. HE WAS PICKED UP BY THE COAST GUARD AND SENT OVER TO THE KROME AVENUE DETENTION CENTER FOR REFUGEES.

IMMIGRATION JUST CALLED TO ASK IF YOU WOULD SPONSOR HIM. APPARENTLY, TO KEEP FROM GETTING DEPORTED, ALPHONSE TOLD THEM YOU WERE HIS FATHER. I KNEW YOU'D WANT ME TO CONFIRM IT, SO I DID.

WRONG AS USUAL. CALL THEM BACK AND..
I'M PROUD OF YOU SIR. A LESS COMPASSIONATE MAN WOULD HAVE SENT HIM PACKING.
GB Trudeau

YOU TOLD IMMIGRATION THAT I WAS PETIT-POIS' FATHER?
YES, SIR. ALPHONSE NEEDS A SPONSOR HE'S RELATED TO TO KEEP FROM BEING DEPORTED..

IT'S THE LEAST WE CAN DO, SIR. AFTER ALL, WE BROUGHT HIM TO THIS COUNTRY. BESIDES, IT'S SUCH A SMALL FAVOR. ONE SIGNATURE AND YOU'D HAVE A FRIEND FOR LIFE!

SAY.. THAT'S RIGHT, I WOULD. IN FACT, HE'D PROBABLY DO ANYTHING FOR ME. IF HE DIDN'T, I COULD BLOW THE WHISTLE ON HIM AND BACK HE'D GO!

HONEY, I THINK WE JUST FOUND OURSELVES A DECKHAND.
I KNEW THE IDEA OF A NEW FRIEND WOULD EXCITE YOU, SIR.
GB Trudeau

HE'S PROBABLY IN THE YARD. WITH ALL THE OVERCROWDING, IT'S GOTTEN HOTTER INDOORS THAN OUT!
THAT RIGHT?

YOUR KID'S LUCKY HE HAD FAMILY HERE. MOST OF THESE PEOPLE ARE GOING TO GET SENT BACK.
SO I HEARD. WHAT A SHAME.

WELL, THERE THEY ARE. WHICH ONE'S YOUR BOY?
HMM.. HARD TO TELL. IT'S BEEN A WHILE SINCE I'VE SEEN HIM.

DAD!
THAT'S HIM.
GB Trudeau

AND WHAT'S THE NAME OF YOUR BUSINESS, SIR?
RUSTY NAIL CHARTERS. LISTEN, HONEY, I'M A BIT PRESSED. WE'VE GOT A TIDE TO CATCH.

I'M ALMOST THROUGH, SIR. WHAT IS THE SPONSOR'S RELATIONSHIP TO THE IMMIGRANT?
I'M HIS LONG-LOST FATHER. WE WERE SEPARATED DURING A TYPHOON 20 YEARS AGO.

HIS FATHER?
RIGHT. TO BE HONEST WITH YOU, I NEVER THOUGHT I'D SEE HIM AGAIN.

IF I MAY ASK, SIR..
HE LOOKS LIKE HIS MOTHER.
HOW IS THE OLD GAL, ANYWAY, DAD?
GB Trudeau

OKAY, AL, I NEED A DECKHAND, SO HERE'S THE DEAL. SINCE PER CAPITA INCOME IN HAITI IS ABOUT $300, I'M PREPARED TO DOUBLE THAT. YOU ALSO GET GRUB AND A BERTH ON THE BOAT.

NOW, IF YOU KEEP YOUR NOSE CLEAN, WE'LL GET ALONG FINE. BUT IF YOU SCREW UP EVEN ONCE, I'LL FEED YOU TO IMMIGRATION SO FAST IT'LL MAKE YOUR HEAD SPIN!

DON'T WORRY, ALPHONSE, IF HE TRIES THAT, YOU CAN ALWAYS TURN HIM IN TO THE POLICE. HE'S ON THE RUN JUST LIKE YOU!
OH?

HONEY!
JUST TRYING TO MAKE IT A FAIR FIGHT, SIR.
HEY, BOSS, COULD I HAVE A RAISE?
©B Trudeau

HEY, ALPHONSE, WHERE'S THE MAN?
HE'S OUT AT SEA, MR. RODRIGUEZ. HE LEFT THREE DAYS AGO.

WHEN'S HE DUE BACK? I GOT A JOB FOR HIM.
SORRY, SIR, MR. DUKE TOLD ME NOT TO ACCEPT ANY NEW BUSINESS FOR HIM. HE'S GOING TO BE GONE AT LEAST FIVE WEEKS.

FIVE WEEKS? WHERE'S HE GOING, COLOMBIA?
NO, SIR, THE FALKLAND ISLANDS. HE'S TAKING A CHARTER OF SIGHTSEERS DOWN TO WATCH THE BRITISH BLOCKADE.

♫ DON'T CRY FOR ME, ARGENTINA! ♫
HA! HA!
EXCUSE ME, SIR. WE'RE OUT OF ICE.
DAMN! WE HAVEN'T EVEN REACHED CUBA YET!
©B Trudeau

HAIL, BRITANNIA! BRITANNIA RULES THE WAVES! ♫
HA, HA!
THEY CERTAINLY ARE A NOISY LOT, SIR.
RUSTY NAIL CHARTERS

OKAY BY ME, HONEY. THEY'RE PAYING PASSENGERS, TWO GRAND A HEAD! ALL WE GOTTA DO IS GET 'EM DOWN TO THE FALKLAND ISLANDS IN TIME FOR THE FIREWORKS.
RUSTY NAIL CHARTERS

I'LL TELL YOU, HONEY, THIS INVASION IS PURE GOLD! NOT TOO MANY WARS THESE DAYS WHERE YOU GET TWO WEEKS' NOTICE, YOU KNOW?
RUSTY NAIL CHARTERS

YES, SIR, IT WAS QUITE A BREAK.
FOR ONCE, WE HAD ENOUGH TIME TO GET A DECENT BROCHURE OUT.
RUSTY NAIL CHARTERS
©B Trudeau

BROCHURE? WE PUT OUT A BROCHURE, SIR?
YOU MEAN YOU NEVER SAW IT? HERE, CHECK IT OUT, HONEY.

"RUSTY NAIL CHARTERS IS PLEASED TO ANNOUNCE AN EXCLUSIVE 35-DAY PLEASURE CRUISE TO THE EMBATTLED FALKLAND ISLANDS. OUR VOYAGE IS SCHEDULED TO COINCIDE WITH THE ARRIVAL OF BRITAIN'S MAGNIFICENT TASK FORCE."

"DON'T MISS THIS UNIQUE OPPORTUNITY TO SEE THE FULL PAGEANTRY OF A ROYAL NAVY OPERATION! WATCH HISTORY IN THE MAKING FROM THE COMFORT OF YOUR OWN DECK CHAIR, WHILE OUR SCANTILY-CLAD ORIENTAL HOSTESS ATTENDS YOUR EVERY NEED.."

SIR! YOU'RE SHAMELESS!
ME? LISTEN, I'M NOT THE ONE RUNNING AROUND WITH NO CLOTHES ON!
©BTrudeau

GOD SAVE THE QUEEN!!
COULD I HAVE YOUR ATTENTION, PLEASE, FOLKS? I HAVE A FEW ANNOUNCEMENTS TO MAKE.

WE'RE A LITTLE BEHIND SCHEDULE, SO WE'LL BE CRUISING AT FULL THROTTLE FROM NOW ON. THOSE WHO WOULD LIKE TO WATER-SKI BEHIND THE BOAT, PLEASE SIGN UP IN THE GALLEY..

OUR RADIO'S DOWN, SO NO NEW POOP FROM THE BBC. I KNOW A LOT OF YOU HOPE THE BRITS WILL BEAT THE STUFFING OUT OF ARGENTINA, BUT REMEMBER, THERE ARE NO WINNERS IN WAR!

NONETHELESS, THE PURSER WILL BE ACCEPTING BETS AFTER DINNER..
ME? SIR, I CAN'T, I'VE GOT TO RUN THE MOVIE.
©BTrudeau

HONEY, WHAT THE HELL IS GOING ON DOWN THERE?
WELL, SIR, WE'RE SCHEDULED TO HIT THE FALKLANDS TOMORROW, SO THE GUESTS ARE HAVING A LITTLE CELEBRATION!
HA, HA! HA!
CLINK!

HMM.. I COULD USE A BREAK MYSELF. TAKE THE WHEEL FOR AWHILE, WILLYA, HONEY?
UM.. I'M SORRY, SIR, I CAN'T LET YOU GO TO THE PARTY LOOKING LIKE THAT.
HA, HA!
HEE!

LOOKING LIKE WHAT?
THE PARTY IS BLACK TIE ONLY, SIR.
CLINK!
CHEERS!

IT'S MY BOAT, DAMMIT!
THEY'RE PAYING GOOD MONEY, SIR. I'LL TRY TO SNEAK YOU UP SOME SANDWICHES.
HA, HA!
HEE!
©BTrudeau

I'M SURPRISED WE HAVEN'T SIGHTED ANY BRITISH SUPPLY VESSELS YET, HONEY. WE'RE RIGHT IN THE MIDDLE OF THE SOUTH ATLANTIC SHIPPING LANES..
WILL WE BE ARRIVING AT THE FALKLAND ISLANDS ON SCHEDULE, SIR?
I THINK SO. LET ME SEE.. OUR LAST RECORDED POSITION WAS HERE.. WE'RE BEARING SOUTHEAST AT 18 KNOTS.. HMM..
WELL, IT LOOKS GOOD. WE MAY POSSIBLY BE OFF BY AN INCH OR TWO, BUT IT'S NOTHING TO GET EXCITED ABOUT..
"ONE INCH EQUALS 1,000 MILES."
SO WE MISS THE OPENING FESTIVITIES. WHO'S GOING TO KNOW THE DIFFERENCE?
GBTrudeau
MAY I HAVE YOUR ATTENTION, PLEASE? THIS IS YOUR CAPTAIN SPEAKING..
THERE'S BEEN A LOT OF IRRESPONSIBLE TALK GOING AROUND TO THE EFFECT THAT WE'RE LOST. NOTHING COULD BE MORE MISLEADING. WE'RE SIMPLY A TAD OFF COURSE, UNDERSTANDABLE ON A 6,000-MILE VOYAGE.
WE'RE ALREADY THREE DAYS LATE!
IF YOU'LL CHECK YOUR CONTRACTS, YOU'LL SEE THAT ACTUAL HOSTILITIES WERE NOT GUARANTEED.
WE'LL MISS THE INVASION!
LIAR!
WE WANT OUR MONEY BACK!
BETTER TRAIN THAT DECK GUN DOWN HERE, HONEY.
THAT'S NOT GOING TO SOLVE ANYTHING, SIR.
GBTrudeau
I THINK I GOT THE PASSENGERS QUIETED DOWN, SIR. I GAVE THEM ALL DRINKS ON THE HOUSE.
WONDERFUL. THERE GOES OUR PROFIT MARGIN.
RUSTY NAIL CHARTERS
IT'S BETTER THAN A FULL-SCALE RIOT, SIR, AND.. HEY! LOOK OUT FOR THAT REEF!
REEF? WHERE?
RUSTY NAIL CHARTERS
CRUNCH!
RUSTY NAIL CHARTERS
SHUDDER!
WE WANT OUR MONEY BACK!
NOW YOU'VE DONE IT, SIR!
IT'S THESE DAMN OUTDATED CHARTS!
RUSTY NAIL CHARTERS
GBTrudeau

I THINK YOU HIT A REEF, SIR.
DAMN! THAT'S ALL WE NEED! GO DOWN AND CHECK OUT THE DAMAGE, WILLYA, HONEY?
RUSTY NAIL CHARTERS

I DON'T BELIEVE THIS! FIRST WE GET LOST, THEN I HAVE TO QUELL A NEAR-MUTINY, AND NOW WE'RE ON A REEF! WHAT THE HELL IS THIS, VOYAGE OF THE DAMNED?
RUSTY NAIL CHARTERS

HONEY! WHAT'S THE STORY ON THE DAMAGE?
RUSTY NAIL CHARTERS

IT DOESN'T LOOK GOOD, SIR.
HOLD ON, I'M GOING TO TRY IT IN REVERSE..
RUSTY NAIL CHARTERS
GB Trudeau

GET THAT OTHER LIFE RAFT OVER THE SIDE! HURRY! WOMEN FIRST!

DUKE? SIR? ANYONE SEEN THE CAPTAIN?
I THINK HE WENT BELOW!

SIR? ARE YOU IN HERE?
YOU KNOW, THIS HAS GOT TO BE ONE OF THE WORST DAYS OF MY LIFE.

SIR! WE'RE GOING DOWN!
I KNOW. I CAN'T GET OVER IT. THANK GOD I'M STONED.
GB Trudeau

HULLO? HULLO?
SIT DOWN, HONEY. I'M SURE THEY'RE ALL OKAY. THERE WERE PLENTY OF LIFE RAFTS TO GO AROUND.
914

I HOPE SO, SIR. THE WELFARE OF THE PASSENGERS IS OUR RESPONSIBILITY.
AH, DON'T WORRY ABOUT IT, HONEY. WHAT'S IN THE COOLER?
914

HMM.. DID YOU BRING ANY WINE TO GO WITH THIS CHICKEN?
914

SIR, ARE YOU SURE YOU WON'T GET IN TROUBLE FOR NOT GOING DOWN WITH THE SHIP?
HELL, NO! IT'S NOT AS ROUGH ON THE INSURANCE COMPANY.
914
GB Trudeau

DID YOU BRING ANY MORPHINE? WHAT ABOUT A FIRST AID KIT? AND COMPASS?
IT'S ALL IN THERE, SIR. DON'T WORRY, WE'LL BE OKAY. IN FACT, THIS TURN OF EVENTS MIGHT TURN OUT TO BE QUITE AN OPPORTUNITY!
701
OPPORTUNITY? WHAT ARE YOU TALKING ABOUT, HONEY?
IT'S A PERFECT CHANCE FOR US TO GET TO KNOW EACH OTHER A LITTLE BETTER!
701
701
WHERE ARE MY GIRLIE MAGS? DID YOU PACK MY GIRLIE MAGS?
I JUST DON'T THINK WE SHOULD LET IT SLIP THROUGH OUR FINGERS.
701
GB Trudeau

SIR? ARE YOU OKAY, SIR?
I'M.. I'M GOING FAST, HONEY. I DON'T KNOW IF I'M GOING TO MAKE IT..
709
DON'T BE SILLY, SIR. OF COURSE, YOU'RE GOING TO MAKE IT..
BEER.. >GASP!< BEER..
709
WHATEVER YOU SAY, SIR. ONE FROSTY COLD BEER COMING UP!
709
ACTUALLY, SIR, WATER IS THE PREFERRED DRINK OF THE DYING.
NONSENSE. GOT ANY PRETZELS TO GO WITH THAT?
709
GB Trudeau

LAND HO!
702
WELL, I'LL BE DARNED..
DIDN'T I TELL YOU I'D BRING US THROUGH THIS? DIDN'T I?
702
BREAK OUT THAT LAST CAN OF BEER, HONEY! THIS CALLS FOR A CELEBRATION!
702
GB Trudeau
ACTUALLY, SIR, WHY DON'T WE HOLD OFF ON THAT?
HELL, NO! WE'RE HOME FREE!

BACK! BACK, YOU UGLY, DISGUSTING CREATURE!
LEAVE THE SHARK ALONE, SIR! WE MADE IT!

GOD, I HATE THOSE THINGS! THEY GIVE ME THE CREEPS!
JUST BE THANKFUL WE MADE IT, SIR.
157°

I CAN'T UNDERSTAND WHAT THIS ISLAND IS DOING HERE! IT'S NOT ON ANY OF THE CHARTS. SEE ANYONE?
NO, SIR. I THINK IT'S DESERTED.
157°

IN THE NAME OF RONALD WILSON REAGAN, PRESIDENT OF THE..
SORRY, SIR, I ALREADY CLAIMED IT FOR CHINA.
157°
GB Trudeau

I GOT SOME MORE FIREWOOD, SIR. WHERE DO YOU WANT IT?
THROW IT ON THE BONFIRE. WE WANT TO BE READY IN CASE A SHIP PASSES.

DO YOU REALLY THINK WE'LL BE RESCUED SOON, SIR?
OF COURSE WE WILL! WE'RE RIGHT IN THE MIDDLE OF THE BUSIEST SEA LANE IN THE SOUTH ATLANTIC!

I HOPE SO, SIR. OUR SUPPLIES ARE GETTING VERY LOW.
I KNOW. LOOK, THAT REMINDS ME. YOU BETTER TAKE THIS AND SEE IF YOU CAN GET US A WILD BOAR OR SOMETHING FOR DINNER.

UM.. AS THE MAN, SHOULDN'T YOU BE BRINGING HOME THE BACON, SIR?
WELL, YEAH, I WOULD IF IT WEREN'T FOR MY BUM KNEE.
GB Trudeau

SIR, I'M AFRAID I'M NOT HAVING MUCH LUCK IN THE WILD BOAR DEPARTMENT. ALL I'VE SEEN SO FAR ARE BIRDS.
KEEP LOOKING, HONEY, THERE'S.. OH, MY GOD!

WHAT IS IT, SIR?
A HUMAN FOOTPRINT! WE'RE NOT ALONE ON THIS ISLAND!

HEY, THAT'S GREAT, SIR, WE..
GREAT? WE'LL HAVE TO BUILD A STOCKADE NOW! THEY COULD BE SAVAGES! CANNIBALS!

BUT IT'S A SNEAKER PRINT, SIR.
MEANS NOTHING! THE VIET CONG WORE TIRE SANDALS!
GB Trudeau

.. AND FROM HERE, A SIMPLE STOCKADE SHOULD BE ABLE TO WITHSTAND ANY ASSAULT THE SAVAGES COULD MOUNT!
IF THERE ARE SAVAGES, SIR.
WE'LL SET OUR PALISADES JUST BELOW THE CLIFF, AND MAYBE PLACE TRIP WIRES AND BOOBY TRAPS IN THE DUNES. AND ON THIS KNOLL, WE'LL PUT YOUR SENTRY TOWER!
FROM HERE YOU'LL HAVE A VIEW OF THE WHOLE BAY!
YES, AND IT'S NICE AND BREEZY HERE. I COULD HANG SOME WIND CHIMES. AND MAYBE BRING A FEW PLANTS UP.
FINE. WOULD YOU LIKE TO LOOK AT SOME FABRICS, TOO?
IT'S THOSE HOMEY TOUCHES WHICH KEEP MORALE UP, SIR.
GB Trudeau

.. AND HERE'S WHERE I WANT THE EMBANKMENTS, WITH THE PALISADES HERE, AND A MOAT DOWN BELOW..
SIR, ISN'T THAT KIND OF AN AMBITIOUS BUILDING PROGRAM FOR THE FIRST DAY?
AMBITIOUS? HONEY, WE'RE TALKING SURVIVAL HERE! IF WE DON'T SECURE OUR PERIMETER SOON, IN A FEW WEEKS THE SEAGULLS WILL BE PICKING SAND FLEAS OUT OF OUR SKULLS!
ON THE OTHER HAND, IT IS TURNING INTO A PRETTY NICE DAY..
WHAT THE HELL. LET'S PARTY.
SIR, I'M WORRIED ABOUT YOUR MOOD SWINGS.
GB Trudeau

SQUAWK!
HEY, LOOK, SIR! A PARROT!
HELLO, JACK! HELLO, JACK!
LISTEN TO THAT, SIR! HE MUST HAVE COME FROM SOME OTHER SHIP!
SQUAWK! DROP DEAD, YOU FILTHY SWINE! TAKE A HIKE, SUCKER! WHAT'S IN IT FOR ME? WHAT'S IN IT FOR ME?
HE TALKS JUST LIKE YOU, SIR!
IT'S UNCANNY.
GB Trudeau

SQUAWK! CHOW'S ON, JACK!
HI, PARROT! WANT A CRACKER?

NO! WE DON'T HAVE ENOUGH FOOD TO BE WASTING IT ON SOME DUMB BIRD! BESIDES, IF THERE'S ONE THING I CAN'T ABIDE, IT'S AN ANIMAL THAT WON'T FEND FOR ITSELF!

THIS BAG OF FEATHERS IS PROBABLY OFF SOME LUXURY LINER. WHERE HE'S BEEN GETTING HANDOUTS HIS WHOLE LIFE!
BUST CAPS, JACK! HUMP THAT PACK! WASTE THAT HOOTCH! HERE'S ONE FOR YO' MAMA! MEDIC!

GOOD LORD! HE'S BEEN TO NAM!
LET'S FRAG THE LIEUTENANT! LET'S FRAG THE LIEUTENANT!
GB Trudeau

SQUAWK! BODY COUNT! BODY COUNT!
HMM.. I DIDN'T NOTICE THAT GOAT PATH BEFORE. WE MAY HAVE A WINDOW OF VULNERABILITY ON OUR HANDS!

INCOMING, JACK!
I BETTER GO DOWN AND CHECK IT OUT. I MIGHT HAVE TO BLOW IT!

HEY, G.I.! HEY, G.I.!
KEEP AN EYE PEELED, BIRD!
SIR? HAVE YOU GOT THE ROPE?

SQUAWK! GOOK AT THREE O'CLOCK!
GOOK? HONEY! HELP!
I THINK HE MEANS ME, SIR.
GB Trudeau

ANY SIGN OF THE BRITISH TASK FORCE, SIR?
NOT YET. THEY MUST HAVE WITHDRAWN SOUTH.

YOU REALLY HAVE YOUR HEART SET ON SEEING THE FLEET, DON'T YOU, SIR?
WHEN YOU'RE THIS CLOSE TO HISTORY, HONEY, YOU DON'T WANT TO MISS IT. EVER BEEN IN A WAR BEFORE?

NO, SIR. I WAS IN A PURGE ONCE.
NOT THE SAME. NOTHING CAN MATCH THE FUROR OF THE REAL THING. I KNOW. I'VE SEEN TWO WARS IN MY LIFETIME, THREE IF YOU COUNT THE BELGIAN CONGO.

YOU FOUGHT IN THE CONGO, SIR?
JUST FOR THE SUMMER. I WAS WORKING MY WAY THROUGH COLLEGE.
GB Trudeau

I WONDER IF WE SHOULD BE TURNING BACK, DICK.
NO, LET'S GO A LITTLE FURTHER, THAD. I'D LIKE TO LOG A PELICAN TODAY IF I COULD.

IT'S NOT OFTEN WE GET TO BIRD IN SUCH PRISTINE SURROUNDINGS. IT'S HARD TO BELIEVE WE'RE SO CLOSE TO CIVILIZATION.

I KNOW. DO YOU REALIZE WE'VE WALKED FIVE HOURS WITHOUT SEEING A SOUL?
INCREDIBLE, ISN'T IT?
GB Trudeau

GREASE 'EM! GREASE 'EM!
SHUT UP, BIRD! THEY'RE NOT IN RANGE!
WHAT TRIBE DO YOU THINK THEY'RE FROM, SIR?

FREEZE RIGHT THERE, GRAMPS!
HO, THADIUS! RUN FOR IT! I'M TAKEN!

HOLD IT, FELLAH! GET BACK HERE, OR YOUR PAL'S A DEAD MAN!

HE OWES YOU A LOT OF MONEY, I ASSUME.
NO, NO, HE'S JUST HARD OF HEARING.
GB Trudeau

..AND YOU WEREN'T SENT HERE BY THE FEDS TO TRACK ME DOWN?
HEAVENS, NO. I'M JUST A TOURIST VISITING THE ISLAND.

TOURIST, HUH? THEN WHAT WERE YOU DOING SNEAKING AROUND THE DUNES?
BY AVOCATION, I'M A BIRD-WATCHER, SIR. BIRDING REQUIRES STEALTH.

I DON'T GET IT, GRAMPS. WHAT'S A BIRD-WATCHER DOING IN THE MIDDLE OF A WAR ZONE?
WAR ZONE? MY DEAR BOY, THIS IS THE ISLAND OF MATAGORDA, OFF OF TEXAS!

TEXAS?
AMERICA, SIR! OUR ORDEAL IS OVER!
NOT NECESSARILY. THERE MAY NOT BE ENOUGH ROOM IN THE BOAT.
GB Trudeau

..AND WHILE I WAS TRYING TO QUELL THE MUTINY, WE HIT THIS DAMN REEF!
IT WASN'T HIS FAULT, THOUGH. THE CHART WAS NEARLY THREE YEARS OUT OF DATE.
AND WHO MIGHT YOU BE, YOUNG LADY?
I MIGHT BE HONEY, SIR. I WAS THE PURSER ON THE "RUSTY NAIL". NOW I'M MR. DUKE'S GAL FRIDAY.
REALLY? ARE YOU SURE YOU'D LIKE TO BE RESCUED, MR. DUKE? MOST MEN DREAM OF BEING SHIPWRECKED ON AN ISLAND WITH A CHARMING YOUNG LADY!
HELL, SO DO I, BUT HONEY AND I WERE THE ONLY SURVIVORS.
COMPLIMENT RECEIVED ON THIS END, SIR.
GB Trudeau
HARD TO BELIEVE, ISN'T IT, HONEY? DOWN TO OUR LAST WEEK'S RATION OF TEQUILA, AND WE'RE RESCUED BY A COUPLE OF BIRD-WATCHERS!
I WAS BEGINNING TO THINK WE WERE DONE FOR, WEREN'T YOU, HONEY?
NOT REALLY, SIR. I WAS PRETTY SURE WE'D MAKE IT.
OH, YEAH? HOW COME?
UM..WELL, ACTUALLY, I HAVE A SMALL CONFESSION, SIR. I SAW THE FERRY COME OVER HERE ABOUT A MONTH AGO.
SAY WHAT?
I JUST THOUGHT IT MORE IMPORTANT THAT WE HAVE SOME TIME TO OURSELVES.
GB Trudeau
HOW MUCH LONGER BEFORE THE FERRY GETS HERE, SIR?
IT SHOULD BE HERE MOMENTARILY. ANXIOUS TO BE LEAVING, ARE YOU?
ACTUALLY, SIR, I'M A LITTLE AMBIVALENT. DUKE AND I HAD SOME WONDERFUL TIMES HERE.
I GUESS I'M ALSO A LITTLE LET DOWN. WHEN WE FIRST ARRIVED, I CLAIMED THE ISLAND FOR CHINA. I THOUGHT I'D DISCOVERED A NEW VACATION SPOT FOR THE MASSES TO COME TO.
YOU CLAIMED MATAGORDA FOR CHINA?
WELL, MOST OF IT. I LOST THE MINERAL RIGHTS TO DUKE IN A POKER GAME.
GB Trudeau

HEY, WHATCHA DOIN' ON MY BENCH, BUDDY?
TAKE A HIKE, GRAMPS, I GOT HERE FIRST.

OH, YEAH? AND WHAT MAKES YOU SO SPECIAL?
YOU HEARD ME, OLD MAN, BEAT IT!

HEY, WAIT A MINUTE.. YOU LOOK AWFUL FAMILIAR! DIDN'T YOU USED TO BE A POLITICIAN OR SOMETHIN'?
AMBASSADOR. I WAS AMBASSADOR TO CHINA.

AMBASSADOR TO CHINA? NO KIDDIN'? WHEN WAZZAT?
IN 1976.

1976? ARE YOU SERIOUS?
YEAH? WHY?

I WAS KING OF FRANCE THAT YEAR! DID YOU KNOW KUBLA? KUBLA KHAN?
I GOTTA START STAYING AT THE "Y"..
©B Trudeau

HI, SAILOR! WELCOME TO THE NEIGHBORHOOD. THE NAME'S ALICE P. SCHWARTZMAN! WHO ARE YOU?
UH.. DUKE, THE NAME'S DUKE.
PLEASED TO MEET YOU, DUCK. WANT PART OF MY PAPER? IT'S ONLY THREE WEEKS OLD!
YEAH.. YOU GOT THE SPORTS SECTION?
SURE. YOU FOLLOW THE PONIES?
NAH. I JUST PUT MY LAST TEN BUCKS ON THE BREWERS.
THIS AIN'T YOUR DAY, DUCKS.
HEY, WHO'S THIS JOHN DE LOREAN GUY WHO'S ALL OVER THE PAPERS?
HE'S A BIG CAR EXECUTIVE WHO GOT BUSTED FOR TRYING TO BUY A TON OF COCAINE.
OH..
HOW A SMART, GOOD-LOOKING FELLAH LIKE THAT COULD GET IN SO MUCH TROUBLE IS BEYOND ME!
WHAT A LIFE HE HAD, DUCKS! A GOLDEN BOY AT G.M., THREE GORGEOUS WIVES, THEN HIS OWN CAR COMPANY! SOMEBODY OUGHT TO MAKE A MOVIE OF HIS STORY. IT'D MAKE MILLIONS!
HELLO? o o
OF COURSE, THAT PERSON WOULD HAVE TO KNOW SOMETHING ABOUT THE DRUG WORLD.
A MOVIE! THAT'S A HELLUVA IDEA, LADY! "THE JOHN DE LOREAN STORY" IS A NATURAL!
TOO BAD YOU DON'T HAVE THE RIGHTS, DUCKY.
I CAN GET 'EM! I'LL CALL HIS LAWYER. I KNOW THIS WORLD — FAST CARS, CHEAP DRUGS, CHEAP CARS, AND FAST WOMEN — THIS IS MY I SCENE!
GOOD LORD, I EVEN KNOW SOME OF THE PRINCIPALS! HETRICK AND ARRINGTON, THE TWO GUYS BUSTED WITH DE LOREAN! WE USED TO DOCK AT THE SAME WHARF IN FT. LAUDERDALE!
HELL, I EVEN ONCE LOANED THEM MY DECK GUN!
OKAY, I'M IN! HERE'S A DIME FOR THE CALL!

YOU WANT TO DO WHAT?
I WANT TO MAKE A MOVIE ABOUT YOUR CLIENT, JOHN DE LOREAN. WE'D LIKE TO CALL IT, "FAST LANES, WHITE LINES."

WHAT? ARE YOU CRAZY?
YEAH, CRAZY LIKE A FOX. IT'S GOT ALL THE ELEMENTS, MAN – CARS, DRUGS, BEAUTIFUL WOMEN! I'M TALKING BOX OFFICE GOLD!

WHAT DID YOU SAY THE NAME OF YOUR MOVIE COMPANY WAS AGAIN?
UM..

HUBCAP PRODUCTIONS.
HUBCAP PRODUCTIONS. WE DO ALL THE BIG DISASTER FLICKS.
GB Trudeau

I'M SORRY, MR. DUKE, I DON'T CARE HOW BIG YOUR PRODUCTION COMPANY IS, MY CLIENT IS NOT INTERESTED IN SELLING HIS STORY!
YOU DON'T UNDERSTAND. A MOVIE LIKE THIS COULD HELP HIS CASE!

OH? HOW SO?
IF WE GET ROLLING RIGHT AWAY, IT'LL CREATE SO MUCH PUBLICITY THAT DE LOREAN COULDN'T POSSIBLY GET A FAIR TRIAL! THEY'LL HAVE TO THROW IT OUT!

HMM.. INTERESTING NOTION.. YES, I LIKE THAT. LET'S SET UP A MEETING..

GREAT! I'LL PUT ON MY SECRETARY!
SHALL I ASK FOR A NET OR GROSS POSITION?
GB Trudeau

BEAUTIFUL! WE'RE TAKING A MEETING ON MONDAY!
HOW EXCITING! HOW LONG DO YOU THINK IT'LL BE BEFORE WE SHOW A PROFIT?

NOT LONG. BUT FIRST I GOTTA IRON OUT A FEW DETAILS, LIKE FINDING $200 TO GET OUT TO LOS ANGELES.
NO PROBLEM, DUCKS. I'VE GOT A LITTLE MONEY STASHED AWAY FOR EMERGENCIES.

YOU'D GIVE ME $200? WHAT'S THE HITCH?
I WANT A $250,000 BONUS AT THE START OF PRINCIPAL PHOTOGRAPHY AND 15% OF THE GROSS AFTER DIRECT COSTS, PLUS A SEQUEL OPTION!

FOR A LOUSY $200 INVESTMENT?
IT WAS MY IDEA. ALSO, I WANT TO STAY AT THE BEL AIR WHEN I COME OUT TO THE COAST.
GB Trudeau

HOW YOU DOING, SID? GOOD TO SEE YOU..
HEY, DUKE! IT'S ME, SID! WHAT'S WITH THE HANDSHAKE? WE GREW UP TOGETHER, REMEMBER?

SO WE GOTTA HUG AND KISS?
HEY, BABE, THIS IS CALIFORNIA, NOT THE OLD NEIGHBORHOOD! WHAT CAN I DO FOR YOU, HUH? TELL ME WHAT YOU WANT!

I'M PUTTING TOGETHER A FEATURE FILM, SID..
SO YOU BRING IT TO THE BEST AGENT IN THE BUSINESS! HEY, NO MOSS GROWING ON YOU, KID. SHOOT IT BY ME!

WELL, IT'S ABOUT A GUY WHO MAKES CARS..
I LOVE IT! BUT IT'S NOT RIGHT FOR US. WHAT ELSE YOU GOT?
GB Trudeau

ANYWAY, THAT'S THE BASIC IDEA. I'M CALLING IT "FAST LANES, WHITE LINES." WHAT DO YOU THINK?
WHAT DO I THINK? GOT A FEATHER? KNOCK ME OVER WITH IT, OKAY?

YOU LIKE IT?
THE JOHN DE LOREAN STORY! DO I LOVE THIS IDEA? DO I LOVE THE MAN WHO BROUGHT IT TO ME? DO I THINK THIS PICTURE IS GOING TO GO THROUGH THE ROOF?

BEATS ME. DO YOU?
YOU KNOW YOU'RE A GENIUS, RIGHT? I MEAN, I DON'T HAVE TO TELL YOU THERE ISN'T AN AGENT IN THIS TOWN WHO WOULDN'T KILL TO GET INTO BED WITH YOU, DO I?

COME AGAIN?
MAGGIE! BRING IN THE STANDARD FORMS! I'M GETTING MARRIED!
GB Trudeau

YOU REALLY THINK MY DE LOREAN PROJECT COULD BE BIG, SID?
THINK? HEY, BUBBY, SID KIBITZ DOESN'T THINK, HE KNOWS! THIS IS VERY BIG, KID – I FEEL IT IN MY GUT! CAPICHE?

LET ME LAY IT OUT FOR YOU, BABE! WE'RE LOOKING AT A PACKAGE THAT'S GOING TO MAKE THIS TOWN WEEP! I'M TALKING SPIELBERG DIRECTING! I'M TALKING DANNY AYKROYD AS THE YOUNG JOHN DE LOREAN..

DAN AYKROYD WOULD PLAY DE LOREAN?
SURE! I SEE A HIGH CONCEPT PICTURE! A KIND OF "ANIMAL HOUSE" ON WHEELS! WHY? YOU LIKE SOMEONE ELSE IN THE ROLE? SELL ME!

UM.. WELL, I WAS THINKING MAYBE WILLIAM HOLDEN.
LOVE IT! I LOVE IT! BILL'S DEAD, BUT I LOVE YOUR THINKING! THAT'S A GREAT DIRECTION TO TAKE IT!
GB Trudeau

WISH YOU'D TOLD ME WE WERE GOING TO A QUICHE JOINT, SID. I'M ALLERGIC TO FERNS.
GOOD SEEING YOU, KIRK! LET'S DO LUNCH SOON!

GOLDIE! WHERE YOU BEEN HIDING, SWEETHEART! HAVE I GOT A VEHICLE FOR YOU! SHOULD SELL A LOT OF POPCORN! CALL ME AND WE'LL TALK PACKAGE!

HEY, WOODY! HOW'S IT GOING, KID? I'VE GOT A PROJECT THAT'S ON FIRE! LET'S TAKE A MEETING AND SEE IF WE WANT TO GET INTO BED TOGETHER OVER AT WARNER'S!

IS THIS ABSOLUTELY NECESSARY?
YOU WANT YOUR MOVIE MADE OR NOT? WARREN! I GOT YOUR NEXT OSCAR, BABE!
GB Trudeau

DID YOU SEE THEIR FACES, BABE? WHEN WORD HITS THE STREETS WE'VE GOT THE DE LOREAN PROJECT, THE MAJORS WILL BREAK DOWN OUR DOORS!
YOU REALLY THINK WARREN BEATTY WOULD DO MY PICTURE, SID?

ARE YOU KIDDING? HE'D KILL TO BE IN IT! HE'D PLAY THE DAMN CAR IF HE HAD TO!
I GUESS THIS WOULD BE A GOLDEN OPPORTUNITY FOR HIM..

WE'RE ON OUR WAY, KID! THIS CALLS FOR A CELEBRATION!
IF YOU INSIST!

YES, SIR?
MAGGIE, RUN DOWN TO THE STOCK ROOM AND SCORE SOME COKE FOR US!
THIS IS GREAT!
GB Trudeau

MISS LANSING FROM FOX ON LINE THREE, SIR!
HOT DAMN! PAY DIRT ALREADY! PUT HER ON.

SIDNEY? SHERRY! I HEAR YOU'RE SITTING ON THE DE LOREAN PROJECT. YOUR CLIENT WANT TO BRING IT TO US?
TALK TO ME, BABE, TALK TO ME! TELL ME HOW MUCH YOU LOVE ME!

WELL, I'D HAVE TO SEE A TREATMENT, OF COURSE, BUT WE COULD BE TALKING THREE MIL, PLUS POINTS!
$3 MILLION? HEY, SHERRY, THIS IS SID! I DIDN'T JUST BREEZE IN FROM ELLIS ISLAND! LET ME GET BACK TO YOU! SAY, NEXT YEAR! CIAO!

UH.. $3 MILLION ISN'T GOOD ENOUGH?
IT'S AN INSULT! MY ANSWERING SERVICE TURNS DOWN OFFERS BETTER THAN THAT!
GB Trudeau

DUCKS! HOW'S OUR PROJECT COMING!
IT'S ON FIRE, ALICE. IT'S REALLY TAKING OFF!

SID'S SO HIGH ON THE PROJECT HE GOT THE AGENCY TO GIVE ME AN OFFICE. THEY'RE EVEN ADVANCING ME PRE-PRODUCTION MONEY!

WE'LL BE MAKING A STUDIO DEAL THIS WEEK, I'LL DO THE SCRIPT NEXT WEEK, AND WE'LL START SHOOTING IN JANUARY. BY NEXT CHRISTMAS, WE'LL BOTH BE MILLIONAIRES!

GREAT! ACQUIRED THE RIGHTS YET?
NO, I'VE BEEN TOO BUSY. THERE'S BEEN A TON OF DETAILS!
GBTrudeau

SO WHEN DO WE MEET WITH THE STUDIO HEADS, SID?
WE START TOMORROW, KID! WE'RE TAKING A LUNCH AT "MA MAISON" WITH MARTY FELBERG!

WHO'S MARTY FELBERG?
AN OLD FRIEND OF MINE. HE'S ABSOLUTELY HOT FOR YOUR PROJECT!

WHAT'S THE POOP ON HIM?
HE'S BIG, VERY BIG. HE CAN MAKE THINGS HAPPEN. BUT IF YOU CROSS HIM, HE'LL CRUSH YOU AND SEND YOU BACK TO KANSAS, WHETHER YOU CAME FROM THERE OR NOT!

HOW ABOUT IF HE LIKES YOU?
SKY'S THE LIMIT! COCAINE, SEX, LOANS AT 1/2% BELOW PRIME..
GBTrudeau

SID, I GOTTA TELL YOU, YOUR BOY IS PUTTING ME AWAY! I'M SITTING HERE LISTENING AND I'M NOT BELIEVING MY EARS!
HOLD ON TO YOUR HAT, MARTY. HE'S SAVED THE BEST FOR LAST!

GO AHEAD, DUKE, LAY IT ON HIM! TELL MARTY YOUR CASTING IDEA!
I'D LIKE TO GET DE LOREAN'S WIFE, CRISTINA FERRARE, TO PLAY HERSELF IN THE MOVIE.

MRS. DE LOREAN.. TO PLAY.. HERSELF? ARE YOU FOR REAL?
IS THAT BOLD, MARTY? WOULD THAT BE A COUP? IS THIS MAN A COMPLETE MANIAC?

HE'S OUTRAGEOUS! GET OUTTA HERE, YOU MANIAC!
DIDN'T I TELL YOU HE GAVE GREAT MEETING?
UH-HUH. I STILL DON'T SEE ANY MONEY ON THE TABLE.
GBTrudeau

OKAY, MARTY, I HATE TO PUT THE ARM ON YOU, BABE, BUT I GOTTA KNOW IF THIS IS A GO PROJECT FOR YOU PEOPLE!
HEY, SID, LIGHTEN UP! I TOLD YOU WE'D BE SWEETHEARTS, DIDN'T I?

THEN WE'RE TALKING GREEN LIGHT? YOU RAN IT UP THE FLAG-POLE AND THE MONEY SALUTED?
THE MONEY LOVED IT! YOUR SCRIPT IS THE TURN-ON OF THE YEAR!

MY SCRIPT?
IT'S SOLID GOLD, KID. EVERYONE AT THE STUDIO ATE IT UP! YOU'VE GOT ONE HELL OF A PAGE-TURNER ON YOUR HANDS!

BUT I HAVEN'T WRITTEN IT YET.
HEY, NO SWEAT. THIS THING WILL WRITE ITSELF!
GB Trudeau

BOTTOM LINE TIME, BABE! WHAT ARE YOU OFFERING MY BOY TO PRODUCE AND WRITE?
HE'LL BE LOOKING AT TWO MIL FIVE, PLUS 3% NET! SWEET, HUH?

SWEET? THIS IS A JOKE, RIGHT, MARTY? YOU'RE PUTTING ME ON, RIGHT? YOU'RE OFFERING ME LESS THAN 20% OF THE GROSS?
OKAY, 5% GROSS! TAKE IT OR YOU'LL NEVER WORK IN THIS TOWN AGAIN!

DON'T PLAY HARDBALL WITH ME, YOU OLD HACK! 15% OF THE GROSS OR WE WALK!
10% OR I'M OUT THE DOOR!

DEAL. WHO LOVES YOU, BABE?
COME TO POPPA, YOU LITTLE MANIAC!
GB Trudeau

BAD NEWS, SID. THE DE LOREAN PROJECT'S DEAD! THE NEW CHIEF OF PRODUCTION HATES IT!
WHAT IS THIS, MARTY! I THOUGHT HE WAS HOT FOR IT!

I THOUGHT SO, TOO, KID, BUT.. HOLD IT, SID.. WHAT, HONEY?.. REALLY? GOOD NEWS, SID! HE'S BEEN FIRED AND THE NEW GUY LOVES THE PROJECT! LET ME CALL HIM AND GET AN OKAY!
I'LL BE HERE.

RING!

YOU REACH HIM?
TOO LATE. HE JUST GOT CANNED.

WHAT DO YOU MEAN, IT FELL THROUGH, DUCKS?
THE STUDIO GOT COLD FEET. IT SEEMS EVERYONE IN TOWN IS DOING A DE LOREAN MOVIE. SID CAN'T GET ANY OF HIS CALLS RETURNED ANYMORE.
BUT AREN'T WE SCHEDULED TO START SHOOTING SOON?
DON'T WORRY, THIS PROJECT MEANS TOO MUCH TO ME TO GIVE UP NOW. I FIGURED OUT ANOTHER WAY TO RAISE THE MONEY.
YOU DID?
SURE. I JUST ASKED MYSELF, "WHAT WOULD JOHN DE LOREAN DO IN A SITUATION LIKE THIS?"
DUCKS.. NO!
RELAX, ALICE, IT'S PERFECTLY SAFE. I'M A PRO.
GB Trudeau
HEY, BABE, DO I HAVE TO PAINT YOU A PICTURE? THE PROJECT IS DEAD! THE MAJORS WON'T TOUCH IT!
SO WE'LL GO INDEPENDENT. I CAN RAISE THE CASH. ALL I NEED IS $50,000 DEVELOPMENT MONEY.
YOU'RE DREAMING, KID.
I SWEAR, SID, THAT'S ALL I NEED. IF I DON'T TURN IT INTO $10 MILLION BY NEXT MONDAY, I'LL PAY YOU BACK DOUBLE!
$10 MILLION BY NEXT MONDAY? HOW DO YOU PROPOSE TO DO THAT?
UH.. ON THE STOCK MARKET.
HEE, HEE! OKAY, I'LL BITE. I'LL HAVE MAGGIE DRAW UP A CHECK.
ACTUALLY, MAN, I NEED IT IN SMALL BILLS. JUST HAVE HER PUT IT IN A PAPER SACK.
GB Trudeau
YOU ROCCO?
MAYBE. WHO WANTS TO KNOW?
DUKE. LEO SENT ME. I UNDERSTAND YOU HAVE SOME MERCHANDISE TO SHOW ME.
YOU GOT THE MONEY?
WOULD I COME ALL THE WAY OUT HERE IF I DIDN'T?
OKAY, ROOM 101. CORAL MOTEL, ACROSS THE STREET. IN TEN MINUTES.
EXCUSE ME, WHAT'S HE SELLING? CAN I GET SOME, TOO?
ABORT.
SORRY. ONE-TIME OFFER.
GB Trudeau

MY, OH MY! ALL THAT NOSE CANDY FOR ME?
THAT'S RIGHT, MAN. 10 KILOS TO YOU FROM BOGOTA WITH LOVE!

10 KILOS? HOLD IT, PAL, IT WAS SUPPOSED TO BE 12 KILOS!
INFLATION, MAN! A HALF MIL JUST DON'T BUY WHAT IT USED TO ..

INFLATION? WHAT SORT OF GARBAGE IS THAT?
IT'S A VERY POPULAR ITEM, MAN. EVERY TIME THERE'S A COKE JOKE ON THE "TONIGHT SHOW," DEMAND JUMPS 10%.

BUT CARSON'S BEEN ON VACATION ALL MONTH!
YEAH, BUT HIS GUEST HOSTS HAVE ALL BEEN DOING DE LOREAN.
GB Trudeau

WELL, EVERYTHING SEEMS TO BE IN ORDER HERE..
WE AIM TO PLEASE, MAN.

HEY, WAIT A MINUTE, PAL! THIS ISN'T ANYWHERE NEAR A HALF MIL!
RIGHT. IT'S FIFTY GRAND, A DOWN PAYMENT. YOU'LL GET THE REST AFTER I MOVE THE STUFF.

WHAT? I DON'T BELIEVE THIS! YOU ARE REALLY DUMB, YOU KNOW THAT, MAN? YOU ARE UNBELIEVABLY DUMB!
TAKE IT OR LEAVE IT, FELLAH.

IF THIS WERE A REAL COKE DEAL, YOU'D BE A DEAD MAN!
A REAL COKE DEAL?
SSHH! NOT YET!
GB Trudeau

IT'S BEEN GREAT DOING BUSINESS WITH YOU, FELLAHS. I'LL SEND YOU TICKETS TO THE PREMIERE!
I WOULDN'T GO COUNTING YOUR OSCARS QUITE YET, MR. DUKE.

WHAT DO YOU MEAN BY THAT, PAL?
LET'S PUT IT THIS WAY. WHAT'S THE WORST POSSIBLE NEWS YOU COULD RECEIVE RIGHT NOW?

YOU BURNED ME! YOU CREEPS SOLD ME 10 KILOS OF SUGAR!
NOPE. WORSE THAN THAT.
GOOD GUESS, THOUGH. TRY AGAIN.

YOU'RE COPS.
CLOSE ENOUGH?
ACTUALLY, FBI. BUT WE'LL GIVE IT TO YOU.
GB Trudeau

MR. MEDEVOY OF ORION PICTURES ON THE LINE, SIR.
THANKS, MAGGIE.. MIKE? SID!
SID! LONG TIME, GUY!
WELCOME BACK, BABE. HOW WAS ASPEN?
OKAY. YOU KNOW, SAME CROWD. HOW'S YOUR DE LOREAN PROJECT GOING?
WELL, THAT'S WHAT I CALLED ABOUT, MIKE. DUKE HAD A RUN OF BAD LUCK WHILE YOU WERE AWAY.
OH, YEAH?
THE STUDIO PULLED OUT AT THE LAST MOMENT. WE WERE TWO DAYS FROM SHOOTING, SO DUKE GOT DESPERATE. HE TOOK THE DEVELOPMENT MONEY AND SET UP A TEN MILLION DOLLAR COCAINE DEAL. UNFORTUNATELY, THE MIDDLEMAN WAS A D.E.A. INFORMANT, AND DUKE WAS BUSTED MAKING THE BUY AT SOME LAGUNA BEACH FLOP HOUSE.
JEEZ.. THAT'S AN INCREDIBLE STORY..
TELL ME ABOUT IT.
IT'D MAKE A HELLUVA MOVIE, WOULDN'T IT?
HEY, MIKE, WHO LOVES YOU, BABE?
GBTrudeau

9 PORT-AU-PRINCE

1984-1987

GO AHEAD, ZONKER. TELL J.J. WHAT YOU JUST TOLD ME.
J.J., YOUR WORRIES ARE OVER. I'VE DECIDED TO GO TO MED SCHOOL.
UH-HUH. AND I'M JOINING THE BOLSHOI.

I'M SERIOUS, J.J. -I'VE APPLIED TO THE BABY DOC COLLEGE OF PHYSICIANS, THE FINEST NEW MED SCHOOL IN ALL OF HAITI!

AND I DON'T WANT TO SOUND COCKY OR ANYTHING, BUT I HAVE EVERY REASON TO BELIEVE THAT I'M A SHOO-IN!
GB Trudeau

I DON'T KNOW, SIR. I'VE NEVER SEEN GRADES LIKE THESE.
I DON'T CARE, DEAN HONEY. WE NEED HIM TO SHORE UP THE VOLLEYBALL SQUAD!

I JUST DON'T THINK WE SHOULD IGNORE HIS GRADES, SIR..
DEAN HONEY, TRUST ME ON THIS ONE. ZONKER HAS MANY COMPENSATING QUALITIES!

BESIDES, WHEN I FOUNDED THE BABY DOC COLLEGE OF PHYSICIANS, I MADE A COMMITMENT TO OFFER THE FINEST IN OFF-SHORE EDUCATION TO ANYONE WITH $12,000!

I CAN'T RENEGE ON THAT COMMITMENT, DEAN HONEY. THIS COLLEGE'S OPEN ADMISSIONS POLICY HAS A PROUD TRADITION THAT GOES ALL THE WAY BACK TO..TO..

LAST THURSDAY.
RIGHT. BY THE WAY, HAS THAT SHIPMENT OF IVY SHOWN UP YET?
GB Trudeau

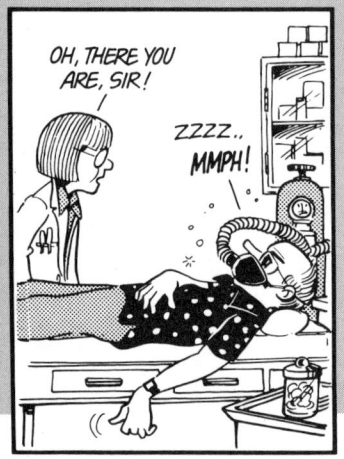
OH, THERE YOU ARE, SIR!
ZZZZ.. MMPH!

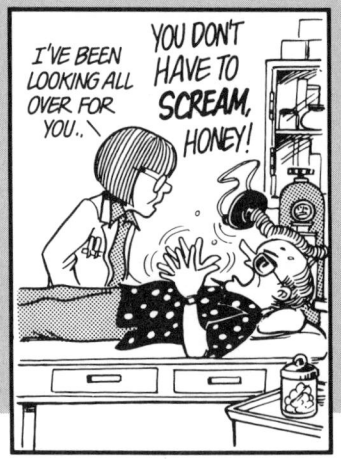
I'VE BEEN LOOKING ALL OVER FOR YOU..
YOU DON'T HAVE TO SCREAM, HONEY!

SORRY, SIR, BUT IT'S INAUGURATION DAY. I DON'T THINK YOU WANT TO MISS YOUR OWN SWEARING IN.
OH.. RIGHT. GIVE ME A MINUTE TO CUT THROUGH THE COBWEBS, OKAY?

WERE YOU UNDER ETHER THE WHOLE NIGHT, SIR?
YEAH, I COULDN'T SLEEP. TOO NERVOUS ABOUT MY SPEECH.
GB Trudeau

..AND CALL THE LABOR MINISTRY. WE'RE GOING TO NEED SCABS TO SERVE LUNCH AFTER THE CEREMONY.
THAT WON'T BE NECESSARY, SIR. I SETTLED THE KITCHEN WORKER STRIKE LAST NIGHT.

YOU DID? NOW, THAT'S THE BEST NEWS I'VE HAD ALL WEEK! GOOD WORK, HONEY!
THANK YOU, SIR. I WONDER IF YOU'D LIKE TO GO THROUGH THE LIST OF TODAY'S HONORARY DEGREE RECIPIENTS.

SURE, WHY NOT? LET'S SEE.. PAUL LUMIÈRE. JEANNE GENOT. PIERRE BERGER. ADRIENNE D'ARCY. IMPRESSIVE LINE-UP, HONEY!
YES, SIR.

WHO THE HELL ARE THEY?
THE KITCHEN STAFF.
GB Trudeau

ARE THE STUDENTS ALL LINED UP FOR THE ACADEMIC PROCESSION, DEAN HONEY?
AS MANY AS WE COULD FIND, YES, SIR.

AS MANY AS YOU COULD FIND?
WELL, SIR, THE HURRICANE LAST WEEK CAUSED SOME BIG SWELLS ON THE NORTH SHORE. A LOT OF THE STUDENTS ARE SURFING.

SURFING? THE MORNING OF MY INAUGURATION? DAMMIT, DEAN HONEY, I WILL NOT TOLERATE THIS KIND OF DISRESPECT TOWARD THE OFFICE OF THE PRESIDENCY!

I WANT THEM EXPELLED! EVERY LAST MOTHER'S SON!
YOU CAN'T DO THAT, SIR. YOU PUT THEIR TUITION INTO FIVE-YEAR BONDS.
GB Trudeau

BEFORE I INTRODUCE THE INAUGURAL SPEAKER, A FEW WORDS. IN THE MONTHS AHEAD, YOU WILL ALL STUDY MEDICINE. YOU WILL PLAY GOLF. YOU WILL LEARN ABOUT TAX SHELTERS. IN SHORT, YOU WILL BECOME DOCTORS!

BUT COME FEBRUARY, LADIES AND GENTLEMEN, YOU WILL DO THE MOST IMPORTANT THING YOU'LL EVER DO IN YOUR LIVES! YOU WILL MEET ST. GEORGE'S IN GRENADA, AND YOU WILL DESTROY THEM IN VOLLEYBALL!

YEAAA!
CLAP!
CLAP!
CLAP!
CLAP!
GB Trudeau

GRENADA SUCKS EGGS! GRENADA SUCKS EGGS!
POINT SPREAD CITY!
THEY SURE HAVE A LOT OF SCHOOL SPIRIT, SIR.

BEAT ST. GEORGE! BEAT ST. GEORGE!
OKAY, OKAY. SETTLE DOWN!
NOW, REMEMBER, PEOPLE, NO PAIN, NO GAIN! I WANT YOU OUT ON THE VOLLEYBALL COURT IN FULL SWEATS EVERY DAY AT 9:00! TO MAKE TIME, I'M CANCELLING DR. NORTH'S IMMUNOLOGY COURSE!
DUUUKE! DUUUKE!
SO LET'S GET OUT THERE AND.. AND..
LOOK AT THAT. THEY'RE DOING THE WAVE.
THEY LOVE YOU, SIR!
GBTrudeau

ROBERT VESCO, AS AN INNOVATIVE FINANCIER OF THE HIGHEST ORDER, YOU HAVE MADE THE CARIBBEAN YOUR OYSTER, EARNING THE RESPECT OF LAW ENFORCEMENT OFFICERS EVERYWHERE.
WHEN YOUR OWN COUNTRY TURNED ITS BACK ON YOU, YOU SKILLFULLY MOVED YOUR ASSETS TO THE BAHAMAS WHERE YOU NOW OPERATE YOUR EMPIRE FROM AN UNDISCLOSED LOCATION.
IN PRIDEFUL RECOGNITION OF ALL YOU'VE GOTTEN AWAY WITH, THE BABY DOC COLLEGE OF PHYSICIANS TAKES GREAT PLEASURE IN CONFERRING ON YOU THE DEGREE OF DOCTOR OF ARTS AND LEISURE!
THANK YOU, PRESIDENT DUKE. I'M VERY PROUD THAT YOU..
OUR PLEASURE. LISTEN, BOBBY, WE NEED A GYM.
GBTrudeau

IN CLOSING, A FEW WORDS ABOUT GREED. KEEP IT IN CHECK. YOU HAVE ONLY TO LOOK TO THE CURRENT ADMINISTRATION TO SEE THE VIRTUE IN THIS!
NUMEROUS REAGAN APPOINTEES HAVE BEEN INVOLVED IN FINANCIAL SCANDAL, BUT MOST OF THEM ARE STILL IN OFFICE. WHY? BECAUSE NO ONE PROFITED BY TOO UNSEEMLY AN AMOUNT.
THE LESSON? DON'T OVERREACH. IF YOU WANT TO PIG OUT, BE DISCREET. THANK YOU VERY MUCH.
YEAA!!
CLAP! CLAP! CLAP!
INSPIRATIONAL, GUY! DAMN INSPIRATIONAL!
WELL, I THOUGHT THERE SHOULD BE SOME MORAL CONTENT.
CLAP! CLAP! CLAP!
CLAP CLAP
GBTrudeau

HONEY, I'M VERY DISAPPOINTED IN YOU. I THOUGHT YOU REACHED A SETTLEMENT WITH THE KITCHEN STAFF!
PATHOLOGY
S3

I DID, SIR. IT WASN'T MY FAULT. THE STUDENTS TOLD THE WORKERS THEY WERE STILL BEING EXPLOITED, SO THEY RENEGED.

AND NOW THE STRIKE HAS SPREAD. THE GROUNDSKEEPERS ARE OUT, AND THE FACULTY AT THE VOODOO CENTER WON'T CROSS THEIR LINES.
WELL, THAT DOES IT! I'M BRINGING IN SCABS! I DON'T HAVE TO TAKE THIS!

DON'T YOU WANT TO TRY ARBITRATION, SIR?
NO WAY! I.. HUUNH!

SIR! WHAT IS IT?
AAIEEK!

AREN'T YOU DOING THAT A LITTLE HARD, MAN?
NAH, I'M JUST GETTING HIS ATTENTION.
THWAP! THWAP! THWAP!
GB Trudeau

BOY, IT'S GREAT TO SEE YOU AGAIN, UNCLE DUKE. IT'S BEEN MUCH TOO LONG!
SURE HAS. GOT THE CERTIFIED CHECK FOR YOUR TUITION?

YUP. HERE YOU GO. I HOPE THIS WORKS OUT. DAD HAD TO TAKE OUT A PRETTY STIFF LOAN..
HE WON'T REGRET IT, BOY. HE'LL BE WATCHING YOU GRADUATE IN THREE SHORT YEARS! FOUR YEARS, MAX.

I DUNNO, UNCLE DUKE. I'VE NEVER EVEN TAKEN BIO BEFORE.
NEITHER HAVE A LOT OF OUR STUDENTS. DEAN HONEY HERE IS TUTORING HALF THE VOLLEYBALL TEAM!

VOLLEYBALL? THERE'S TIME FOR VOLLEYBALL?
MOST OF THE GAMES ARE FIXED, BUT IT'S STILL GOOD FUN.
WELCOME TO CLUB PRE-MED, SIR!
GBTrudeau

TO THE MEDICAL COLLEGE! ON THE DOUBLE!

OUI, MONSIEUR!
WHAT A QUAINT WAY TO GET AROUND!
NICE, HUH?

IF THERE'S ONE THING I LOVE, IT'S A GOOD SERVICE ECONOMY. THEY DON'T ALWAYS DO IT WELL HERE, BUT THEY DO IT FOR NEXT TO NOTHING!

I DIDN'T EVEN KNOW THEY HAD RICKSHAWS IN HAITI.
THEY DON'T. I HAD IT SHIPPED IN. YO, HONEY! YOU STILL WITH US?
YES, SIR! PANT! PANT!
GBTrudeau

..AND IN ADDITION TO BEING FULLY EQUIPPED, ALL OUR LABS HAVE SHAG CARPETING!
THIS IS INCREDIBLE!

I HAD NO IDEA THAT BABY DOC WAS SO OPULENTLY APPOINTED! I EXPECTED PALM FROND ROOFS AND CANVAS TENTS!

THIS PLACE HAS ALL THE OLD WORLD CHARM OF A TROPICAL OXFORD. ONE CAN ALMOST SEE THE DONS SIPPING PORT ON THE VERANDA!

ACTUALLY, THREE MONTHS AGO, IT WAS A BROTHEL.
I MEAN, HOW MANY CLASSROOMS STILL HAVE RED VELVET WALLPAPER?
GBTrudeau

AND THEN WHAT?
WELL, ONCE I BOUGHT THE BROTHEL, I GOT THE LOCAL AUTHORITIES TO RAZE MOST OF THE SURROUNDING SHANTIES.

AFTER THAT, IT WAS JUST A MATTER OF PUTTING IN THE TENNIS COURTS AND SENDING OUT BROCHURES. THE REST IS OFF-SHORE EDUCATION / HISTORY!

IT'S AN AMAZING STORY, UNCLE DUKE, SIMPLY AMAZING!
THANKS. WELL, I BETTER GET BACK TO THE O.R. I WAS IN THE MIDDLE OF SURGERY WHEN YOU CALLED.

SURGERY? BUT..BUT YOU'RE NOT A DOCTOR.
I KNOW, BUT IT'S AN EMERGENCY. AND OUR REGULAR CUTTER IS OUT SNORKELING.
©B Trudeau

CURTIS, THIS IS YOUR NEW ROOMMATE! SAY HELLO TO..UH..JOE SMITH!

HI, JOE! WELCOME TO BABY DOC.. HEY, DID ANYONE EVER TELL YOU YOU LOOK LIKE ZONKER HARRIS?
YEAH. I GET THAT ALL THE TIME.

WAIT A MINUTE! YOU **ARE** ZONKER HARRIS! I SAW YOU TAN AGAINST GEORGE HAMILTON IN THE '81 SUN SPRINTS! I GREW UP ON YOU, MAN! I CAN'T BELIEVE YOU'RE **HERE!**

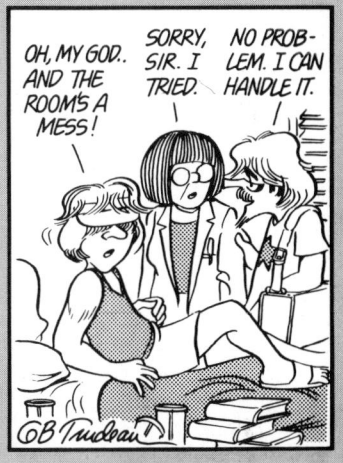
OH, MY GOD.. AND THE ROOM'S A MESS!
SORRY, SIR. I TRIED.
NO PROBLEM. I CAN HANDLE IT.
©B Trudeau

GOOD LORD, CURTIS. YOU ACTUALLY **OWN** A ZONKER HARRIS SIGNATURE MODEL TANNING REFLECTOR?
YES, SIR, MR. HARRIS!

HEY, HEY, WHAT'S THIS "MR. HARRIS" STUFF, CURTIS? WE'RE ROOMIES, FOR GOD'S SAKE!
YES, SIR. COULD YOU SIGN THIS, PLEASE? IT'S NOT FOR ME. IT'S FOR..UH.. MY AUNT.

GLAD TO. WHAT'S YOUR AUNT'S NAME?
HER NAME? UH..CURTIS. AUNT CURTIS. I WAS NAMED AFTER HER.. REALLY.

IF YOU SAY SO.
GOD, THIS IS SO UNCOOL! WHAT AM I **DOING?**
©B Trudeau

CURTIS, DEAN HONEY TELLS ME YOU BEGAN YOUR MEDICAL EDUCATION IN GRENADA.
THAT'S RIGHT, MAN. ST. GEORGE'S. I WAS ONE OF THE GUYS WHO GOT RESCUED.
GOOD THING, TOO. IT WAS ABOUT TWO DAYS BEFORE FINALS, AND I HADN'T CRACKED A BOOK IN WEEKS!
TALK ABOUT BEING SAVED BY THE BELL! I WAS SO RELIEVED THAT WHEN I GOT HOME, I LITERALLY KISSED THE GROUND.
YOU KNOW, I WONDERED ABOUT THAT.
THAT'S WHAT I LIKE ABOUT THIS PLACE, MAN. YOU DON'T HAVE THAT KIND OF INSANE ACADEMIC PRESSURE.
HERE AT BABY DOC, THERE'S SOME PERSPECTIVE. YOU STRIKE JUST THE RIGHT BALANCE BETWEEN ACADEMICS AND SURFING.
WELL, THAT'S SO IF YOU PUNT YOUR BOARDS, YOU CAN ALWAYS GET WORK AS A LIFEGUARD.
SEE? THAT TAKES VISION. YOU'RE AN AWESOME EDUCATOR, MAN.
GB Trudeau

GOOD AFTERNOON. PRESIDENT DUKE'S RESIDENCE.
DEAN HONEY? IT'S ZONKER.
YES, YOUNG SIR. WHAT CAN I DO FOR YOU?
IS UNCLE DUKE IN? I NEED ANOTHER EXTENSION.
I'M SORRY, YOUR UNCLE CAN'T COME TO THE PHONE RIGHT NOW.
STILL ASLEEP?
NO, HE'S HOSTING A TEA FOR FACULTY MEMBERS AND THEIR SPOUSES.
HE'S TRYING TO MAKE SOME TENURE DECISIONS, AND FRANKLY, HE DOESN'T KNOW ALL THE DOCTORS AS WELL AS HE SHOULD.
GB Trudeau
SO! HONEY TELLS ME YOU USED TO WORK FOR THE GESTAPO.
HEE, HEE! WELL, YES..
NOW, DEAR, NONE OF YOUR OLD WAR STORIES.

YOU GOT BACK JUST IN TIME, HONEY. I'M GOING TO NEED YOUR HELP DURING THE MEDICAL CONFERENCE WE'RE HOSTING THIS WEEK.
THE COLLEGE IS HOSTING A MEDICAL CONFERENCE, SIR?
YEAH, ON ECSTASY. THE D.E.A., IN ITS WISDOM, HAS JUST DECLARED ECSTASY A BIG, BAD, SCHEDULE I NO-NO!
I DON'T THINK I'M FAMILIAR WITH THAT DRUG, SIR.
SHRINKS HAVE BEEN USING IT FOR YEARS, BUT THE KIDS, AS USUAL, RUINED IT FOR EVERYONE. THEY TURNED MDMA INTO A DAMN PARTY DRUG!
MDMA? OH, YOU MEAN METHYLENEDIOXYMETHAMPHETAMINE!
KNOCK IT OFF, HONEY.
YOU SEE, HONEY, ECSTASY IS A VERY PROMISING PSYCHOTHERAPEUTIC TOOL. BUT THANKS TO THE FEDS, THE WORK OF TOP MDMA RESEARCHERS HAS BEEN NIPPED IN THE BUD!
WHAT I'LL BE PROPOSING AT THE CONFERENCE IS THAT SOME OF THESE PEOPLE JOIN OUR FACULTY AND CONTINUE THEIR IMPORTANT WORK RIGHT HERE!
I SEE.
SIR, I HOPE THIS ISN'T JUST A FRONT FOR..
EVERY PENNY WILL GO TO SCHOLARSHIPS, HONEY.
SO WHAT'S THE HOLD-UP, DEAN HONEY?
THE STEWARDESS SAYS THEY WON'T GET OFF THE PLANE, SIR. THEY CLAIM THEY'RE HAPPY WHERE THEY ARE.
DAMN! I KNEW THIS WOULD HAPPEN!
WHENEVER YOU PUT A BUNCH OF HOT-SHOT DRUG DESIGNERS TOGETHER, THE FIRST THING THEY DO IS SWAP COMPOUNDS!
ANYONE HERE WANT TO HELP ME PROMOTE GOOD?
I DO! LET ME GET MY THINGS! IS THIS HOME OR ABROAD?

ON BEHALF OF BABY DOC COLLEGE OF MEDICINE, I'D LIKE TO WELCOME YOU ALL TO THE OPENING SESSION OF "ECSTASY: WHITHER THE FUTURE?"
BABY DOC COLLEGE

I KNOW YOU SHARE MY OUTRAGE OVER THE OUTLAWING OF MDMA. WITHOUT UNFETTERED RESEARCH, WHERE WILL THE NEXT LITHIUM COME FROM, THE NEXT SACCHARINE?
BABY DOC COLLEGE

SURE, THERE ARE RISKS, BUT THAT'S A SMALL PRICE TO PAY FOR PROGRESS!
BABY DOC COLLEGE

SURE, THERE ARE RISKS, BUT THAT'S A SMALL PRICE TO PAY FOR PROGRESS! SURE..
UH-OH.
BABY DOC COLLEGE
©B Trudeau

GREAT KEYNOTE SPEECH, PRESIDENT DUKE. ALL OF US ARE LOOKING FORWARD TO A VERY ILLUMINATING SYMPOSIUM.

LISTEN, AFTER THE PANEL TONIGHT, I WANT YOU TO TRY A LITTLE SOMETHING I'VE BEEN WORKING ON. I CALL IT MDMA, JR.!

THANKS, DOC. YOU KNOW, I FEEL AS IF I'VE KNOWN YOU MOST OF MY ADULT LIFE. SURE, IT'S A CRAZY FEELING, BUT I WANTED TO SHARE IT WITH YOU.

YOU'VE ALREADY BEEN SNACKING, HAVEN'T YOU, SIR?
HOLY SMOKES! LOOK AT THE MOLECULAR STRUCTURE ON THIS BABY!
©B Trudeau

..AND I'D LIKE TO THANK DR. STAN FILBURN FOR ORGANIZING THE "MOONLIGHT WITH MDMA" THEME PARTY ON THE BEACH LAST NIGHT. WELL DONE, STAN!
BABY DOC COLLEGE

OKAY, NOW, TODAY FROM 9:00 TO 9:15, DEAN HONEY WILL BE HOSTING A ROUNDTABLE ON THE ETHICS OF DRUG DESIGNING, AFTER WHICH WE'LL BREAK FOR LUNCH.
BABY DOC COLLEGE

AT 2:30, THE MAIN EVENT. THOSE BRILLIANT TWINS FROM USC, DRS. ALBIE AND BUNNY GORP, WILL DEMONSTRATE HOW THEY BEAT THE FEDS WITH THEIR HOT, NEW, TOP 40 HYBRID — "INTENSITY"!
BABY DOC COLLEGE

..AND WE JUST REMOVE THIS MOLECULE AND.. VOILA!
LEGAL AS SEA SALT!
POP!
©B Trudeau

WITH THAT SIMPLE CHEMICAL RECONFIGURATION, "INTENSITY" CAME KICKING INTO THE WORLD.
WE JUST FIGURED WHY GO WITH TWO OXYGEN MOLECULES WHEN ONE WILL DO?
THE DRUG, BY THE WAY, IS INSANELY GREAT. WE FORESEE MYRIAD APPLICATIONS IN PSYCHIATRY AND PROFESSIONAL FOOTBALL.
ANY SIDE EFFECTS, DR. GORP?
YES, BUT INTRIGUING ONES. FOR EXAMPLE, "INTENSITY" GIVES THE ILLUSION OF SUBSTANCE TO YOUR ALTER EGO.
UH..HOLD IT, ALBIE. ARE YOU IMPLYING I'M ONLY A SIDE EFFECT?
IT'S ONLY TEMPORARY, THOUGH.
GB Trudeau
DR. GORP, ARE THERE ANY OTHER SIDE EFFECTS ASSOCIATED WITH "INTENSITY" WE SHOULD BE AWARE OF?
WELL, YES, "INTENSITY" SEEMS TO SHARE SOME OF THE MILD UNPLEASANTNESS ATTRIBUTED TO ITS CHEMICAL COUSINS..
..LIKE NAUSEA, TIGHTENING OF THE JAW, SOME DIZZINESS..
BAD NEWS, ALBIE. TRICKY DICK GOT THE G.O.P. NOMINATION!
..AND, OF COURSE, FLASHBACKS.
GB Trudeau
DR. GORP, HAVE YOU WORKED OUT THE ETHICAL RAMIFICATIONS OF MARKETING A DESIGNER DRUG AS UNTESTED AS "INTENSITY"?
NO, BUT MY TWIN BROTHER BUNNY HAS, RIGHT, BUNNY?
THAT'S RIGHT, ALBIE..
I'VE DONE A LOT OF RESEARCH ON THE MATTER, AND I CAN ASSURE YOU, MORALS-WISE, WE'RE ON TERRA FIRMA.
SIR, IF YOU HIRE THE SIDE EFFECT, I'M QUITTING.
NOW, DEAN HONEY, I CAN'T BREAK UP THE ACT.
GB Trudeau

A FIRST-RATE PRESENTATION, GORP, FIRST-RATE!
THANK YOU, PRESIDENT DUKE.
HAVE YOU THOUGHT OVER MY OFFER TO MOVE YOUR OPERATION DOWN HERE TO BABY DOC?
YES, I HAVE. I MIGHT BE INTERESTED.
GREAT. WHAT DO YOU SAY WE GO DOWN TO THE BEACH AND TALK TERMS?
SOUNDS GOOD.
YEAH, I COULD USE A DIP.
NOW, BUNNY, YOU KNOW YOU'RE WATER-SOLUBLE.
HI, MOM, IT'S ME. DEAN HONEY JUST TOLD ME YOU'VE BEEN TRYING TO REACH ME. IS EVERYTHING OKAY AT HOME?
EVERYTHING'S FINE, DEAR. I CALLED ABOUT THE LOTTERY TICKET AUNT SOPHIE SENT YOU FOR YOUR BIRTHDAY.
OH, YEAH? DID I WIN SOMETHING?
YOU WON $23 MILLION, DEAR.
GET THIS, HONEY. I WON $23 MILLION.
HOW NICE, SIR. JUST IN TIME FOR HOLIDAY SHOPPING.
23 WHAT?
YOU COULD ALSO PAY YOUR BAR BILL.
$23 MILLION! MOM, ARE YOU SURE THERE HASN'T BEEN SOME MISTAKE?
THAT'S CERTAINLY A REMARKABLE LOTTERY PRIZE, SIR.
MOM, I WANT YOU TO HAVE HALF OF IT, OKAY? NO, NO, I ABSOLUTELY INSIST! 50%!
THAT'S VERY GENEROUS OF YOU, SIR.
WHAT? NO, MOM.. NO..
I JUST HOPE IT ALL WORKS OUT FOR YOU..
OKAY, 60%, BUT THAT'S MY FINAL OFFER!
THEY SAY MONEY CAN REALLY CHANGE PEOPLE.

DEAN HONEY, NOT A WORD OF MY WINDFALL TO ANYONE UNTIL I THINK THIS THROUGH, OKAY?
NOT EVEN YOUR UNCLE DUKE, SIR?
ESPECIALLY MY UNCLE DUKE! IT'S A SECRET, UNDERSTAND? A SECRET!
A SECRET. YES, SIR. YOU CAN COUNT ON ME.
$23 MILLION! I MUST BE DREAMING..
IT'S SORT OF A SECRET, SIR.
YOU WERE RIGHT TO BRING THIS TO ME, HONEY.
GBTrudeau
ZONK! HOW'S IT GOING, STRANGER? LONG TIME!
I SAW YOU THIS MORNING AT BREAKFAST, UNCLE DUKE.
THAT WAS YOU? YOU LOOK DIFFERENT! DONE SOMETHING WITH YOUR HAIR?
WHAT DO YOU WANT, UNCLE DUKE?
WELL, I'VE SOME BAD NEWS, SON. THE NEW HEATING OIL BILL CAME IN. I'M GOING TO HAVE TO RAISE ROOM AND BOARD TO $1,000 A DAY.
WHAT?
STRICTLY ON AN ABILITY-TO-PAY BASIS, OF COURSE.
I'LL KILL HER.
HE USED HIS LOVER'S WILES ON ME, SIR.
GBTrudeau
WELL, BOY, YOUR LIFE'S COURSE HAS TAKEN A DANGEROUS, HAIRPIN TURN. LIKE IT OR NOT, YOU NOW HAVE TO ANSWER TO AN AWESOME NEW MASTER-MONEY!
NO WAY, UNCLE DUKE. MONEY DOESN'T CHANGE A THING. I'M CONTINUING TO STUDY TO BE A DOCTOR!
NEPHEW, THINK FOR A MOMENT. WHY IS IT YOU WANTED TO BE A DOCTOR?
WELL, TO MAKE..
GOOD POINT.
ZONKER, DON'T BE AFRAID TO ASK FOR HELP IN THE DAYS AHEAD.
GBTrudeau

SIR! WAKE UP! YOU'RE MISSING ALL THE EXCITEMENT!

WHAT?.. >SNORT!< WHAT EXCITEMENT?
ZONKER'S PRESS CONFERENCE ON HIS LOTTERY PRIZE!

HE GOT SO MANY CALLS FROM THE MEDIA THIS WEEKEND, HE DECIDED TO READ A PREPARED STATEMENT ABOUT HIS PLANS.
GB Trudeau

"..AND, OF COURSE, I'LL BE DATING SHOW GIRLS."
BEFORE THE CHECK CLEARS?

ZONKER! HOW DID YOU FEEL WHEN YOU HEARD THE GOOD NEWS?
YEAH, WHAT WERE YOUR FEELINGS?
COULD YOU DESCRIBE THEM?

WELL, AT FIRST I DIDN'T FEEL ANYTHING. I JUST WENT NUMB.

THEN I FELT A RUSH OF GIDDINESS, FOLLOWED BY FEELINGS OF DISORIENTATION, QUEASINESS, SHORTNESS OF BREATH..

..HUNGER, RAGE, SEXUAL LONGING, VERTIGO, BOREDOM, AND FINALLY, A TINGLING SENSATION.
WHAT ABOUT AFTER THE NEWS SUNK IN?
GB Trudeau

LADIES AND GENTLEMEN, THE BOTTOM LINE HERE IS THAT NO AMOUNT OF MONEY COULD EVER INTERFERE WITH MY DREAM OF ESTABLISHING A PRIVATE MEDICAL PRACTICE IN SOUTHERN CALIFORNIA.

WHAT ABOUT CHARITY, ZONKER?
HOW DOES YOUR FAMILY FEEL?
WHAT'S THE TAX BITE?

HEY, HEY, YOU NETWORK BOYS HAVE BEEN HOGGING ALL THE QUESTIONS. LET'S LET THE SUPERMARKET MEDIA GET IN A FEW, OKAY?

ZONKER, ABOUT YOUR LOVE-CHILD WITH MRS. GORBACHEV..
ZONKER, WILL YOU BE SLAYING MOM, CO-ED, SELF?
GB Trudeau

THAT'LL HAVE TO BE THE LAST QUESTION, BOYS! I HAVE TO GET BACK AND HIT THE BOOKS!
SO SAID LOTTERY WINNER ZONKER HARRIS THIS MORNING AS HE RETURNED TO CLASSES HERE AT THE ACADEMICALLY GRUELING BABY DOC COLLEGE OF PHYSICIANS.
$23 MILLION JUST DOESN'T SEEM TO HAVE CHANGED THIS UNAFFECTED YOUNG MAN AND HIS BOYHOOD DREAM OF BECOMING A DOCTOR.
YO, BABE! I'LL GIVE YOU TEN GRAND TO TAKE MY BIO-CHEM EXAM!
OKAY.
GB Trudeau
I GOT THE RICKSHAW ALL WARMED UP TO TAKE YOU TO THE AIRPORT, LAD!
UNCLE DUKE, I DON'T WANT A RICKSHAW.
THEN I'LL HAVE THE LIMO SENT ROUND. LET ME GIVE YOU A HAND HERE.
YOU CERTAINLY ARE BEING CONSIDERATE, UNCLE DUKE.
THANKS, NEPHEW.
A TEENY BIT OUT OF CHARACTER, WOULDN'T YOU SAY?
YOU'RE RIGHT. WANT ME TO SEE A SHRINK? I WILL IF YOU'RE WORRIED.
GB Trudeau
HAVE A GREAT CHRISTMAS HOLIDAY, NEPHEW. HERE'S A LITTLE SOMETHING TO SLIP UNDER THE OL' TREE!
BABY DOC
I.. I DON'T KNOW WHAT TO SAY, UNCLE DUKE.
IT'S A BABY DOC SCHOOL TIE. SO YOU WON'T FORGET ABOUT US, GUY!
BABY DOC
UNCLE DUKE, DO I DETECT A NEW NOTE OF OBSEQUIOUSNESS FROM YOU SINCE THE LOTTERY, OR IS IT JUST MY IMAGINATION?
YES.
BABY DOC
YES WHAT?
YES, SIR.
BABY DOC
GB Trudeau

..AND THE FACULTY VOTE WAS SEVEN TO TWO, WITH BUNNY ABSTAINING.
UH-HUH. GET ME SOME COFFEE, WILL YA, HONEY?

EXCUSE ME, SIR?
COFFEE. BLACK.

SIR, IN CASE YOU'VE FORGOTTEN, I AM THE DEAN AT THIS MEDICAL COLLEGE! NOT A SECRETARY, NOT A SERVING GIRL, THE DEAN!

ASKING ME TO GET COFFEE IS JUST SO TYPICAL OF YOUR EXPLOITATIVE ATTITUDE TOWARDS YOUR LOYAL SUBORDINATES!

ALL YOU DO IS ORDER ME AROUND AND OGLE ME LIKE NOBODY'S BUSINESS, ESPECIALLY WHEN MY LAB COAT SUGGESTIVELY FALLS OPEN!
GET TO THE POINT, WILL YA, HONEY?

SIR, I'M TIRED OF BEING YOUR LOVE SLAVE!
DOES THAT MEAN I'M NOT GOING TO GET MY COFFEE?
GB Trudeau

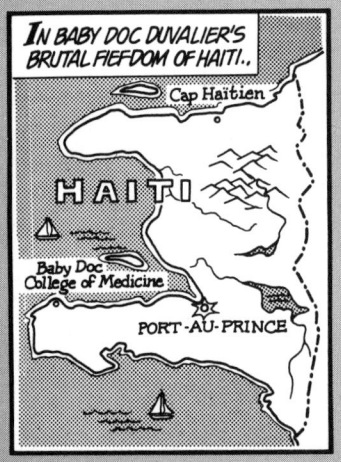
IN BABY DOC DUVALIER'S BRUTAL FIEFDOM OF HAITI..
Cap Haitien
HAITI
Baby Doc College of Medicine
PORT-AU-PRINCE

..WHERE THE SECRET RITES OF VODOUN ARE PRACTICED MUCH AS THEY WERE 200 YEARS AGO..

.. A SOUL-SEARING SCREAM PIERCING THE STILL OF THE NIGHT..
AAIEE!

..HARDLY RAISES AN EYEBROW.
KEEP IT DOWN, SIR!
GB Trudeau

CARRIED ALONG BY GENTLE TRADE WINDS OFF HAITI..

..A SOLITARY FLY..

..BEGINS HIS DAY.
BZZZZZ!

SIR? SIR?
GB Trudeau

GOOD MORNING, SIR. TIME FOR YOUR VITAMIN PICK-ME-UP!

YOU'RE LOOKING MORE INERT THAN USUAL THIS MORNING, SIR.. HEY, WHERE'S YOUR VEIN?..

HMM.. NO PULSE, EITHER. PALLID COMPLEXION, DILATED PUPILS.. SIR, IF I DIDN'T KNOW YOU BETTER, MEDICALLY SPEAKING, I'D SAY YOU WERE..

.. DEAD.
GB Trudeau

YUP. THE OLD MAN'S DEAD, ALL RIGHT.
ARE.. ARE YOU SURE, CURTIS?

POSITIVE. BUT I'M JUST A SECOND-YEAR STUDENT. YOU NEED AN ACTUAL DOCTOR TO PRONOUNCE HIM DEAD. ASK DR. JANATA.
DR. JANATA LOST HIS LICENSE YEARS AGO.

OH. HOW ABOUT DR. VON WICK? OR DR. KINKAID?
DR. VON WICK IS A PARAPSYCHOLOGIST. KINKAID IS A FORMER PRO HOCKEY TRAINER.

AREN'T THERE ANY REAL DOCTORS AT THIS MED SCHOOL?
WE'VE NEVER NEEDED ONE BEFORE.
GB Trudeau

WELL, HERE'S YOUR DEATH CERTIFICATE..
THANKS FOR COMING OUT, DR. PHILLIPE.
I CAN'T BELIEVE IT..

I'M NOT SURE ABOUT THE CAUSE OF DEATH. IT COULD BE AN OVERDOSE.
THE HELL YOU SAY!

WE'LL HAVE TO WAIT FOR THE CORONER'S REPORT. ANY IDEA WHAT KIND OF DRUGS HE MAY HAVE BEEN USING?

DUKE? NO WAY, MAN. THE DUDE WAS AS CLEAN AS..
SIGH.. I'LL GET THE ROLODEX.
GB Trudeau

DEAN HONEY?
ADIEU, DU

DEAN HONEY, I'M SORRY IF I'M DISTURBING YOU, BUT I WANTED TO PASS ON THE CONDOLENCES OF THE ENTIRE SECOND-YEAR CLASS. WE KNOW HOW CLOSE YOU WERE TO THE DECEASED.
THANK YOU, CURTIS.
ADIEU, DU

WE'D LIKE YOU TO CONSIDER, THOUGH, A POTENTIAL SILVER LINING IN THIS TERRIBLE TRAGEDY..
SILVER LINING? HOW COULD THERE POSSIBLY BE A SILVER LINING?
ADIEU, DU

WELL, IT CONCERNS OUR CADAVER SHORTAGE..
NO! GET AWAY! VULTURES!
SLAM!
CIAO, DU
GB Trudeau

WELCOME BACK, ZONK. I WANT TO TELL HOW DEEPLY SORRY I AM ABOUT YOUR UNCLE'S DEMISE.
BABY DOC
THANK YOU, CURTIS. I APPRECIATE THAT.
IT'S A TERRIBLE LOSS, MAN. DUKE WAS SO.. SO.. WELL, LET ME PUT IT THIS WAY..
BABY DOC
WHEN ALL'S SAID AND DONE, AFTER THE DUST HAS SETTLED AND THE BODIES HAVE BEEN COUNTED, DUKE WILL BE REMEMBERED AS.. AS.. UH.. WELL YOU KNOW.
BABY DOC
NO, WHAT? I'VE GOT TO SAY SOMETHING AT THE SERVICE.
THAT'S IT! SOMETHING! HE WAS REALLY SOMETHING!
BABY DOC
GBTrudeau

DEAN HONEY? IT'S ME, ZONKER.
OH, SIR, YOU'VE COME..
ADIEU
OF COURSE I'VE COME. HOW ARE YOU HOLDING UP, FRIEND?
TO BE HONEST, SIR, NOT SO WELL.
CIAO, DU
HAVE YOU EVER HAD AN AFFAIR OF THE HEART, SIR, WHERE AFTER YEARS OF DENIAL AND LOVING FROM AFAR, THE DOORS OF PASSION WERE FINALLY FLUNG OPEN, ONLY TO HAVE YOUR LOVER CRUELLY SNATCHED AWAY BY THE FATES?
S'LONG
UM.. WELL, LET ME SEE..
ME NEITHER. BUT WE CAME THAT CLOSE!
GOOD RU
GBTrudeau

".. I WILL FEAR NO EVIL: FOR THOU ART WITH ME; THY ROD AND THY STAFF, THEY COMFORT ME."
WE'LL NOW HAVE THE EULOGISTIC READING. CURTIS?
YOU GOT IT, YOUR GRACE.
"WHAT CAN YOU SAY ABOUT A 25-YEAR-OLD GIRL WHO DIED? THAT SHE WAS BEAUTIFUL. AND BRILLIANT. THAT SHE LOVED MOZART AND BACH. AND THE BEATLES. AND ME."
CURTIS, WHAT THE HELL IS THAT?
IT'S FROM "LOVE STORY." IT WAS THE CLOSEST I COULD FIND IN THE LIBRARY.
GBTrudeau

AN OVERDOSE JUST DOESN'T MAKE SENSE, CURTIS. DUKE KNEW HIS LIMITS.
LET'S GO OVER IT AGAIN, DEAN HONEY. WHEN DID YOU LAST SEE HIM?
AROUND 10 P.M. HE'D JUST HAD HIS MASSAGE AND HE WAS UNWINDING WITH A FIFTH OF..
WAIT A MINUTE, A MASSAGE? WHO GAVE HIM THE MASSAGE?
JUST A BURSARY STUDENT FROM THE VOODOO CENTER..
VOODOO? THAT'S IT! DUKE ISN'T DEAD, HE'S A ZOMBIE! WE BURIED HIM ALIVE!
THIS HAS GOT TO BE THE WORST HANGOVER OF MY ENTIRE LIFE..
GBTrudeau
THE MASSEUSE FROM THE VOODOO CENTER HAS MYSTERIOUSLY DISAPPEARED!
THEN I WAS RIGHT, DEAN HONEY! DUKE HAS BEEN ZOMBIFIED!
HOW EXACTLY IS THAT DONE, SIR?
THE VICTIM IS POISONED TOPICALLY WITH THE TOXIN OF A PUFFER FISH..
IT REDUCES HIS METABOLIC RATE TO THE POINT WHERE HE APPEARS DEAD! HE'S THEN BURIED, AND LATER DUG UP AND REVIVED BY A VOODOO SORCERER..
SOUNDS LIKE SOME CRAZY FRATERNITY STUNT.
..AND THEN SOLD INTO SLAVERY!
GBTrudeau
ARE YOU SURE ABOUT THIS ZOMBIE STUFF, SIR?
POSITIVE! COME ON, WE'VE GOT TO GET BACK TO THE GRAVEYARD BEFORE THE BOKOR!
THE WHAT?
THE VOODOO SORCERER WHO DID HIM IN! WHO KNOWS WHAT EVIL PURPOSE HE HAS IN STORE FOR DUKE!
I DUNNO, SIR. DUKE WOULD NEVER SUBMIT TO SOME WITCH DOCTOR!
HE WILL AFTER HE'S FED THE BOKOR'S PASTE! IT CRUSHES THE FREE WILL AND SPIRIT OF THE ZOMBIE!
HOW DO YOU KNOW ALL THIS STUFF, SIR?
I'M DATING ONE. THEY'RE REAL EASY TO TALK TO.
GBTrudeau

HONEY? GET IN HERE! I CAN'T FIND THE LIGHTS! HONEY?
DAMN! WHAT IS IT WITH THAT CHICK? SHE TAILS ME DAY AND NIGHT, BUT WHEN I REALLY NEED HER, I MIGHT AS WELL BE.. BE..
THUMP! THUMP!
UH-OH.
GB Trudeau
BUT WHY, SIR? WHY WOULD ANYONE WANT TO DO THIS TO DUKE?
WELL, HE MUST HAVE OFFENDED A PRIEST FROM ONE OF THE LOCAL BIZANGO SECRET SOCIETIES..
WHO KNOWS WHAT THE OLD BOY DID? ZOMBIFICATION IS CAPITAL PUNISHMENT IN VODOUN SOCIETY. MAYBE HE WAS CAUGHT MESSING WITH THE WRONG LOCAL TALENT.
DUKE?.. DATING AROUND?
IT HAPPENS, DEAN HONEY.
I'LL KILL HIM.
THAT COULD BE A TAD REDUNDANT, HONEY.
GB Trudeau
THERE'S THE CEMETERY!
SCREECH!
H-308
HANG ON, SIR!
TOO LATE!
TOO LATE, INDEED.
GB Trudeau

THE INTERVIEW'S ON? FANTASTIC!

ANY GROUND RULES? WHAT'S HE PREPARED TO COVER?

UH-HUH.. RETIREMENT, RIGHT.. HIS PLACE IN HISTORY.. UH-HUH.. NO, I DON'T HAVE ANY PROBLEMS WITH THAT.

TIP O'NEILL?
BABY DOC.
GB Trudeau

LOOK AT THOSE FACES. ARROGANT TO THE END! WOULDN'T YOU LOVE TO KNOW WHAT THE DUVALIERS SPIRITED OUT WITH THEM THE NIGHT THEY FLED?

WELL, YES AND NO..
FRIDAY, FEB
Duvalier Lea
The final drive to the airport.
"powerful as a monkey's tail." U.S. of-
decided to give up his auth-
Baby Doc has

SOMETIMES, THE REAL STORY CAN BE..

..UNSPEAKABLY HIDEOUS!
GB Trudeau

..AND RICK'S ALREADY LEFT TO VISIT HIM IN EXILE. IT'S ONE OF THE FEW INTERVIEWS DUVALIER'S EVER GIVEN!

GOODNESS! THAT IS A REMARKABLE ASSIGNMENT!

IT SHOULD YIELD SOME ABSOLUTELY FASCINATING INSIGHTS INTO THE GENESIS OF EVIL!

..AND THEN THE OTHER KIDS STARTED CALLING ME "BASKETHEAD."
SO THAT'S WHEN YOU DECIDED TO GET EVEN?
GB Trudeau

MR. EX-PRESIDENT-FOR-LIFE, ALMOST EVERYONE WAS SHOCKED BY HOW QUICKLY YOUR REGIME SEEMED TO COLLAPSE..
WERE YOU YOURSELF SURPRISED AT HOW FAST THINGS CAME UNRAVELLED?
NOT AT ALL. I KNEW THERE WERE SUBVERSIVES IN HAITI.
JUST LAST JULY, WE HAD A DEMOCRATIC REFERENDUM ON MY RULE. THE VOTE FOR ME WAS 4,500,000 TO 2.
SO YOU HAD AN INKLING..
ALL IT TAKES IS A COUPLE OF BAD APPLES.
GBTrudeau
MR. DUVALIER, DO YOU THINK YOUR WIFE'S ILL-TIMED EXTRAVAGANCES CONTRIBUTED TO YOUR FINAL DOWNFALL?
HOW DO YOU MEAN?
WELL, FOR INSTANCE, HER LEAVING FOR A $1.7 MILLION SHOPPING SPREE IN PARIS WHILE HAITI WAS IN THE MIDST OF A SEVERE ECONOMIC CRISIS.
$1.7 MILLION? SHE SPENT $1.7 MILLION IN PARIS?
REPORTEDLY.
WHAT'D SHE DO WITH THE REST OF IT!
UM.. I DON'T KNOW. I'D RATHER NOT GET CAUGHT IN THE MIDDLE HERE.
GBTrudeau
I'M AFRAID YOU'LL HAVE TO EXCUSE ME NOW, MR. REDFERN. I HAVE ANOTHER ENGAGEMENT.
OF COURSE, MR. DUVALIER.
I'LL HAVE MY MAN DRIVE YOU TO THE AIRPORT.
THAT'S OKAY. I DON'T WANT TO TROUBLE ANYONE..
NO TROUBLE AT ALL! LÉGUME!
"LÉGUME"?
YOU BELLOWED, YOUR PARIAHSHIP?
GBTrudeau

LÉGUME! TAKE MR. REDFERN TO THE AIRPORT!
THIS GUY LOOKS VERY FAMILIAR..
WHO?
MR. REDFERN! THE GENTLEMAN IN FRONT OF YOU!
WHAT ABOUT HIM? IS HE BOTHERING YOU, BOSS?
NO, SIMPLETON! I WANT YOU TO DRIVE HIM TO THE AIRPORT!
RIGHT AWAY, YOUR HEINOUSSHIP! I'M TO DRIVE TO THE.. TO THE.. WHERE?
THE AIRPORT!
HEY, WHY DON'T I JUST GRAB A CAB?
RIGHT! I'M TO DUMP HIM NEAR THE AIRPORT!
GB Trudeau
YOU'RE AN AMERICAN, AREN'T YOU? WHAT ARE YOU DOING WORKING FOR DUVALIER?
I DON'T HAVE ANY CHOICE. I'M UNDER HIS CHEMICAL CONTROL.
HOW'S THAT?
I'VE BEEN ZOMBIFIED. I'M HIS SLAVE.
A SLAVE, HUH?
YEAH.
SO WHAT'S THAT LIKE?
NOT SO GOOD. IT'S HARD TO GET CREDIT.
GB Trudeau
A SLAVE? I DON'T UNDERSTAND. WHAT'S KEEPING YOU FROM JUST LEAVING?
THE BOSS FEEDS ME THIS MUSH CALLED THE ZOMBIE'S CUCUMBER. IT NEUTRALIZES FREE WILL.
IT'S NOT A BAD LIFE. YOU DON'T HAVE TO TAKE RESPONSIBILITY FOR ANY OF YOUR ACTIONS. BUT I MISS THE DANGER, THE ADRENALINE, THE SENSE OF BEING RIGHT OUT THERE ON THE..
HOOOONK!
RRUMBBLE!
..EDGE. SAY, WHICH SIDE OF THE ROAD DO THEY DRIVE ON HERE?
LEFT..
GB Trudeau

YOU KNOW, LÉGUME, YOU LOOK VERY FAMILIAR TO ME. WHAT DID YOU DO BEFORE YOU PASSED INTO BONDAGE?
I'M NOT REALLY SURE..

THE ZOMBIE'S CUCUMBER IS A VERY DISORIENTING DRUG. EVERY TIME I START TO THINK ABOUT THE PAST, I GET ALL CONFUSED.

ALL I CAN REALLY REMEMBER IS JUST BITS AND PIECES.

LIKE WHAT?
WELL, LIKE, I'M ALMOST POSITIVE I USED TO HAVE HAIR.
GB Trudeau

WELL, THANKS FOR THE RIDE, LÉGUME. I'M SORRY ABOUT YOUR ENSLAVEMENT.
CAN'T YOU HELP ME, PAL? I'D BEG, BUT I'M INCAPABLE OF PASSION.

I THINK IT'S ONE OF THOSE DEALS WHERE YOU KIND OF HAVE TO HELP YOURSELF, LÉGUME.
HOW ABOUT BUYING ME? I COULD PAY YOU BACK LATER.

THANKS, BUT I CAN'T REALLY USE A SLAVE. THAT'S WHAT COPY BOYS ARE FOR.
COPY BOYS, EH? SO THAT'S THE COMPETITION!

ARE YOU GOING TO BE OKAY?
MAYBE. I THINK I'LL GO WANDER AROUND FOR AWHILE. I REALLY LIKE WANDERING AROUND.
GB Trudeau

ANYWAY, WHEN I GOT HOME, IT FINALLY CAME TO ME. "LÉGUME" HAD TO BE YOUR UNCLE DUKE!
THIS IS SUCH A RELIEF, RICK..

NOW WE'VE JUST GOT TO GET HIM HOME! ANY SUGGESTIONS, COUNSELOR?
WELL, I SUPPOSE I COULD CONTACT THE FRENCH POLICE..

TOO MESSY. WE COULD BE TIED UP IN COURT FOR YEARS. HOW ABOUT IF YOU NEGOTIATE DIRECTLY FOR HIM.
YOU MEAN, BUY HIM?

SURE! JUST SAY YOU'RE LOOKING FOR A NANNY.
A ZOMBIE NANNY?
GB Trudeau

MR. DUPUIS? YES, THIS IS MR. HARRIS. I UNDERSTAND YOU REPRESENT EX-PRESIDENT-FOR-LIFE DUVALIER.

GOOD, GOOD. I'LL TELL YOU WHY I CALLED. I'M VERY INTERESTED IN ACQUIRING ONE OF HIS ZOMBIE SLAVES, A MR. LÉGUME.

WHY? SENTIMENTAL REASONS, MOSTLY. MAY WE NEGOTIATE? GREAT. I'M GOING TO PUT ON MY HIGH-POWERED LEGAL COUNSEL, MS. JOANIE "JAWS" CAUCUS.

"JAWS" HERE.
RING! RING! HEY, JAWS! THE ATTORNEY GENERAL ON LINE TWO!
GB Trudeau

HOW FAR DO YOU WANT TO GO WITH THIS?
AS FAR AS WE HAVE TO. I'M A RICH MAN.

MR. DUPUIS? SINCE THE PURCHASE OF HUMAN BEINGS IS FORBIDDEN OUTSIDE OF PRO SPORTS, MY CLIENT HAS ADVISED ME TO OFFER YOU A "FINDER'S FEE" FOR MR. DUKE'S RETURN.

WHAT DO WE HAVE IN MIND? WELL, THAT'S DIFFICULT TO SAY, MR. DUPUIS. HOW CAN WE MEASURE THE VALUE OF A PERSON? IS IT POSSIBLE TO SET A PRICE FOR A HUMAN LIFE?

$10 MILLION. TAKE IT OR LEAVE IT.
PASS. WE'RE NOT TALKING MOTHER TERESA HERE.
GB Trudeau

EXCUSE ME, SIR. THERE'S A RUMOR IN THE SLAVE QUARTERS THAT I'M ON THE BLOCK.
THAT'S RIGHT, LÉGUME. A RICH AMERICAN WANTS TO BUY YOU. HE CLAIMS TO BE YOUR NEPHEW.

NEPHEW? YOU MEAN, ZONKER? OH, PLEASE, YOUR MALIGNANCY, NOT HIM! ZONKER'S A MONSTER! CRUELTY INCARNATE! HE'S EVIL ON THE HOOF!

OR IS THAT MY COUSIN ALFREDO? I GET THEM MIXED UP..
IT DOESN'T MATTER. THE DEAL IS AS GOOD AS DONE!

COULDN'T YOU SELL HIM ONE OF THE OTHER GUYS?
SORRY. I ALREADY SENT HIM YOUR BROCHURE.
GB Trudeau

.. AND THOSE ARE DUKE'S HEALTH CERTIFICATES. I HAD THEM POUCHED OVER FROM FRANCE.
GOOD THINKING, JOANIE.

LET'S SEE HERE.. HIS WEIGHT IS 145.. THAT'S ABOUT RIGHT. BLOOD PRESSURE IS 20 OVER 30.. GOOD, GOOD..

20 OVER 30 IS GOOD?
IT'S NORMAL FOR A ZOMBIE. THEY'RE PRETTY MELLOW. AHA! HIS DENTAL X-RAY! YUP, IT'S DUKE, ALL RIGHT!

HOW CAN YOU TELL?
HIS MOLARS. THAT'S OLD MICRO-FILM FROM HIS SMUGGLING DAYS.
GB Trudeau

$4.5 MILLION? THAT DOESN'T WORK FOR US. HOW ABOUT 4.2 ON A 15-YEAR SCHEDULE WITH COLAS? WHAT? NO.. THAT WON'T DO..

WE'RE WASTING VALUABLE TIME HERE, COUNSELOR. LET ME GIVE IT A SHOT..
UM.. MR. DUPUIS, MY CLIENT WOULD LIKE TO TALK TO YOU PERSONALLY..

DUPUIS? HARRIS HERE! THIS ISN'T AN ARAB BAZAAR, MON AMI! ALL I'VE GOT IS $17 MIL CASH! TAKE IT OR LEAVE IT!

DONE. SEE, YOU JUST HAVE TO BE FORCEFUL.
OH, ZONKER..
GB Trudeau

IT WAS 3:45 A.M. WHEN THE NIGHT PORTER SIGNED FOR THE CRATE FROM MARSEILLES...

SAR? SAR?
HUNKLE DOOOKE?

SIR? CAN YOU HEAR ME?
HE DOESN'T LOOK SO GOOD...
GB Trudeau

SIR? DO YOU REMEMBER ME? DEAN HONEY?
NO...I CAN'T...I... COUGH!

I'LL BE RIGHT BACK.
TAKE IT EASY, BIG GUY.
WHAT'S GOING ON? WHERE... WHERE... AM I?

YOU'RE BACK AT THE COLLEGE. YOU'VE BEEN UNDER THE INFLUENCE OF A ZOMBIE COMPOUND. WE'RE GOING TO TRY TO DRY YOU OUT. SO JUST RELAX, OKAY?

REMEMBER NOW, SIR?
HONEY! YOU'LL FRIGHTEN HIM!
AAAG..
GB Trudeau

UM... HONEY, I THINK WE MIGHT BE OVERLOADING UNCLE DUKE'S CIRCUITS A LITTLE HERE. MAYBE IF I COULD BE ALONE WITH HIM...

YOU? BUT YOU DON'T HAVE THE SAME INTIMATE RAPPORT THAT...
WHAT ARE YOU TALKING ABOUT? I'VE KNOWN UNCLE DUKE MOST OF MY LIFE!

MAYBE, BUT I'M HIS SECOND-IN-COMMAND HERE, AND I...
HONEY, I PAID FOR HIM!

THAT'S IT, LORD IT OVER ME!
I DON'T TRUST THIS CHICK. SHE'S GOT PATERNITY SUIT WRITTEN ALL OVER HER.
GB Trudeau

ANY PROGRESS?
NAW. HE'S STILL PRETTY OUT OF IT.

HE'S BEEN ON THAT ZOMBIE PASTE FOR WEEKS, THOUGH. IT'LL PROBABLY BE SOME TIME BEFORE HE REALLY SHAKES IT.

WHAT HE REALLY NEEDS NOW IS A GOOD NIGHT OF Z'S. I JUST LEFT STRICT ORDERS HE ISN'T TO BE DISTURBED!

TRY TO REMEMBER, SIR! WE WERE DEEPLY IN LOVE!
DON'T YOU EVER KNOCK?
GB Trudeau

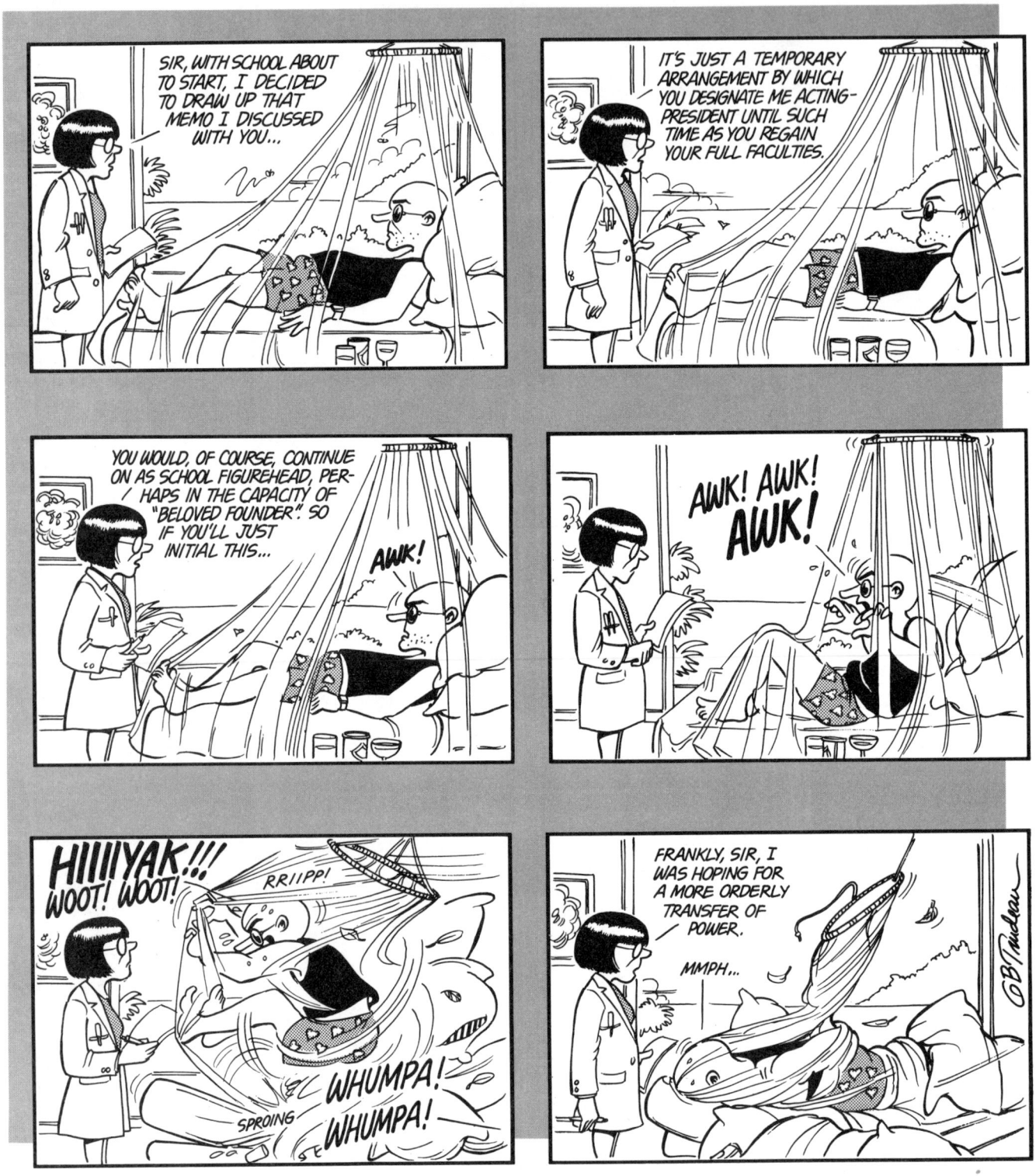
SIR, WITH SCHOOL ABOUT TO START, I DECIDED TO DRAW UP THAT MEMO I DISCUSSED WITH YOU...
IT'S JUST A TEMPORARY ARRANGEMENT BY WHICH YOU DESIGNATE ME ACTING-PRESIDENT UNTIL SUCH TIME AS YOU REGAIN YOUR FULL FACULTIES.
YOU WOULD, OF COURSE, CONTINUE ON AS SCHOOL FIGUREHEAD, PERHAPS IN THE CAPACITY OF "BELOVED FOUNDER". SO IF YOU'LL JUST INITIAL THIS...
AWK!
AWK! AWK! AWK!
HIIIIYAK!!! WOOT! WOOT!
RRIIPP!
SPROING
WHUMPA! WHUMPA!
FRANKLY, SIR, I WAS HOPING FOR A MORE ORDERLY TRANSFER OF POWER.
MMPH...
GBTudeau

WHAT'S THE WORD FROM THE FRONT, DON?
IT'S CATCHING ON, SIR. CANDIDATES ALL OVER THE COUNTRY ARE ENLISTING IN YOUR WAR AGAINST DRUGS!

UNFORTUNATELY, AS A CAMPAIGN ISSUE, IT SEEMS TO HAVE ONE DRAWBACK: EVERYONE'S ON THE SAME SIDE OF THE ISSUE.

IF ONLY WE COULD FIND A STRAW MAN, SOME HIGH-PROFILE LIBERTARIAN CRAZY OR STUPID ENOUGH TO TAKE A STAND FOR DRUG ABUSE!
GB Trudeau

I'M NEEDED, HONEY.
SIR! YOU SAID SOMETHING!

...AND THE FOLLOWING PARTS OF THE BILL OF RIGHTS HAVE BEEN SUSPENDED...
SOME WAR ON DRUGS! IT'S SCORCHED EARTH TIME! I'VE GOT TO GET HOME, PRONTO!

THEY'LL LISTEN TO ME! I'M PRESIDENT OF A RESPECTED MEDICAL COLLEGE!
UH...YOU WERE, SIR. LAST WEEK, JUDGE DUPUIS RULED YOU INCOMPETENT.

DUPUIS? THAT TREACHEROUS OLD CROCK OF SLIME! I'VE HAD HIM ON RETAINER FOR TWO YEARS! YOU CAN'T TRUST ANYONE THESE DAYS!

LISTEN, HONEY...
PRESIDENT HONEY.
GB Trudeau

HELP ME FIND MY SNEAKERS, HONEY! MY COUNTRY NEEDS ME!
IT'S TOO LATE, SIR. EVERYTHING HAS CHANGED SINCE YOU'VE BEEN GONE.

GONE? I DIDN'T GO ANYWHERE! DID I?
PEOPLE ARE NO LONGER TOLERANT OF DRUG USE. THE COST HAS BEEN TOO HIGH. A LOT OF US NOW THINK IT WAS WRONG TO LOOK THE OTHER WAY!

AFTER NANCY REAGAN'S SPEECH, I REALIZED THAT I'D BEEN REMISS, THAT BY STANDING IDLY DURING YOUR SELF-DESTRUCTIVE BINGES, I'D LET YOU DOWN AS A FRIEND.

YEAH, WELL, DON'T LOSE ANY SLEEP OVER...
I'VE TURNED YOU IN, SIR.
HEY, DID YOU GUYS KNOW THE HOUSE WAS SURROUNDED?
GB Trudeau

WHAT IS THIS, A SHAKEDOWN? I'M NOT GREASING THE COLONEL ENOUGH AS IT IS?

I DON'T KNOW WHAT YOU'RE TALKING ABOUT, MONSIEUR.
OKAY, OKAY, SO I'M A LITTLE BEHIND IN MY PAYMENTS. YOU'VE MADE YOUR POINT. TAKE THESE THINGS OFF!

JE REGRET, MONSIEUR...
YOU CAN'T HOLD ME! YOU HAVEN'T A SHRED OF EVIDENCE!
FOUND IT, OFFICER. MUST BE A KILO.

I'LL TAKE YOU DOWN WITH ME, HONEY. I SWEAR IT.
I'M DOING THIS OUT OF LOVE, SIR.
GB Trudeau

THIS IS INSANE! SINCE WHEN DO YOU CARE ABOUT DRUGS IN THE THIRD WORLD? IT'S PART OF THE ECONOMY, FOR GOD'S SAKE!
SO'S AMERICAN AID.

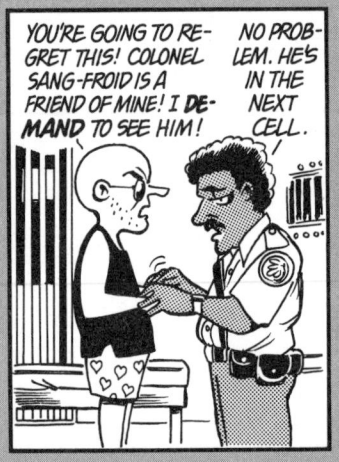
YOU'RE GOING TO REGRET THIS! COLONEL SANG-FROID IS A FRIEND OF MINE! I DEMAND TO SEE HIM!
NO PROBLEM. HE'S IN THE NEXT CELL.

HUH?
I'M SURE YOU HAVE A LOT TO CATCH UP ON.

WATER... WATER...
OH, RIGHT. AND WHERE THE HELL ARE YOU WHEN I NEED YOU?
GB Trudeau

SIR, I KNOW YOU'RE PROBABLY THINKING I'VE ACTED DISLOYALLY IN TURNING YOU IN TO THE AUTHORITIES.

BUT TRY TO UNDERSTAND. YOU HADN'T COMPLETED A SENTENCE IN FOUR MONTHS. I DID IT OUT OF DESPERATION!

I MISSED YOU, SIR. I MISSED THE GRACEFUL, SPIRITED MAN WHO FIRST WALKED INTO MY LIFE TEN YEARS AGO. SO I TOOK MATTERS INTO MY OWN HANDS.

IN TIME, I THINK YOU'LL THANK ME FOR...
I'VE PAID A LARGE MEXICAN $50 TO KILL YOU.
GB Trudeau

A JAILHOUSE ALTERCATION.
UNH!
A 5" NINJA BUTTERFLY KNIFE CATCHES THE LIGHT...
THWIPP!
AIIEE!!
...AND DUKE'S WHOLE LIFE STARTS TO FLASH BEFORE HIS EYES!
DAY ONE.
WAAAH!
MY GOD, HE'S...HE'S WEARING RAY-BANS!
GBTrudeau
THE EARLY YEARS ARE FLASHING BEFORE DUKE'S EYES...
YO! MOMMY!
PUT A CORK IN IT, KID!
WEDNESD
Duke, following incid
Local Youth
7, held for
by a staff reporter
AKRON, Oct. 5-
SILENT NIGHT, HOL...
AAIEE!
LOANS
UP TO 50¢
"PAY me back LATER"
"OUR FRIEND THE AMPHETAMINE," OR, "WHY JOHNNY CAN'T BLINK."
amacus
date
Feb
GBTrudeau
AS DUKE STARES DEATH IN THE FACE, MEMORIES OF EARLY MANHOOD FAN OUT THROUGH HIS MIND...
...AND WE'RE PROUD TO SAY WE'RE STILL SEGREGATED.
BOY! THIS IS THE COLLEGE FOR ME!
DARNIT, BROTHER DUKE! THAT'S OUR LAST KEG OF BREWSKI!
ARE YOU SURE YOU'RE A TEACHING ASSISTANT, DUKEY?
GRATEFUL ALUMNI, EH?
JUST KEEP THE POINT SPREAD TO FIVE, GOT IT?
ONE OF THREE MEN I USED TO KNOW WOULD BE VERY PROUD OF YOU, DEAR!
DON'T TRY ANYTHING STUPID! I'M A COLLEGE GRADUATE!
GBTrudeau

DUKE'S RECENT PAST FLICKERS THROUGH HIS MIND LIKE A KINETOSCOPIC LOOP...
I'M A REASONABLE MAN, MAC. SO I KNOW THIS ISN'T SNOW.
SPEAKING OF VEGETABLES, HOW'S THE CHAIRMAN?
MY GOD! HE'S ATTACKING THE REF!
FETCH MY DART GUN, BOY.
$250,000! AND THAT'S MY FINAL OFFER!
SIR! WE'RE GOING DOWN!
I KNOW. THANK GOD I'M STONED.
SIR, I'M WORRIED ABOUT YOUR MOOD SWINGS.
WILLIAM HOLDEN? I LOVE IT! BILL'S DEAD, BUT I LOVE YOUR THINKING!
WELL, I'M ALMOST POSITIVE I USED TO HAVE HAIR.
GBTrudeau
JAGGED SHARDS OF MEMORY SPIN MADLY OUT OF DUKE'S OVERHEATED FORNIX...
STRUGGLING YOUNG PORNOGRAPHER...
AIEEE!
ERP!
WHE THE HEL
GOT A DEAL?
THUNK!
BLAM!
...ONE OF THEM LODGING UNDER THE THUMBNAIL OF HIS TORMENTOR!
OW! DAMN!
GBTrudeau
THE GUARD SAYS YOU WERE VERY LUCKY, SIR. APPARENTLY, THE GENTLEMAN YOU PICKED A QUARREL WITH HAS KILLED FIVE PEOPLE!
I KNOW. YOU WERE SUPPOSED TO BE THE SIXTH. THAT'S WHAT THE FIGHT WAS ABOUT. HE WAS TRYING TO WELSH ON OUR DEAL.
I'LL JUST LEAVE THE FLOWERS WITH THE NURSE.
YOU CAN RUN, HONEY, BUT YOU CAN'T HIDE.
GBTrudeau

HI. I'M SAL DOONESBURY, AND I'D LIKE TO WELCOME YOU TO THE INSTITUTE FOR IMMACULATE CONTRACEPTION, POPULARLY KNOWN AS WHOOPEE U.!

AS DISTRICT SALES MANAGER TRAINEES, YOU ARE HERE TO LEARN THE WHOOPEE WAY OF LIFE. IT MAY BE THE MOST IMPORTANT COURSE OF INSTRUCTION YOU EVER TAKE!

WHEN YOU SELL DR. WHOOPEE, YOU ARE SELLING HOPE. YOU BECOME PART OF THE SOLUTION. YOU'LL BE SAYING NO TO A MYRIAD OF SOCIAL PROBLEMS!

OF COURSE, YOU'LL ALSO BE WINNING FABULOUS PRIZES!
SAL, HOW MANY POINTS FOR THE CATCHER'S MITT?
©BTrudeau

BEFORE WE START, LET'S TAKE A LOOK AT THIS MOTIVATIONAL VIDEO MESSAGE FROM DR. WHOOPEE'S FOUNDER AND CHAIRMAN!
CLIK!

YOU KNOW, WHEN I FOUNDED DR. WHOOPEE LAST YEAR, I SWORE MY PRODUCTS WOULD BE THE FINEST AVAILABLE ON THE MARKET! WELL, I DELIVERED ON THAT PLEDGE.

HOW DO YOU KNOW? HOW DO YOU KNOW OUR LINE IS ALL I SAY IT IS? HOW DO YOU KNOW WE USE ONLY THE FINEST MATERIALS CURRENTLY AVAILABLE ANYWHERE IN THE CARIBBEAN BASIN?

TRUST ME.
©BTrudeau

AN INSPIRATIONAL VIDEO FOR DR. WHOOPEE TRAINEES...
AS FOUNDER OF DR. WHOOPEE, I KEEP AN EAGLE EYE ON OUR PRODUCT FROM START TO FINISH!

"DR. WHOOPEES ARE STILL MADE BY HAND BY LOCAL HAITIAN CRAFTSPEOPLE USING THE SAME TIME-HONORED METHODS I DEVELOPED BACK IN 1986."
Dr. Whoopee

"BY CONTRAST, OUR DISTRIBUTION IS STATE-OF-THE-ART. ORDERS ARE RELAYED BY SATELLITE AND PROCESSED BY COMPUTER!"

MEANWHILE, IN RESEARCH AND DEVELOPMENT...
EUREKA! PLAID!
©BTrudeau

WHY DO WE DO IT? WHY DO WE POUR SUCH CARE AND QUALITY INTO EACH AND EVERY DR. WHOOPEE?

WELL, TO GENERATE SHORT-TERM PROFITS, OF COURSE, BUT ALSO BECAUSE... BECAUSE...

...UH... BECAUSE...

BECAUSE WE CARE, SIR.
NO, THAT'S NOT IT. THERE'S SOME TAX ANGLE...
©B Trudeau

A FINAL WORD OF CAUTION: ONLY ONE IN 15 OF YOU WILL ACTUALLY GRADUATE. BUT FOR THOSE OF YOU WHO MAKE IT, THE REWARDS ARE BOUNDLESS!

AS A DISTRICT SALES MANAGER, YOU'LL EARN HEFTY COMMISSIONS, EVEN AS YOU ENJOY THE PRESTIGE OF BEING THE DR. WHOOPEE REP FOR YOUR AREA!

SO DREAM BIG AND NEVER FORGET THE THREE PILLARS OF DR. WHOOPEE'S PLEDGE TO THE PUBLIC: CONVENIENCE, SAFETY, AND ATTRACTIVE DESIGNER COLORS!

OKAY, CLASS, WHAT ARE THE THREE PILLARS?
COMFORT! SAFETY! ATTRACTIVE DESIGNER COLORS!
CLIK!
©B Trudeau

DR. WHOOPEE. FIRST IN SALES...
YES, MA'AM, WE CATER ROCK CONCERTS. DO YOU HAVE AN ACCOUNT WITH US?

...SUBSCRIPTIONS...
GOOD MORNING, MR. JONES!
IT'S THE CONDO BOY, DEAR!

...SERVICE...
THANK GOODNESS YOU'RE HERE! WE CAN'T GET THE WRAPPER OFF!
NO PROBLEM, MA'AM!

...AND COUNSELING.
SEE! SHE SAID IT AGAIN!
MARY? DID YOU REALLY MEAN TO SAY "NO"?
I DON'T KNOW. I'M SO CONFUSED, DOCTOR WHOOPEE.
©B Trudeau

DOONESBURY! WHY THE HELL HAVEN'T YOU MOVED THAT LAST CONSIGNMENT OF DR. WHOOPEES?
SORRY, SIR...
...BUT TWO OF MY TOP GUYS TOOK OFF FOR THE HARMONIC CONVERGENCE.
WHAT?
LISTEN, SAL, NO MORE HIPPIE HOLIDAYS! IF YOUR PEOPLE WANT TO CAVORT WITH SPOOKS, LET THEM DO IT ON THEIR OWN TIME! GOT IT?
GBTrudeau
EXCUSE ME, SIR, THERE'S A WILLIAM CASEY HERE TO SEE YOU.
UH... LET ME GET BACK TO YOU, SAL...
BILL... BILL CASEY... MY GOD, IT IS YOU!
LONG TIME, DUKE.
THIS IS ABSOLUTELY INCREDIBLE...
I MEAN, YOUR BEING HERE IN HAITI! AND LOOKING SO WELL! I MEAN, CONSIDERING THAT, YOU KNOW... I MEAN, THIS IS HARD TO... TO...
LET'S CUT THE CRAP, BILL. YOU'RE DEAD.
A LEADING THEORY, IT'S TRUE.
GBTrudeau
HOW... HOW'D YOU PULL IT OFF, BILL? THE WHOLE WORLD THINKS YOU'RE DEAD!
I'M A SPOOK, DUKE. DECEIT HAS BEEN MY LIFE.
BUT... WHY?
TO PROTECT THE COVERT OPERATIONS SLUSH FUND, THE MISSING MILLIONS. I KNEW IT WOULD COME OUT IN THE HEARINGS, AND I DIDN'T WANT TO BE AROUND TO ANSWER ANY QUESTIONS!
IT'S TOO BRILLIANT A PLAN TO GIVE UP, DUKE. SINCE THE MONEY ISN'T APPROPRIATED, THE PRESIDENT WOULD HAVE A COMPLETELY DISCRETIONARY, ALBEIT ILLEGAL, COVERT CAPABILITY!
SO WHERE DO I FIT IN?
AS I SAY, IT'S ILLEGAL.
GBTrudeau

THE POSSIBILITIES ARE FANTASTIC, DUKE! WE COULD FUND THE CONTRAS, BUY THE AFGHANS NUKES, TERMINATE PANAMA'S PRESIDENT!
EXCUSE ME A MINUTE, WILL YOU, BILL?
HONEY!
YES, SIR?
©BTrudeau
AM I ON ANYTHING RIGHT NOW?
LET ME CHECK YOUR BOOK, SIR...
DUKE, LET ME COME RIGHT TO THE POINT...
I'M ALL EARS, BILL!
THIS COVERT ACTION SLUSH FUND IS THE GREATEST INNOVATION IN U.S. INTELLIGENCE IN A GENERATION. I'M PROUD OF IT. I DON'T WANT TO SEE IT DIE WITH ME!
NOR I, BILL.
I NEED YOUR HELP, DUKE. I NEED SOMEONE WHO CAN LEAD THE ILLEGAL COVERT OPERATIONS OF THIS COUNTRY INTO THE TWENTY-FIRST CENTURY!
GEE, I DUNNO, BILL. I GOT A LOT ON MY PLATE AND...
CLIK!
FOR AN OBSCENE FEE, OF COURSE.
OBSCENE? HOW OBSCENE? HAITI HAS DIFFERENT COMMUNITY STANDARDS.
©BTrudeau
OBVIOUSLY, DUKE, I CAN'T USE COMPANY PERSONNEL ANYMORE. THAT'S WHY I NEED YOU TO ASSEMBLE A COVERT ACTION TEAM!
HERE'S THE COMPLETE FINANCIAL RECORD. TAKE A LOOK, SO YOU KNOW WHAT YOU'VE GOT TO WORK WITH. I'LL GIVE YOU THE ACCOUNT NUMBER WHEN YOU'RE READY TO GO!
THERE'S NO TIME TO WASTE, DUKE. I'M NOT A WELL MAN. IN FACT...>COUGH!< I MAY NOT...
TOP SECRET
>COUGH!<
>COUGH!<
HACK!
HACK!
CRASH!!
JEEZ, BILL, THIS IS ONE HELLUVA HAND-OFF.
©BTrudeau

...AND I PUT DOWN A HEAVY DEPOSIT ON 2 C-14S. AS FOR PERSONNEL, I'VE RETAINED NEARLY 40 CONTRACT PLAYERS, MOSTLY GERMAN MERCS.
OKAY, BILL?
WHEEZE!

GOOD. SO ALL I NEED NOW IS YOUR SIGNATURE AND BANK ACCOUNT NUMBER. YOU DO RECALL THE NUMBER, DON'T YOU, BILL?

BILL?

LOOK, BILL, I'M OUT-OF-POCKET OVER 200 G's HERE, SO I'D APPRECIATE...
CROAK.
©B Trudeau

NO! NO WAY! I WILL NOT BE CHEATED! YOU WILL NOT DIE, CASEY!

WHAT IS THIS? ONE SECOND, I HAVE MILLIONS IN MY GRASP, THE NEXT, ALL I'VE GOT IS A DEAD C.I.A. DIRECTOR IN MY BED!

GET ME THE "NATIONAL ENQUIRER."
©B Trudeau

..AND FOR 50 GRAND, IT'S A BARGAIN!
WHAT EXACTLY ARE YOU OFFERING THE "ENQUIRER," MR. DUKE?

ALL THE COLOR PIX YOU WANT, PLUS MY EXCLUSIVE STORY!
AND YOU'RE SURE YOU HAVE THE BODY?

OF COURSE I HAVE THE BODY! I JUST SENT MY ASSISTANT OVER TO MY BUNGALOW TO PACK IT IN ICE!

EXCUSE ME, SIR, WHAT BODY?
SHALL WE SAY ALL THE MONEY UP FRONT?
©B Trudeau

GONE? WHAT DO YOU MEAN THE BODY'S GONE?
IT MIGHT HAVE BEEN THE MED STUDENTS, SIR. AS YOU KNOW, THERE'S STILL A CADAVER SHORTAGE. OR IT COULD HAVE BEEN STOLEN BY LOCAL VOODOO-ISTS FOR THE BONES!
BUT I NEED THAT BODY! I HAVE PLANS FOR IT!
FRANKLY, SIR, I THINK THE BIGGER PROBLEM NOW IS ALL THE EXPENSES YOU'VE RUN UP.
YOU'RE RIGHT. THE CORPSE IS SPILT MILK.
ELEGANTLY PUT, SIR.
TWO MINUTES! ALL THAT OLD DIRTBAG HAD TO DO WAS HOLD ON FOR TWO MORE LOUSY MINUTES!
INSTEAD, I'M LEFT WITH AN UNSIGNED BANK AUTHORIZATION CARD AND $230,000 IN UNRECOVERABLE CAPITAL OUTLAYS!
SIR, IF I MAY ASK, WHERE DID YOU GET THAT KIND OF FINANCING? I THOUGHT THE COMPANY WAS STILL IN THE RED.
>BZZZ!<
YEAH?
MR. GOTTI'S PEOPLE ON THEIR WAY UP, SIR.
WE'LL USE THE BALCONY! GET THE WET SUITS!
THE MOB? YOU BORROWED FROM THE MOB?
HONEY, THE ONLY DIFFERENCE BETWEEN THE MOB AND THE BANKS IS YOU DON'T HAVE TO FILL OUT ANY FORMS. THEY BOTH ROB YOU BLIND!
SIR, DO YOU REALIZE THAT SINCE I MET YOU, THIS IS THE FIFTH TIME I'VE JOINED YOU ON THE LAM?
SO WHAT? IT'S NOT LIKE YOU'VE BEEN DOING IT FOR LOVE!
SIR, I WANT A RAISE.
WE'LL TALK ABOUT IT WHEN WE GET TO THE DOMINICAN REPUBLIC.

10 NEW YORK

1987-1988

I'M A MAN OF RESPECT. I EXPECT TO BE TREATED LIKE ONE. YOU FOLLOW ME?

WHEN I SPOT SOMEONE $230,000, I EXPECT TO SEE IT AGAIN. I'M A BUSINESSMAN. IF I GET STIFFED, I LOSE FACE. AND THAT'S BAD FOR BUSI-NESS.

HEY, YOU WANT A NEW SUIT? YOU WANT I SHOULD HAVE YOU MEASURED FOR A SUIT, TOO?

UH... SURE. WOOL?
CONCRETE. YOU'RE IN A WORLD OF TROU-BLE, DOG MEAT.
GB Trudeau

LOOK, I WAS **GOING** TO PAY YOU BACK! I **SWEAR** IT! BUT WHAT COULD I DO? WHO KNEW MY MOTHER WOULD NEED SURGERY?

PSST, SIR! DON'T YOU THINK YOU SHOULD LEVEL WITH THIS GUY? HE COULD BE A FEDERAL AGENT!
SHUT UP, HONEY. HE'S JOHN GOTTI, HEAD OF THE GAM-BINO FAMILY!

OH.

CARRY ON, SIR.
YOU'VE GOT A MOTHER, RIGHT, BIG GUY? RIGHT?
GB Trudeau

LEMME TELL YOU SOMETHING, DUKE. I'M AN ACQUITTED MAN. I LIKE THE ACQUITTED LIFE VERY MUCH. I'M THE ROSE OF HOWARD BEACH!

SO I GOTTA BE CAREFUL, UNDER-STAND? THAT'S WHY I'M GONNA LET YOU GUESS WHAT I WANT FROM YOU, AND WHAT'LL HAPPEN TO YOU IF I DON'T GET IT.

YOU WANT 10% OF MY BUSINESS OR I GET MY HANDS BROKEN?
GUESS AGAIN.

YOU GET 90% OR I GET STUFFED INTO A CAR COM-PACTER?
IS THAT A **GUESS?** HOW COME YOUSE GUYS DON'T GUESS THAT GOOD?
HEY, C'MON, BOSS, HE GOT LUCKY!
GB Trudeau

ALL THE BEST, DUKE!
I WON'T LET YOU DOWN, JOHNNY...
CLINK!

DR. WHOOPEE IS NOW RIDING A WAVE OF UNPRECEDENTED CONSUMER ACCEPTANCE...

... AND I CAN'T THINK OF ANY REASON WHY YOUR ORGANIZATION SHOULDN'T GET A TASTE!

PSST! SIR! BECAUSE IT'S WRONG!
WHO IS THIS BROAD, JIMINY CRICKET?
GB Trudeau

DAMN!

GOT A STORY, PAL?
YEAH. I JUST SOLD OUT TO THE MOB. THE MOB GIVES ME MIGRAINES. END OF STORY.

MIGRAINES, EH? BOY, THEY CAN BE WICKED! I USED TO GET 'EM DURING MY FIRST MARRIAGE.

OVER-THE-COUNTER?
UNDER. JOIN ME?
GB Trudeau

I KNOW WHAT YOU'RE GOING THROUGH, PAL. MY INDUSTRY'S RIFE WITH HOODS! YOU CAN'T BELIEVE WHAT THEY DO TO HORSES!

HORSES? YOU IN RACING?
PET FOOD. THE BUSINESS IS OWNED OUTRIGHT BY THE KANSAS CITY MOB.

GEEZ! HOW COULD I TELL THAT TO A TOTAL STRANGER? HEY, YOU'RE NOT WIRED, ARE YOU?

TOTALLY. BUT THANKS.
COULD YOU CUT ME DOWN? I GOT A TRAIN.
GB Trudeau

SURE YOU'LL BE OKAY, PAL?
I'M FINE! I'M FINE!
WHOA... SURE YOU ARE! BETTER FIND SOMEPLACE TO DROP ANCHOR...
KFWUMP!!!
HEY! FIND YOUR OWN BED, JACK!
DAMN HOMELESS. THEY ALWAYS TAKE THE GOOD SPOTS.
GB Trudeau

YOU'RE COPS, AREN'T YOU? THAT'S WHY YOU'RE STARING AT ME! WELL, THREE CAN PLAY THAT GAME!
THERE HE IS...
WHAT THE...
EASY DOES IT, BROTHER.
WE'RE HERE TO HELP YOU.
PROPERTY
GRAND CEN
HELP ME? RIGHT! AND WHO ARE YOU?
NOT TO WORRY...
WE'RE SOCIAL WORKERS.
SHOOT ME! FOR GOD'S SAKE, SOMEBODY SHOOT ME!
GIVE HIM A SANDWICH. I'LL CALL FOR THE VAN.
GB Trudeau

YES, THIS IS LORD ZONKER.
SIR! IT'S DEAN HONEY! THANK GOODNESS I FOUND YOU!
OXFORD
I JUST GOT A CALL FROM THE AUTHORITIES! DUKE WAS CAUGHT UP IN THE CITY'S SWEEP OF THE MENTALLY INCOMPETENT! HE'S BEEN COMMITTED TO BELLEVUE HOSPITAL!
UNCLE DUKE'S BEEN COMMITTED? REALLY?
YES, SIR!
THEN OUR LONG NATIONAL NIGHTMARE IS OVER.
YES, SIR. DO YOU WANT TO COME IN ON SOME FLOWERS WITH ME?
GB Trudeau

ORDERLY! ORDERLY!
HEY, HEY, WHAT'S ALL THE HUBBUB, BUB?
THIS IS ALL A FREAKISH MISTAKE! I GOTTA GET OUTA HERE!
I SEE.
LISTEN, FRIEND, THERE ARE HUNDREDS OF DERANGED FOLKS ON THE STREETS OF NEW YORK. BELLEVUE ONLY HAS 28 BEDS FOR THEM. YOU SHOULD BE GRATEFUL YOU WERE CHOSEN FOR ADMISSION!
BUT I'M NOT DERANGED!!
THEN YOU SHOULDN'T BE FAKING IT. WE NEED THE BED.
©B Trudeau
OFF ATLANTIC CITY, ABOARD THE "TRUMP PRINCESS"...
...DONALD TRUMP'S NEW $37 MILLION FLOATING PLAYPEN...
...WHERE THE BATHROOM FIXTURES ARE GOLD, AND EACH OF THE 11 SUITES HAS CHAMOIS WALLS.
©B Trudeau
...A NEW CAPTAIN IS BEING HIRED.
AND YOU SAY YOU'RE DISCREET?
I'M YOUR MAN, MR. TRUMP!
AND THIS IS MY PRIVATE SUN DECK! IT HAS BULLET-PROOF GLASS, A CIRCULAR POOL, AND A HYDRAULICALLY LIFTED SUN BED!
AMAZING, MR. TRUMP!
QUALITY MEANS EVERYTHING, CAPTAIN! THE GOLD FIXTURES! THE TORTOISE SHELL CEILING! IT'S UNBELIEVABLE THIS MUCH QUALITY EXISTS OUTSIDE MY IMAGINATION!
AND LOOK, MORE QUALITY! THE ONYX DESK, HAND CARVED BY A WHOLE VILLAGE OF ARTISANS!
INCREDIBLE!
AND OVER THERE, THAT'S MY WIFE! LOOK AT THE QUALITY!
VERY IMPRESSIVE!
©B Trudeau

LOOK AT THE QUALITY! CHAMOIS LEATHER WALLS! BIRD'S EYE MAPLE TRIM! HAND-CARVED ONYX BATHROOMS! WE'RE TALKING QUALITY! A LEVEL OF QUALITY THAT'S HARD TO EXPLAIN!
TRUMP PRINCESS
LOOK HERE, MORE QUALITY...
EXCUSE ME, SIR. BY "QUALITY", YOU MEAN IT COSTS AN OBSCENE AMOUNT, RIGHT?
UH... RIGHT.
GBTrudeau
THERE ARE OTHER DEFINITIONS?
NONE THAT MATTER. I WAS JUST CHECKING.
LOOK AT THE PERFORMANCE QUALITY OF THIS BOAT! 17.5 KNOTS CRUISING SPEED! 8,500 MILES WITHOUT REFUELING! YOU CAN'T JUST BUY THIS KIND OF QUALITY, YOU HAVE TO WILL IT!
DO YOU THINK YOU CAN HANDLE HER, CAPTAIN?
NO PROBLEM, MR. TRUMP!
OKAY, SEE THAT LITTLE OUTBOARD OVER THERE?
WITH THE KIDS? YEAH, I SEE IT.
SWAMP IT.
PIECE OF CAKE.
GBTrudeau
ON THE BOARDWALK.
MAGNIFICENT, ISN'T SHE?
YEAH. IF YOU'RE A LITTLE BOY INTO GIGANTIC TOYS.
TAKES YOUR BREATH AWAY, DOESN'T IT?
I'LL SAY. YOU DON'T OFTEN SEE VULGARITY ON THAT SCALE.
QUITE A SIGHT, EH?
DO YOU REALIZE TRUMP COULD HAVE BUILT 800 UNITS OF LOW-INCOME HOUSING WITH WHAT HE PAID FOR THAT THING?
LATER...
WELL?
AS YOU SUSPECTED, BIG GUY! THEY LOVE YA!
GBTrudeau

GOOD EVENING, BILLY!
OH, GOOD EVENING, MR. TRUMP!

WHERE'S OUR NEW CAPTAIN?
HE WENT BELOW, SIR. TO ENTERTAIN SOME OF THE HIGH ROLLERS FROM YOUR CASINO.

NOW THAT'S INITIATIVE! I THINK CAPTAIN DUKE IS GOING TO WORK OUT JUST FINE!

A SOLID GOLD FAUCET? WHERE'D YOU GET IT?
NEVER MIND. ARE YOU IN OR NOT?
GB Trudeau

YES, MR. TRUMP?
FIRE HER UP, CAPTAIN. I WANT YOU TO TAKE HER TO NEW ORLEANS!

NEW ORLEANS, SIR?
THE G.O.P. CONVENTION—WHERE THE ACTION IS! HAVE OUR ON-BOARD PUBLICIST GET ON IT!

BY SHOWING UP IN THE "TRUMP PRINCESS," WE CAN SEND AMERICA AN IMPORTANT MESSAGE ABOUT THE LAST EIGHT YEARS!
WHICH MESSAGE IS THAT, SIR?

TAX BREAKS FOR THE RICH WORK!
A GOOD MESSAGE, SIR! A TIMELY MESSAGE!
GB Trudeau

LADIES AND GENTLEMEN, BEFORE WE SET SAIL FOR NEW ORLEANS, A FEW WORDS ABOUT CREW DISCIPLINE!

THIS IS A TRUMP BOAT, AND LIKE ANY OTHER TRUMP OPERATION, IT SHALL BE RUN WITH A GLEAMING, STAINLESS STEEL FIST!

TO DEMONSTRATE HOW TOTAL MY AUTHORITY IS, I'VE DECIDED, IN HONOR OF MRS. TRUMP, TO FIRE EVERYONE WHOSE NAME BEGINS WITH "I"!

DUKEY... NO!
UH... EXCEPT FOR MISS IVEY, MY CABIN BOY.
GB Trudeau

...AND WHILE EVERYONE ELSE WAS WAITING FOR THE PRICE TO GO DOWN, I STEPPED IN WITH $30 MILLION CASH AND SNAPPED UP A BOAT WHOSE REPLACEMENT VALUE IS $180 MILLION!
IT WAS A NEGOTIATING TRIUMPH! THE "TRUMP PRINCESS" IS A FLOATING TRIBUTE TO THE ART OF MAKING A DEAL!
HEE, HEE!
WHAT'S SO FUNNY, CAPTAIN?
NOTHING'S FUNNY, SIR. I JUST LOVE THAT YOU CALL DEAL-MAKING AN "ART."
CLASSY, HUH? IT WAS MY WIFE'S IDEA.
IT REALLY PUTS PAINTING AND LITERATURE IN THEIR PLACE.
GB Trudeau
I GUESS COMING DOWN HERE WAS A GOOD IDEA, MR. TRUMP! LOOK AT THE RECEPTION YOU'RE GETTING!
WELL, OF COURSE, CAPTAIN! WHETHER IN ATLANTIC CITY OR NEW ORLEANS, THERE WILL ALWAYS BE AN AUDIENCE FOR QUALITY!
THESE ARE MY PEOPLE, CAPTAIN, THE STRIVERS, THE WANNA-BES, THE LITTLE PEOPLE WITH BIG DREAMS!
YOO-HOO! DONALD! OVER HERE!
WARNING!
GB Trudeau
YOU SEEN THE VICE PRESIDENT, SENATOR?
NO, HE DIDN'T MAKE IT. FROM WHAT I HEAR, HIS HANDLERS ARE KEEPING HIM UNDER WRAPS UNTIL TOMORROW.
THEY FIGURE REAGAN'S RECEPTION IN THE BOWL TONIGHT COULD PROVE EMBARRASSING.
EMBARRASSING? THAT'S PUTTING IT MILDLY.
GB Trudeau
FOUR MORE YEARS! FOUR MORE YEARS!
SIGH...

IS THE BUSHMAN ON YET?
IN A MOMENT...

HIS SON IS INTRO-DUCING HIM NOW.

HIS SON MADE A VIDEO?
IT'S NOT A VIDEO. IT'S A SLIDE SHOW.
GB Trudeau

SLIDE SHOW?
NEXT, PLEASE. OKAY, THIS IS MY DAD'S 25-YEAR-OLD GOLF CART...

...AND SO GEORGE BUSH HAS SPELLED OUT WHAT HE CALLS "THE VISION THING."

IT IS, LARGELY, A VISION OF MORE OF THE SAME, ONLY WITH FEWER PEOPLE GOING TO JAIL. STILL NO WORD ON WHO'S PAY-ING FOR IT.

AND NOW, AT THE MOMENT OF GEORGE BUSH'S GREATEST POLITICAL TRIUMPH, HE IS JOINED AT THE PODIUM BY THE ENTIRE BUSH CLAN!

NEAT SPEECH, DAD!
I KICKED TAIL! I KICKED TAIL!
WASN'T THAT UNCLE SKIPPY?
GB Trudeau

THE RETURN VOYAGE OF THE "TRUMP PRINCESS" FROM NEW ORLEANS WAS UNEVENTFUL...
MORE CAVIAR TOPSIDES!
AYE, AYE, SIR!

...UNTIL THE FATEFUL MORNING WHEN THE PURSER SPOTTED A FAMILIAR FIGURE LEANING AGAINST THE RADIO MAST.
MY GOD! IT CAN'T BE!

LATER, THE NIGHT MAID CONFIRMED THE SIGHTING.
IT'S...YOU!

THE CAPTAIN WAS DULY NOTIFIED.
SIR? ELVIS IS ON BOARD.
OH, YEAH? BOOK HIM FOR TO-NIGHT.
SPORTS
GB Trudeau

IT'S TRUE, SIR. ELVIS IS ON BOARD.
YOU DON'T SAY...
HOW'D HE GET ON BOARD?
WE DON'T KNOW, SIR. HE APPEARS TO BE A STOW-AWAY!
WHERE'S HE NOW?
HE'S ON THE POOL DECK. HITTING ON THE TOWEL GIRL.
HEY, BABY! EVER HEAR OF THE KING?
PLEASE.
GB Trudeau
GOOD TO MEET YA, CAPTAIN...
I KNEW YOU WERE ALIVE, KING. I NEVER GAVE UP HOPE.
I APPRECIATE THAT, MAN. I DON'T KNOW WHAT I WOULD HAVE DONE WITHOUT MY FANS. THEY KEPT ME GOIN'. I COULDN'T HAVE MADE IT WITHOUT 'EM!
SO WHERE **HAVE** YOU BEEN ALL THESE YEARS, KING?
WELL, BELIEVE IT OR NOT, THEM TABLOID PAPERS ACTU-ALLY GOT IT RIGHT!
NO! ON A U.F.O.?
THEY HAD LITTLE RICHARD FOR A WHILE, TOO. DID SOME TESTS ON HIM.
GB Trudeau
TRUMP, NOTIFIED OF ELVIS' PRE-SENCE ON HIS YACHT, CHOPPERS TO THE "TRUMP PRINCESS" AT ONCE.
I DON'T CARE WHAT IT COSTS! I WANT ELVIS TO PLAY MY ATLANTIC CITY CASINOS!
I HEAR YOU, MR. T!
PUT HIM IN THE DIAMOND SUITE! AND TAKE CARE OF HIM! WHAT ELVIS WANTS, ELVIS **GETS!**
I'M WAY AHEAD OF YOU, SIR.
AMPHETAMINES, SIR! COMPLI-MENTS OF THE CAPTAIN!
Y'ALL ARE GREAT, MAN.
GB Trudeau

TRUMP AND PRESLEY! WE'RE TALKING COMEBACK MAGIC AT THE **HOTTEST** CASINO VENUE IN THE WORLD! WHAT DO YOU SAY, KING?

DONNY, I WOULDN'T BE HERE IF I DIDN'T BELIEVE IN YOU AS A QUALITY PROMOTER. EVERYTHING ABOUT YOU SCREAMS QUALITY.
THANK YOU.

BUT IT'S GOING TO TAKE MORE THAN $2 MILLION A WEEK, MAN. I'VE GOT A LOT OF RESPONSIBILITIES.
NAME YOUR PRICE, KING! WRITE YOUR OWN TICKET!

I MEAN, I GOT 1,200 ILLEGITIMATE CHILDREN TO SUPPORT.
SAY NO MORE.
WE'VE ALL BEEN THERE, KING. WHAT AGES?
GB Trudeau

... AND I ONLY WANT TO DO THREE SHOWS A WEEK. AND I'M NOT DOING ANY SETS OF MORE THAN 30 MINUTES, OKAY, MAN?

HEY, YOU'RE THE KING.
GOOD. ONE OTHER THING. I ONLY SING JOHN DENVER MATERIAL NOW.

IS THAT A PROBLEM?
WE COULD DROP HIM OVERBOARD. WHO'D KNOW? HE'S DEAD.
©B Trudeau

LADIES AND GENTLEMEN, **TRUMP PRODUCTIONS**, IN ASSOCIATION WITH **DONALD TRUMP PROMOTIONS**...

...IS PROUD TO ANNOUNCE A **DONALD TRUMP** CONCERT-OF-THE-CENTURY TO BE STAGED RIGHT HERE IN THE **TRUMP PLAZA HOTEL AND CASINO!**

AHEM...
OH... FEATURING **ELVIS PRESLEY!**
©B Trudeau

EVERYTHING'S ALL SET, MR. TRUMP. ELVIS IS PRIMED AND READY TO GO!
GOOD. HAVE ALL THE QUALITY CELEBRITIES ARRIVED?

YES, SIR. TYSON AND DON KING ARE HERE, AND I JUST SEATED SINATRA AND HIS BODYGUARDS UP FRONT.
HOW ABOUT THE VICE PRESIDENT?

HE'S STILL IN HIS DRESSING ROOM. HAVING HIS COSTUME FITTED.
COSTUME?
©B Trudeau

LET'S SHOW A LITTLE MORE SHOULDER.
"I PLEDGE ALLEGIANCE..."
ON IN FIVE, POPPY!

LADIES AND GENTLEMEN, THERE ARE SUPERSTARS AND THERE ARE SUPERSTARS, BUT THERE'S ONLY ONE SUPERSTAR'S SUPERSTAR!

LET'S BRING HIM OUT! LADIES AND GENTLEMEN, I GIVE YOU THE KING OF ROCK 'N' ROLL, MR. ELVIS PRESLEY!
CLAP!
YEA!
CLAP!
CLAP!

THANK YOU! Y'ALL ARE BEAUTIFUL! I LOVE YOU!
YOU'RE FACING THE WRONG WAY, KING.

THANK YOU! Y'ALL ARE BEAUTIFUL! I LOVE YOU!
YOU TOOK THEM ALL AT ONCE, DIDN'T YOU?
©B Trudeau

LADIES AND GENTLEMEN, BEFORE I GET STARTED, I WANT TO BRING OUT A CAT WHO'S NOT AFRAID TO STAND UP FOR OL' GLORY. LADIES AND GENTLEMEN, MR. GEORGE BUSH!

THANKS, ELVIS. IT'S GREAT TO BE HERE!
I DIG WHERE THIS CAT IS COMING FROM ON EVERY ISSUE, PEOPLE! PATRIOTISM, GUNS, EVERYTHING BUT DRUGS!

ELVIS, MY PAL NORIEGA FELT THE SAME WAY. IT'S AN HONEST DIFFERENCE!
HEY, IS THIS OL' BOY OKAY OR WHAT? LET'S HEAR IT, PEOPLE!

I PLEDGE ALLEGIANCE...
SEE, THIS IS WHY I GOT OFF DRUGS. WHO CAN TELL THE DIFFERENCE ANYMORE?
©B Trudeau

THANK YOU VERY MUCH, LADIES AND GENTLEMEN. IT'S GOOD TO BE BACK.

THE PEOPLE HERE AT TRUMP PLAZA TOLD ME Y'ALL WANTED TO HEAR MY OLD HITS, SONGS LIKE "HEARTBREAK HOTEL" AND "DON'T BE CRUEL..."

BUT I TOLD 'EM, I GOTTA BE ME. TONIGHT I WANNA PLAY SOMETHIN' DIFFERENT FOR Y'ALL. LADIES AND GENTLEMEN, THE MUSIC OF MY GOOD FRIEND, MR. JOHN DENVER!
GB Trudeau

DAMN... DID YOU CALL THE RIOT POLICE?
THEY'RE ON ALERT.
ROCKY MOUN-TAIN HIIIGH!

IT'S AN OUTRAGE! FIRST THE GUY CHARGED $1500 A TICKET FOR A 90-SECOND FIGHT! NOW HE'S RIPPED OFF $2500 A HEAD TO SEE SOME BLIMPO ELVIS IMPOSTER SING "ROCKY MOUNTAIN HIGH"!

I'M ROLAND HEDLEY. IT'S A BAD NIGHT FOR CASINO OPERATOR DON TRUMP AS HIS MUCH BALLY-HOOED RETURN OF ELVIS HAS ERUPTED INTO UGLY MAYHEM.

ANOTHER CLEAR LOSER HERE TONIGHT: GEORGE BUSH, WHOSE CAMPAIGN APPEARANCE HAS BEEN COMPLETELY UPSTAGED BY THE VIOLENT REACTION TO THE ABORTED CONCERT.
GB Trudeau

...AND IF I'M ELECTED, I DARN SURE WON'T BURN THE FLAG!
KILL TRUMP! KILL TRUMP!

THE BOSS SUMMONS DUKE FOR THEIR WEEKLY CONFAB.
...AND MY WIFE WILL BOARD TODAY. SEND A LITTER.
CHECK.

OH, ONE MORE THING. I'VE HIRED A NEW SOCIAL DI-RECTOR.
SOCIAL DIRECTOR?

YEAH. I'D LIKE YOU TO MEET HER. MARILYN, SEND IN MISS HUAN.

HOLD IT...
FATE! THERE'S NO OTHER WORD FOR IT, SIR!
GB Trudeau

CAN YOU BELIEVE IT, SIR? THE WINDS OF DESTINY HAVE TOSSED US TOGETHER AGAIN!
ISN'T IT GREAT, SIR? A FRESH START! A CHANCE TO SHIP OUT AND SHAPE UP TOGETHER! WHO SAYS THERE ARE NO SECOND ACTS IN AMERICA? SIR? HELLO?
CAPTAIN, YOU DON'T SEEM TOO THRILLED TO SEE THIS YOUNG WOMAN...
SHE'S JUST A FLASHBACK, SIR. SHE'LL GO AWAY.
NO, SIR, IT'S REALLY ME! TOUCH ME! DISCREETLY, OF COURSE.
GB Trudeau

SO MUCH HAS HAPPENED SINCE WE SAW EACH OTHER LAST, SIR...
I WAS AFRAID OF THAT.
FIRST, WE HAD A LABOR DISPUTE AT DR. WHOOPEE, AND A DISGRUNTLED FORMER EMPLOYEE ATTACKED ME IN THE EXECUTIVE WASHROOM WITH A SPATULA...
AFTER THAT, I HAD A TORRID PLATONIC RELATIONSHIP WITH A CAPO FROM THE GAMBINO FAMILY, WHICH ENDED WHEN I TOLD HIM I WANTED HIS BABY. THEN I HAD A SELF-DESTRUCTIVE CRUSH ON...
HEY! DID I ASK? DID I ASK?
NO, SIR. AND FRANKLY, I'M A LITTLE HURT.
GB Trudeau

...AND THEN A FRIEND OF A FRIEND INTRODUCED ME TO MRS. TRUMP'S PERSONNEL DIRECTOR!
SO EVERYTHING TURNED OUT GREAT, ALTHOUGH FOR A WHILE THERE THINGS LOOKED PRETTY GRIM...
IT TOOK ME A LONG TIME TO GET OVER BEING ATTACKED BY THAT MADMAN WITH A SPATULA. THE POLICE NEVER IDENTIFIED HIM.
IT WAS ME.
WELL, I THOUGHT SO, BUT I COULDN'T FIND YOU IN THE MUG BOOK.
GB Trudeau

11 PANAMA CITY

1990

DAY 20.
IT'S A MESS DOWN THERE SIR. WE'RE BASICALLY BUILDING ALL OF PANAMA'S GOVERNING INSTITUTIONS FROM SCRATCH!
WHAT WE URGENTLY NEED IS A CIVILIAN ADMINISTRATOR, SOMEONE ON THE GROUND WHO CAN DIRECT THE RECONSTRUCTION OF THE COUNTRY!
GOT ANYONE IN MIND?
YES, SIR. A RETIRED FOREIGN SERVICE OFFICER WITH GOOD COLONIAL EXPERIENCE. HE'LL DO IT IF WE CAN SETTLE ON A TITLE.
OKAY, HOW ABOUT "MAXIMUM PROCONSUL"?
DONE! FAX MY CONTRACT TO SOUTHERN COMMAND!
SORRY, DUKE, I CAN'T SPARE YOU. I'M GONNA HOLD YOU TO YOUR CONTRACT!
BUT MR. T, THIS APPOINTMENT TO PANAMA IS A MAJOR OPPORTUNITY...
PANAMA CITY IS THE NEXT HAVANA, THE NEXT SAIGON! IT'S WIDE OPEN, AND AS PROCONSUL, I'LL BE MAKING THE DECISIONS ON DEVELOPMENT—HOUSING, HOTELS, CASINOS, THE WORKS!
DON'T BE A STRANGER.
AYE, AYE, SIR!
SIR, MAY I BE THE FIRST TO CONGRATULATE YOU ON YOUR APPOINTMENT TO MAXIMUM PROCONSUL OF PANAMA. I ONLY WISH I COULD JOIN YOU!
UNFORTUNATELY, SINCE OUR DIVORCE, I'VE DEVELOPED ROOTS AND COMMITMENTS RIGHT HERE IN NEW JERSEY. I HAVE A NICE HOME THAT I'VE JUST DECORATED...
...AND I HAVE TWO CATS AND FOUR PLANTS THAT NEED ME. I ALSO HAVE A JOB I LOVE, FOR WHICH I AM BOTH APPRECIATED AND WELL-COMPENSATED!
WHAT A SHAME. I NEED SOMEONE TO TASTE MY FOOD.
I'LL GO BACK.

DAY 24. PROCONSUL DUKE MEETS THE PRESS ON A SWELTERING HOWARD AIR FORCE BASE TARMAC.
I'M ONLY GOING TO SAY THIS ONCE...

MY MISSION HERE IS TO REBUILD A BASICALLY DYSFUNCTIONAL NATION, A COUNTRY WITH NO POLICE FORCE, NO CALL-WAITING, AND NOT A SINGLE DECENT MEXICAN RESTAURANT!

I DON'T WANT TO PUT ANY TIMETABLES ON THIS, BUT MY GUESS IS WE'LL BE OUT OF HERE WELL BEFORE THE '92 NEW HAMPSHIRE PRIMARY. ANY QUESTIONS?

YES, YOU WITH THE TENTACLES AND MELTING EYEBALLS.
MR. DUKE, HAVE YOU LICKED YOUR DRUG PROBLEM YET?

MAN, LOOK AT THE NEIGHBORHOOD NEAR THE COMANDANCIA!
THEY SAY HUNDREDS OF CIVILIANS LOST THEIR LIVES, SIR.

YEAH, WELL, BUSH SAID THE BODY COUNT WAS WORTH IT, SO THAT'S GOOD ENOUGH FOR ME!
YES, SIR.

LOOK, HONEY! IF PEOPLE LIKE YOU HADN'T CALLED HIM A WIMP, WE WOULDN'T EVEN BE HERE!
I KNOW, SIR. WE ALL BEAR RESPONSIBILITY.

SO HOW'S THE NEW PROCONSUL WORKING OUT?
MIXED REPORTS, SIR.

AT LAST WEEKEND'S EMBASSY RECEPTION, HE SPILLED A PITCHER OF DAIQUIRIS ON VICE PRESIDENT CALDERON AND LATER FELL INTO THE POOL...

ON THE OTHER HAND, HE'S GOTTEN PERSONALLY INVOLVED IN RESTORING CIVIL PEACE. HE'S EVEN BEEN TEACHING CLASSES AT THE NEW "PUBLIC FORCE" ACADEMY!

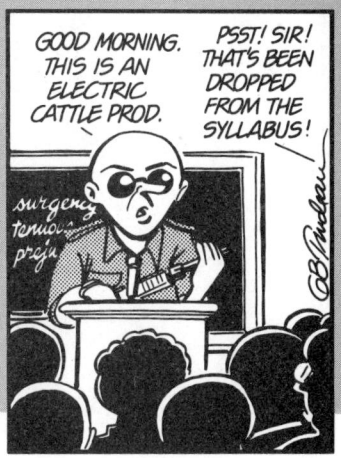
GOOD MORNING. THIS IS AN ELECTRIC CATTLE PROD.
PSST! SIR! THAT'S BEEN DROPPED FROM THE SYLLABUS!

PROCONSUL DUKE TALKS TO PANAMA'S NEW "PUBLIC FORCE."
THE IMPORTANT THING FOR YOU TO REMEMBER IS THAT IN THE NEW PANAMA, YOU GOTTA GO BY THE BOOK— OUR BOOK!
NOW, I DON'T LIKE IT ANY MORE THAN YOU, BUT THAT'S THE DOWN SIDE OF A REAL DEMOCRACY— FOR SOME REASON, CRIMINALS HAVE RIGHTS!
WHAT KIND OF RIGHTS, SEÑOR PROCONSUL?
UM... WELL, FOR STARTERS, YOU CAN'T DO ANYTHING CRUEL OR UNUSUAL.
BUT YOUR SOLDIERS MADE NORIEGA LISTEN TO RAP MUSIC FOR A WEEK!
THAT WAS STILL PART OF THE INVASION. DOESN'T COUNT.
SEÑOR, WILL WE GET TO WEAR ITALIAN SPORTS JACKETS?
GB Trudeau
MEN, AS PANAMA'S NEW PEACE OFFICERS, IT'LL BE UP TO YOU TO MAKE THIS A COUNTRY WE CAN ALL BE PROUD OF!
PANAMA'S BEING GIVEN ONE MORE CHANCE TO EMULATE THE AMERICAN MODEL OF DEMOCRACY. YOU HAVE A FREELY ELECTED PRESIDENT, YOU HAVE A CONSTITUTION, YOU HAVE FOUNDING FATHERS...
WHAT FOUNDING FATHERS?
THE 82ND AIRBORNE. REVERE THEM.
HOW ABOUT A DECLARATION OF INDEPENDENCE?
DON'T GET CUTE. CLASS DISMISSED.
No
GB Trudeau
LISTEN, COLONEL, AFTER WE CLEAR OUT OF HERE, YOU CAN GO BACK TO YOUR OWN WAY OF KEEPING ORDER! BUT UNTIL THEN, I'VE GOT A DEMOCRACY TO RUN!
YOU'VE GOT TO FIND A FEW MEN FOR THE PUBLIC FORCE WHO WEREN'T IN THE P.D.F.! EVERYONE THINKS ALL WE'VE DONE IS CHANGE THE SHOULDER PATCHES!
SI, SEÑOR PROCONSUL, BUT THE PEOPLE RESPECT MY MEN!
ARE YOU KIDDING? THEY LOATHE THEM! 92% OF THE PANAMANIAN PEOPLE SUPPORT THE INVASION!
IF YOU SAY SO, SEÑOR. SHOULD WE DETAIN THE OTHER 8%?
YOU STILL DON'T GET IT, DO YOU?
GB Trudeau

THE PROCONSUL GETS A CALL.
MR. DUKE? THIS IS THE PRESIDENT! HOW'S DANNY MAKING OUT?
WELL, HE'S MAKIN' A HELLUVA IMPRESSION, SIR!

I WAS AFRAID OF THAT. WHAT'S HE DOING NOW?
INSPECTING THE INVASION FORCE, SIR. HE'S WORRIED ABOUT THEIR UNIFORMS.

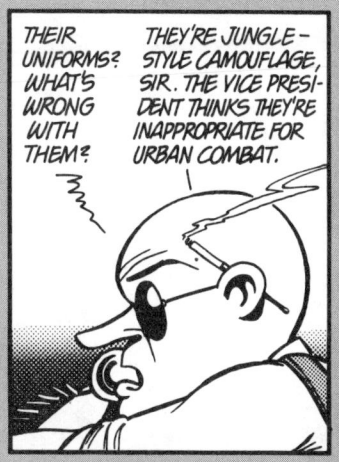
THEIR UNIFORMS? WHAT'S WRONG WITH THEM?
THEY'RE JUNGLE-STYLE CAMOUFLAGE, SIR. THE VICE PRESIDENT THINKS THEY'RE INAPPROPRIATE FOR URBAN COMBAT.

CAN WE GET UNIFORMS WITH LITTLE BUILDINGS ON THEM?
WE'LL TRY, SIR!

SO HOW ARE THE TROOPS, MR. VICE PRESIDENT?
GOOD! THEY LOOKED TAN, RESTED, NOT AT ALL LIKE THEY'D BEEN IN AN INVASION!

THE ONLY PROBLEM IS THEY'RE STILL HERE. THE WHOLE REASON I CAME DOWN HERE WAS TO REASSURE OUR FRIENDS THAT THIS WAS A SHORT-TERM, ONE-TIME INTERVENTION!

IT'S NOT EASY CARRYING A MESSAGE LIKE THAT ALL OVER LATIN AMERICA—TO COUNTRIES LIKE... LIKE... WHAT'S THAT ONE WITH THE BEACHES?

WHATEVER.
RIGHT. ESPECIALLY IF YOU DON'T SPEAK A WORD OF LATIN!

PRESIDENT VARGAS? PROCONSUL DUKE HERE! LISTEN, I GOT DAN QUAYLE HERE SITTING IN MY OFFICE...

HE'S MADE A HECK OF AN EFFORT TO GET DOWN HERE. AND I THINK MORE OF YOU GUYS SHOULD BE HEARING HIM OUT...

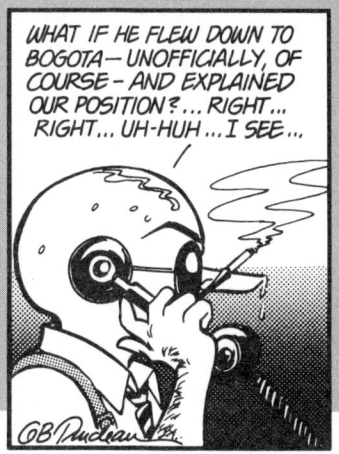
WHAT IF HE FLEW DOWN TO BOGOTA—UNOFFICIALLY, OF COURSE—AND EXPLAINED OUR POSITION?... RIGHT... RIGHT... UH-HUH... I SEE...

HE'S AFRAID YOU'LL BE DRAGGED FROM YOUR LIMO AND BEATEN WITH PIPES.
DAMN... OKAY, LET'S TRY THE PRESIDENT OF PUERTO RICO!

LOOK, PRESIDENT ARIAS, I APPRECIATE YOUR POSITION, BUT COME ON, THE INVASION WASN'T DANNY QUAYLE'S CALL! **NOTHING** IS! WHY TAKE IT OUT ON HIM?

BECAUSE THE NATIONS OF THIS REGION HAVE HAD ENOUGH, MR. PROCONSUL.
ENOUGH? ENOUGH OF WHAT?

IN 1901, THE U.S. SENT TROOPS TO COLOMBIA; IN 1902, TO PANAMA; IN 1903, HONDURAS, DOMINICAN REPUBLIC AND PANAMA; IN 1904, DOMINICAN REPUBLIC AND PANAMA; 1906, CUBA; 1907, HONDURAS; 1910, NICARAGUA; 1911, HONDURAS; 1912...

WELL? WELL?
BAD LUCK. HE'S A HISTORY NUT.
GB Trudeau

LOOK, PRESIDENT GARCIA PEREZ, YOU'VE GOT TO TAKE THE LONG VIEW HERE! SOONER OR LATER, BUSH IS GONNA SEND QUAYLE TO PERU WHETHER YOU LIKE IT OR NOT!

WHY NOT JUST GET IT OVER WITH? WHAT?...UH-HUH...RIGHT... HOW WOULD THAT WORK? UH-HUH... OKAY, LET ME FLY IT BY HIM.

HE SAYS YOU CAN COME IF YOU SLIP ACROSS THE BOLIVIAN BORDER, DON A DISGUISE AND RIDE BY BURRO 250 MILES TO A REMOTE MONASTERY OUTSIDE OF CUZCO, WHERE YOU WOULD MEET WITH A RANKING GOVERNMENT OFFICIAL.

A **RANKING** OFFICIAL? WOW...
ALERT THE MONKS.
GB Trudeau

WERE YOU ABLE TO OPEN ANY DOORS FOR THE VEEP, SIR?
YEAH, POSSIBLY PERU.

GARCIA PEREZ SAYS HE CAN COME AS LONG AS HE'S WILLING TO PUT ON A DISGUISE AND RIDE A DONKEY THROUGH THE ANDES FOR A SECRET MEET AT A MONASTERY.

DANNY'S GAME, BUT HE'S STILL GOTTA RUN IT BY THE BIG GUY.

DANNY, COME HOME.
AW, SIR! I ALREADY GOT MY DISGUISE!
GB Trudeau

DID MR. QUAYLE EVER MAKE IT TO PERU, SIR?
NOPE...

HE GOT CALLED BACK TO WASHINGTON AT THE LAST MINUTE.

MY GUESS IS THEY WANT HIM IN PLACE IN CASE THE CHIEF GETS WAXED ON HIS WAY DOWN TO THE DRUG CONFERENCE.
GB Trudeau

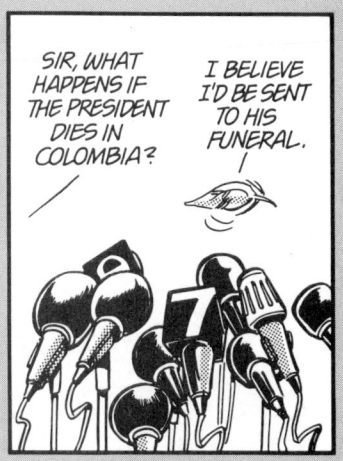
SIR, WHAT HAPPENS IF THE PRESIDENT DIES IN COLOMBIA?
I BELIEVE I'D BE SENT TO HIS FUNERAL.

IN PANAMA, THE BLOOM IS OFF THE INVASION...
WHAT DID BUSH BRING US BUT MORE POVERTY AND DEATH?

THOUSANDS OF OUR HOMES WERE DESTROYED, BUT STILL WE SEE NO AID! WE MUST TAKE OUR COUNTRY BACK! WE MUST SEND THE PROCONSUL PACKING!

YANQUI GO HOME!
YANQUI GO HOME!
YANQUI GO!

NOT MUCH OF A LIKENESS.
CLOSE ENOUGH, SIR.
GB Trudeau

ANTI-U.S. RIOTS! AFTER ALL I'VE DONE FOR THIS RAT-HOLE OF A COUNTRY!
I CAN IMAGINE HOW THAT MIGHT BE DEMORALIZING, SIR...

BUT LOOK AT IT FROM THE PANAMANIAN PERSPECTIVE. JUST TO ARREST A DRUG DEALER, U.S. FORCES MANAGED TO INFLICT $2 BILLION WORTH OF DAMAGE ON THE COUNTRY.

IN THE ABSENCE OF NO AID WHATSOEVER, THOUSANDS ARE STILL HOMELESS. SOME ARE EVEN LIVING UNDER CLUSTERS OF PARACHUTES ABANDONED BY THE VERY SOLDIERS WHOSE ARRIVAL LEFT THEM HOMELESS!

CHEAP, THIRD WORLD IRONY! I WON'T STAND FOR IT!
THEY CALL IT "SCREAMING EAGLE ESTATES."
ZIP!
GB Trudeau

I DON'T BELIEVE IT! YOU WERE RIGHT, HONEY! THERE ARE PEOPLE LIVING UNDER PARACHUTES!
YES, SIR. FOR FOUR MONTHS NOW.
THIS IS INCREDIBLE! LIKE SOME NIGHTMARISH POST-MODERN WHITE SALE.
ACTUALLY, SIR, IT'S INVASION LITTER...
...BUT WITHOUT IT, THESE PEOPLE WOULD HAVE NO SHELTER AT ALL! IT MEANS A LOT YOUR COMING DOWN HERE, SIR. IT SHOWS YOU CARE!
YEAH, BUT I DON'T. THIS WOULD MAKE A HELLUVA THEME PARK, WOULDN'T IT?
YOU CAN'T FOOL ME, SIR.
SEÑORA! I'M TOLD YOU AND OTHERS MAKE YOUR HOMES HERE AMONG THE PARACHUTES! HOW REMARKABLE!
THERE'S SOMETHING VISIONARY HERE! PARACHUTE DOMICILES! COOL, DRY, STRONG, ILLUMINATED BY SOFT, FILTERED LIGHT! THIS IS THE FUTURE! IT WORKS!
I SEE A CITY, SEÑORA! A SILK CITY! 1,000 SHIMMERING UNITS STRUNG ACROSS THE HILLS! WHAT DO YOU SAY TO THAT?
LAST NIGHT, WE BURNED YOU IN EFFIGY.
OKAY, 2,000! BUT ANY MORE AND YOU'LL ATTRACT RODENTS.
CITIZENS OF PANAMA! WHAT YOU HAVE BUILT HERE IS NOTHING SHORT OF FANTASTIC! FROM THESE DISCARDED SHROUDS YOU HAVE FASHIONED YOUR OWN SALVATION!
IT IS NOW MY PRIVILEGE TO DEDICATE "SCREAMING EAGLE ESTATES" TO THE MEMORY OF YOUR FOUNDING FATHERS — THE 82ND AIRBORNE! CHEERS!
C'MON, HONEY, LET'S GET TO OUR NEXT APPOINTMENT! BY GOD, I'M GLAD I SAW THIS WITH MY OWN EYES!
SIR, WHAT'D WE HAVE FOR BREAKFAST?
NOTHING SPECIAL. ONE DAY, THIS WILL ALL BE YOURS, HONEY!

THIS IS ABOUT MONEY AGAIN, RIGHT, EXCELLENCY?
NO, MR. PROCONSUL. IT IS ABOUT HOPE...

WHEN THE U.S. INVADED US LAST YEAR, PANAMANIANS HAD EVERY REASON TO BELIEVE THAT YOU WOULD DO RIGHT BY US...
GLUB!

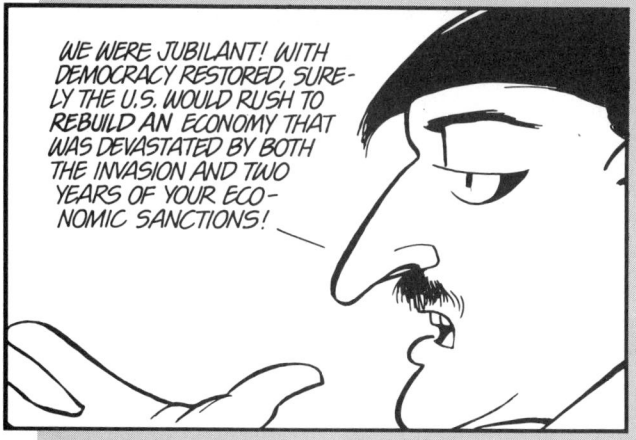
WE WERE JUBILANT! WITH DEMOCRACY RESTORED, SURELY THE U.S. WOULD RUSH TO REBUILD AN ECONOMY THAT WAS DEVASTATED BY BOTH THE INVASION AND TWO YEARS OF YOUR ECONOMIC SANCTIONS!

NO SUCH LUCK! WHEN IT COMES TO ITS NEIGHBORS, THE U.S. ALWAYS SEEMS TO HAVE PLENTY OF MONEY TO INVADE, BUT NEVER ENOUGH TO CLEAN UP AFTER!

YEAH, WELL, YOU GOTTA UNDERSTAND, EXCELLENCY. INVASIONS ARE PAID FOR OUT OF THE PRESIDENT'S DISCRETIONARY FUND...
I KNOW, I KNOW. AND CONGRESS IS IN NO MOOD TO REBUILD SOMEBODY ELSE'S MORIBUND ECONOMY.

RIGHT! SO WHAT DO YOU WANT?
RE-INVADE US! RESTORE A LITTLE HOPE!
©B Trudeau

12 KUWAIT CITY

1991

BROUGHT IN ANOTHER EPW YESTERDAY...
MAN, YOU'D THINK THEY ALL WOULD HAVE GOTTEN THE WORD BY NOW!
KUW

ANY HOMERS STILL HOLED UP IN K-CITY?
NOT THAT I'VE HEARD. I THINK THE AREA'S BASICALLY SECURE.
MBROOM!

HOW THEY DOING WITH SERVICES?
NOT SO GOOD ON THE ELECTRICITY AND WATER, BUT SOME DUDE'S ALREADY OPENED UP A NIGHTCLUB!
VROOM!
©B Trudeau

GENTLEMEN! WELCOME TO CLUB SCUD!

BOYS AND GIRLS, IF I COULD JUST HAVE YOUR ATTENTION, PLEASE!

WELCOME TO CLUB SCUD! I'M DUKE, YOUR HOST AND FORMER U.S. PROCONSUL TO PANAMA. BEHIND ME IS YOUR BARGIRL FOR THE EVENING. HER NAME IS UNPRONOUNCEABLE, BUT SHE ANSWERS TO "HONEY"!

LET ME JUST ADD HOW PROUD WE ARE OF ALL OF YOU! YOU'RE A MAGNIFICENT BUNCH OF WARRIORS! I CAN'T TELL YOU WHAT AN HONOR IT IS TO HELP YOU CELEBRATE THE LIBERATION OF KUWAIT! ANY QUESTIONS?
©B Trudeau

YES, SIR. WHY'D YOU LEAVE PANAMA?
ARE YOU KIDDING? THE COUNTRY'S IN RUINS!

DRINK UP, SOLDIER! EVERY TENTH BREW IS ON THE HOUSE!
THANKS, BUDDY. THIS YOUR PLACE?

IT IS!
MAN, I'D ALMOST FORGOTTEN WHAT BEER TASTED LIKE! IN THE FIELD WE'VE BEEN DRINKIN' HOOCH MADE FROM GLASS CLEANER!

HEE, HEE! THAT'S CUTE!
"CUTE"?
CLUB SCUD
©B Trudeau

MR. DUKE STARTS EVERY DAY WITH A QUART OF AVIATION FUEL.
AND THAT'S IN PEACETIME!

I THINK WE SHOULD JUST LAY IN SOME CHARGES AND BLOW THE SUCKER UP!
CAN WE CONTAIN THE COLLATERAL DAMAGE?

HE WILL NEVER GIVE UP POWER! NEVER, I SAY!
THEN WE MUST SEIZE IT! TONIGHT!

THEY WERE DRAGGED OFF LAST NIGHT. WE FEAR THE WORST...
I'LL TELL THE PRINCE MYSELF!
GB Trudeau

WE SEEM TO BE ATTRACTING A VERY INTERESTING CLIENTELE, SIR.
YEAH, TOO INTERESTING. CASH ONLY, GOT IT?

LOOK AT THIS ROOM, WILLYA, HONEY? WE GOT ROYALISTS, REFORMISTS, MILITIA, MARINES, ENGINEERS, FIREFIGHTERS, WEAPONS SALESMEN, BUILDERS, JOURNALISTS...

WE DON'T EVEN HAVE A LICENSE, AND ALREADY CLUB SCUD IS THE HOTTEST HANGOUT IN THE GULF! ALL WE NEED ARE SOME EXOTIC, SULTRY BABES TO COMPLETE THE SCENE!

AHEM.

I SAID, AHEM.
WHAT? ONE JUST COME IN?
GB Trudeau

HEY... AREN'T THOSE THE BOYS FROM BECHTEL SITTING AT TABLE TWO?
YES, SIR. WE SEEM TO BE DRAWING EVERY HEAVY-HITTER IN TOWN.

SPEAKING OF WHICH...
'LO, EVERYBODY!

NORM!
GB Trudeau

HOW'S IT GOING, GENERAL?
AHEAD OF SCHEDULE! WHICH IS MORE THAN I CAN SAY FOR THAT BEER!

HOW WE MAKING OUT, SIR?
LIKE GANG-BUSTERS, HONEY! DOUBLING THE COVER CHARGE DIDN'T HURT A BIT!

I SEE YOU HIRED A NEW BAR-TENDER...
HAD TO. WE'RE DOING SERIOUS VOLUME NOW. WE CAN'T GET CAUGHT SHORT-HANDED.

BESIDES, THE GUY'S A REAL PRO. HE KNOWS HIS INVENTORY, AND HE KNOWS HOW TO LISTEN.

...AND, OF COURSE, IN A TANK, YOU CAN'T SMOKE AT **ALL!**
YOU POOR KID!
©B Trudeau

HONEY, LET'S ADMIT IT, WE'RE ON A ROLL – BIG TIME! AND IT AIN'T GONNA QUIT SOON!

WE GOT A BUILT-IN CLIENTELE FOR **YEARS** TO COME – THE ENGINEERS, THE CONTRACTORS, THE WEAPONS SALESMEN, THE DIPLOMATS, THE PRESS!

HELL, THE CITY'S **SWARMING** WITH RANK, SWEATY OPPORTUNISTS HERE ONLY TO FEED OFF THE DETRITUS OF THIS COUNTRY'S TRAGEDY!
©B Trudeau

SORT OF LIKE US.
EXACTAMENTO! DID YOU PAY OFF THE MILITIA THIS WEEK?

SO HOW'S THE TILL LOOK TONIGHT, HONEY?
EXCEL-LENT, SIR.

THE BOYS FROM THE HOUSTON FIRE-FIGHTING COMPANIES GOT PAID TODAY. THEY'RE SPENDING MONEY LIKE THEY'VE NEVER EVEN **HEARD** OF ALIMONY BEFORE!

I MUST SAY, THEY LOOK QUITE GLAMOROUS IN THEIR OIL-SOAKED JUMPSUITS. I JUST WISH THEY WOULDN'T START SO MANY FIGHTS...

HEY, **JERK-FACE!** WATCH THE SPARKS, OKAY?
OH... SORRY.
©B Trudeau

GOOD EVENING, FOLKS! I'D LIKE TO WELCOME YOU TO CLUB SCUD, ESPECIALLY THE OIL WELL CAPPERS FROM RED ADAIR AND THE OTHER TEXAN OUTFITS!

I THINK YOU'LL FIND OUR ESTABLISHMENT AN OASIS OF GOOD CHEER AND REFRESHMENT IN THE OTHERWISE DRY AND BLASTED LANDSCAPE THAT IS POST-WAR KUWAIT!

WHETHER IT'S THE IMPECCABLY MIXED COCKTAILS OR THE CRISPLY STARCHED TABLECLOTHS, WE HAVE SPARED NO EFFORT IN MAKING YOUR CLUB A PLACE OF DISTINCTION AND CLASS!
GB Trudeau

NOW THEN, SOMEONE ASKED ME ABOUT OUR MISS DESERT STORM WET T-SHIRT CONTEST...
THAT WAS ME. I WAS JUST CURIOUS.

SORRY THE BOYS AIN'T SCRUBBED TODAY. OUR WATER LINE WENT DOWN...
FINE WITH ME, SIR. I LIKE THE MANLY SCENT OF SWEET CRUDE!

WELL, YOU KINDA HAVE TO IF YOU'RE GONNA HANG WITH WELL-KILLERS! WE DO GET DOUSED WITH JUICE! SOMETIMES OUR OWN WIVES CAN'T TELL US APART. HEE, HEE!

HEE...

PROBABLY WHY I'M ON MY FIFTH MARRIAGE.
I WAS GOING TO SAY.
GB Trudeau

MAN... WHAT A DAY! RAN OVER ANOTHER LAWN DART!
WHAT'S A LAWN DART, SIR? SOUNDS DANGEROUS.

UNEXPLODED CLUSTER BOMB. BLEW A TREAD CLEAN OFF MY BULLDOZER!
WOW... YOU KNOW, YOU GUYS ARE THE HEROES NOW!

UH-HUH... HEY, LISTEN, KID, YOU WANT A FRIENDLY PIECE OF ADVICE?
FROM YOU, SIR? I'D BE HONORED!

GET A HAIRCUT. YOU LOOK LIKE A GIRL.
THANK YOU, SIR.
GB Trudeau

KUWAIT HIGH SCHOOL 1991 YEARBOOK

What a year it's been for the seniors! First, classes were suspended for the fall and winter. Most of us left for Cairo or Gstaad. Then, liberation! What a hoot! As Prince Tariq "Disco" Al-Amiri put it, "Saddam Hussein can eat my shorts!" Even with no classes, five guys got into Princeton and three into UCLA, so the year wasn't a total loss. Also, there was the senior prom -- talk about a blast! Thanks to Sheik al-Sabah for letting us use his townhouse in London, and to the whole class for showing so much spirit. Go, Scorpions!

YOUSSEF AL-MIAZ
"Al" "The Man"
Class President... Slept through the invasion... Treasurer for neighborhood resistance cell... "Grow up!"...Quote: "Down with the dens of treason and shame, as mentioned in our previous communique."

HAMED AL-MESBAH
"Ham" "Pee-Wee"
Vice President... illegal editorial... weenie reforms ... boycotted Emir's party... working at McDonald's... "sweet spot" on a baseball... Ambition: "to move Kuwait into the 15th century."

ABDEL AL-SABAH
"Prince" "Your Majesty"
Class Treasurer... "I'm outa here!"... Christmas in Aspen... Waterbombing his bodyguard... CNN freak... Bootsie in Bahrain... Trying to grow a mustache...Gold sneaker eyelets... Polo I, II.

AHMAD SALMAN
"Stinky" "Traitor"
Class Secretary... P.L.O. donation boxes... Only guy in school who could fix the air conditioning... "Go, Intifada!"... Soccer I, II... Uncle Hussein... Missing for two months.

Compliments of your local Rolls-Royce Dealer.

SENIORS: COME SEE US FOR YOUR FIRST CAR!

Compliments of

BECHTEL

For the very best in infrastructure.

SEE YOU TOMORROW NIGHT, SIR?
NO. I'M JUST PASSING THROUGH ON A PILGRIMAGE.
FRESHEN YOUR DRINK, SIR?
NO, MY BUSINESS HERE IS DONE...
HOPE WE'LL SEE YOU GENTLEMEN AGAIN!
AFRAID NOT. WE'RE BEING ROTATED HOME TOMORROW.
SO WHAT'S YOUR NAME, SIR?
DON'T HAVE A NAME. I PREFER IT THAT WAY.
SEE YOU AGAIN, SIR?
DOUBT IT. I'LL PROBABLY BE DEAD IN THE MORNING.
SIR, DOES IT EVER DEPRESS YOU THAT WE DON'T HAVE REGULARS?
NAH. THEY ALWAYS WANT TABS.
G.B. Trudeau

HEY, DUKE! IS THIS RIGHT? YOU ONLY WANT ONE CASE OF LAGER?
YEAH, THAT'S RIGHT.

WHAT'S HAPPENED TO BUSINESS, MY FRIEND?
ALL THE CAPPERS LEFT. SAME WITH THE BUSINESSMEN. THEY GOT FED UP.

WELL, I SUPPOSE THAT WAS BOUND TO HAPPEN SOONER OR LATER. MIGHT BE TIME FOR A CHANGE, DUKE.

I'M ALREADY ON IT!
GLUG!
GLUG!
SPLAT!

HONEY! I'VE MADE A BUSINESS DECISION!

YOU HAVE, SIR?
WE'RE CLOSING DOWN! WITH THE FIRE FIGHTERS GONE, WE CAN'T TURN A PROFIT! IT'S TIME TO TORCH THE BUILDING AND PICK UP THE INSURANCE!

ARE YOU SERIOUS, SIR?
YEAH. BETTER PACK YOUR STUFF.

UM... HOW MUCH TIME DO I HAVE?
NOT MUCH. I'LL BE IN THE CAR.

SIR! WHAT HAVE YOU DONE?
I'VE MADE A SHREWD BUSINESS DECISION, HONEY!

BUT... BUT, BURNING DOWN THE CLUB?
WE'D LOST PROFITABILITY, HONEY! I HAD TO ACT!

THERE WAS NO FUTURE FOR US HERE, HONEY, NO OPPORTUNITY! THE NEW, PROSPEROUS KUWAIT WAS A VICIOUS LIE!

BUT... BUT, MY PERSONAL EFFECTS! MY LACEY UNMENTIONABLES...
OH, HELL, HONEY! WITH THE INSURANCE MONEY, YOU CAN BUY A TRUCKLOAD OF PANTIES!

HOW COULD YOU, SIR? THE CLUB... OUR DREAM... UP IN SMOKE!
GAS

YOU'VE DESTROYED A LEGEND, SIR! A MYTHICAL CROSS-ROADS, WHERE FLAXEN-HAIRED A-10 PILOTS—TEN FEET TALL—STRADDLED THE BARSTOOLS AND RE-LIVED THE HEROICS OF K-DAY!

A PLACE WHERE WELL CAPPERS AND EARTHMOVER SALESMEN AND KUWAITI PREPPIES DRANK AND LAUGHED AND PLANNED FOR A BRIGHTER TOMORROW FOR ALL OF ALLAH'S CHILDREN!

WE ALSO HOSTED TWO BOMBINGS AND AN ASSASSINATION.
NOT ON MY SHIFT. THE CLUB SCUD I SAW WAS MAGIC!
GB Trudeau

EXCUSE ME? YOU ARE THE OWNER OF THIS BUILDING?
DEPENDS. WHO'S ASKING?

I'M THE FIRE INSPECTOR. WE FOUND A FIRE BOMB. IT LOOKS LIKE ARSON.
ARSON? GOOD GOD! ARE YOU SURE?

AM I SURE? WELL, YES AND NO. LET ME PUT IT THIS WAY...
GB Trudeau

500 CASH TURNS IT INTO A GREASE FIRE.
A GREASE FIRE! GOOD GOD! HEAR THAT, HONEY?
I'LL SPEAK TO THE COOK, SIR.

EXCUSE ME? MISS? WHAT HAPPENED TO THE CLUB?
IT WAS TORCHED. BY ITS OWNER...

WHAT? WHY?
FOR THE INSURANCE. DOESN'T IT MAKE YOU SICK? THE ONLY OUTPOST OF CIVILITY AND CULTURE WITHIN 500 MILES AND IT'S GONE! GONE FOREVER!

THIS IS TERRIBLE. A GREAT LOSS.
YOU KNOW WHAT THE GREATEST LOSS IS, SIR? MY INNOCENCE! THAT'S GONE FOREVER, TOO!

IT HAPPENS. ANY UNEXPLODED BEERS AROUND?
IT TOOK A GREASE FIRE TO MAKE ME A WOMAN.
GB Trudeau